Rattling the Gates

Rattling the Gates

ROLAND R. HEGSTAD

Review and Herald Publishing Association
Washington, D.C. 20012

Library of Congress Catalog Card No. 73-87488.

Copyright © 1974 by
Review and Herald Publishing Association

Editor: Raymond H. Woolsey
Cover and Design: Alan Forquer

Printed in U.S.A.

Contents

11
Rattling the Gates

In his book *High Adventure,* Businessman George Otis, a Presbyterian active in the neo-pentecostal movement, tells of speaking one night in a Unity church in Los Angeles.

" 'I had,' " he says, " 'a vague impression of Unity as being a sterile old denomination—something like a big religious club. My own idea of the thinking of some of their ministers went like this: Love and positive thinking are the big things! The Bible is a wonderful literary treasure, but not necessarily all really God's Word, of course. Jesus was a great Teacher and remarkable Prophet—but not necessarily virgin-born of God. Very good people—strong on social works with a little reincarnation woven in here and there.' " [1]

Otis was not intimidated. He told them of having experienced an unexpected baptism with the Holy Spirit that opened the door to a completely new existence. Afterward he met in the chapel with those who wanted to be sure they knew Jesus as Saviour and to learn more about the baptism with the Holy Spirit.

"That cool Los Angeles night," says Otis, "more than ninety people in the ornate old Unity chapel prayed for forgiveness of their sins . . . and some thirty stayed behind to meet Christ as Baptizer with the Holy Spirit.

"God was rattling the gates of that great old denomination as He is now rattling the gates of every manner of church. Some gates may be guarded by well-meaning 'defenders of the doctrines and traditions' of the institution, but Jesus' voice out there at the gates is being heard by certain responding hearts inside of each. *And the Spirit and the bride say, Come. And let him that heareth say, Come. And let him that is athirst come. And whosoever will, let him take the water of life freely* (Rev. 22:17)." [2]

Otis, a millionaire industrialist, is one of many thousands of Protestants, Catholics, and others who today are witnessing to the work of the Holy Spirit through neo-pentecostalism, or the charismatic movement. "Charismatic" comes from the Greek *charisma,* and refers to gifts of extraordinary power given by the Holy Spirit to followers of Christ for the benefit of the church. Participants witness to gifts of healing, signs, wonders, and ecstatic tongues speaking. It was Otis who brought the gift of tongues to movie star and television personality Pat Boone. Defenders "of the doctrines and traditions" of Pat's church subsequently dropped him from membership. Denominational gates are, indeed, being rattled.

Oral Roberts, who reports that Jesus Christ appeared to him in 1968 with a "mantle of leadership" [3] to bring the charismatic ministry into the mainline churches, describes the encounter between the movement and the institutional church as a "confrontation":

"The Church of Jesus Christ, whatever name it goes by— Pentecostal, Nazarene, Presbyterian, Baptist, Methodist, Mennonite, Congregational, Catholic—is having a confrontation with the men and women of this age who are filled with the Holy Ghost and faith." [4]

Neo-pentecostals—and old-time pentecostals as well— look on the movement as a miracle-working Third Force commissioned by Christ to bring Protestantism, Catholicism, and ultimately the religious world under the mantle of the Holy Spirit's charismatic cape. David J. DuPlessis, for ten years head executive of the Pentecostal World Conference, describes the movement as "spiritual ecumenicity," in contrast to the "institutional ecumenicity" represented by the World Council of Churches.[5] "The Spirit bade me go" to the major denominations with this message, he says.[6]

Pentecostalism—as distinguished from neo-pentecostalism—received its "baptism" on January 1, 1901, at a small Bible school in Topeka, Kansas. A young Methodist minister, Charles Parham, laid his hands on the head of a student, Miss Agnes Osman, who received an ecstatic utterance. The emerging movement came to national attention in 1906 through reports of healings and other wonders at the Azusa Street Mission in Los Angeles.[7] Most Pentecostal bodies trace their spiritual heritage to one or the other of these places. Their deeper roots sprang from the pietistic revivals of the seventeenth and eighteenth centuries.

Until 1960 pentecostalism went its shouting, jerking, hand-clapping, tongues-talking, fundamentalist way, glorying in possession of spiritual gifts long ignored by the historic churches. Then, in 1960, through an Episcopal priest, it nudged at the gates of mainline Protestantism. On Sunday morning, April 3, Dennis J. Bennett, then pastor of the eminently respectable suburban St. Mark's Episcopal church, Van Nuys, California, startled parishioners by telling of his "baptism in the Holy Spirit," which had taken place the previous October.

Said Bennett: "The Holy Spirit did take my lips and tongue and form a new and powerful language of praise and power that I myself could not understand."[8]

Reaction was immediate. An associate priest removed his vestments, publicly resigned, and walked down the aisle and out of the church.[9] With the parish of 2,500 divided over the matter, Bennett resigned, and later that year transferred to St. Luke's Episcopal church in Seattle, a virtually defunct congregation that has grown since to several hundred members. *Time* reported the event, and the country became aware of a developing pentecostalism within historic Protestantism.

Today neo-pentecostalism has penetrated more than 100 denominations, and 480 groups in America and the other four continents.[10] Size of the world movement is somewhere between 8 and 14 million members.[11] In Latin America pentecostalism now numbers 63.3 per cent of all Protestants.[12] On the continent as a whole 5 or 6 million people may be linked with the movement.[13] In Chile pentecostalism has doubled itself every ten years since 1930.[14] In Brazil pentecostals in 1930 represented 9.5 per cent of the Protestant population; in 1964 they constituted 73.6 per cent of all Protestants in that country.[15] In the United States some 2,000 ministers of churches affiliated with the National Council of Churches have received the gift of tongues and are emphasizing charismatic gifts.[16] Healing services are no longer unusual. Church councils and local congregations alike are struggling with the question of tongues. Ministers have been dismissed and transferred, and congregations have split over the issue.

In 1967 neo-pentecostalism slipped through the gates of the Roman Catholic Church, and before the bishops could cry, "Katie, bar the door!" (to employ an unecclesiastical colloquialism), charismatic phenomena were breaking out all over. Today, estimates of Catholic charismatics range up to 300,-000, almost surely a highly inflated figure.[17] In June of 1973 the *National Catholic Reporter* quoted membership estimates "ranging upward and downward from 100,000," still an impressive growth. Another measure of development can be found in the *Directory of Catholic Charismatic Prayer Groups,* which in 1971 listed some 350 in the United States and abroad, and in 1972, 625, an incomplete listing, with 539 in the United States. In June of 1973 charismatic leaders had records of more than 1,200 prayer groups in the United States, increasing by one a day. In 1970 attendance at the International Conference on Charismatic Renewal, held at Notre Dame, was 1,250; in 1971, 5,500; in 1972, 11,000; in 1973,

RELIGIOUS NEWS SERVICE PHOTO

Worshipers raise their hands as they "speak in tongues" at a Church of God (Pentecostal) meeting in Dallas, Texas.

20,000. Ralph Martin, director of the International Communications Office for The Catholic Charismatic Renewal, reports "Thousands are involved" in Mexico and Australia. Half of "Puerto Rico's 73 towns have prayer groups; there are 30 such groups in France and more than 20 in Taiwan, where Catholic Charismatic Renewal literature is being translated into Chinese." [18]

The Jesus movement is largely charismatic. William F. Willoughby, religious news editor of the Washington *Star*, sets the percentage between 70 and 85 per cent, with most of these having spoken in tongues. A former missionary who is in contact with 100 Jesus people ministries in 48 States reports that most of the centers are charismatic. [19]

An interesting and perhaps prophetic aspect of the charismatic movement is its interdenominational character. Barriers dating to the Reformation are crumbling before the sweep of charismatic wonders. Protestants, Catholics, and other Christians are meeting together, kneeling together, praying together, and receiving gifts that they believe to be the Holy Spirit's good churchkeeping seal of approval.

John A. Mackay, president emeritus of Princeton Theological Seminary, suggests the potential of the movement:

"In a time of revolutionary change—when all institutional structures are crumbling in the secular and religious order, when the churches of historical Protestantism are becoming increasingly bureaucratized, when more and more church members are meeting in cells in an un-ecclesiastical underworld, when the Roman Catholic Church is developing evangelical concern and a deepening sense of what it means to be Christian, when the charismatic movement is growing across all ecclesiastical boundaries—might it not happen that, unless our Protestant churches rediscover dimensions in thought and life that they are losing or disdaining, the Christian future may lie with a reformed Catholicism and a matured pentecostalism?" [20]

Dr. Albert Outler, leading Methodist theologian, and an official observer at Vatican Council II, expressed a similar, but more colorfully phrased, appraisal:

"This [seeking charisma] isn't my bag . . . but I think I know some of the gifts and fruits of the Spirit when I see them, and I am convinced that much of what I have seen is for real and just may be a portent of something very much more. . . . It just might be these odd-ball Catholics with their evangelical concerns for conversion, with their charismatic baptisms and tongues and with their courageous commitments to reform in both church and society who may turn out to have been the vanguards in the third great awakening this country has seen. . . ." [21]

Pentecostal "visions" of the movement, as one would expect, are more gossamer, woven with threads of ethereal bliss. One writer says his "spirit discerns the future and reaches out to touch the heart of mankind and the desire of God." He describes a "new manifestation" of the Holy Spirit coming from heaven. God will strike lightning through the souls of men, there will be a great struggle between the children of God and the children of darkness, and Jesus will destroy the antichrist. [22]

Suggesting that the new movement is the missing line of the ecclesiastical triangle, he draws the following picture. The church is divided into three streams. Catholics form one stream, as they emphasize the formal church and sacraments. Protestants form the second stream, with emphasis upon the Bible, but Protestantism is broken up into many denominations, each with its own interpretation of the truth. "The third stream or force," he says, "is the most recent to emerge, as we have been seeing, the Pentecostal, with its emphasis upon experience of the Spirit and His gifts." [23] The solution to Christianity's problems, he believes, is for these three competing streams to merge and complement each other.

If my—Adventist—vision of Christendom's need corresponds with reality, the church does, without question, need everything—every gift, every weapon, every word of reproof and reconciliation—God has placed at its disposal. And, again, if my vision is correct, revival will come.

"Before the final visitation of God's judgments upon the

earth there will be among the people of the Lord such a revival of primitive godliness as has not been witnessed since apostolic times. The Spirit and power of God will be poured out upon His children. At that time many will separate themselves from those churches in which the love of this world has supplanted love for God and His word. Many, both of ministers and people, will gladly accept those great truths which God has caused to be proclaimed at this time to prepare a people for the Lord's second coming." [24]

This revival will not be confined to the Seventh-day Adventist Church. It will reach all those "other sheep," of whatever fold, whose hearts reach out to the Good Shepherd. Order, doctrine, experience, all will blend in the lives of the true disciple. The crucified and risen Christ will be presented as the Great Physician come with healing in His wings to seek and save that which was lost. In His disciples the law of God will be magnified and made honorable (see Isa. 42:21); truth will be prized above life itself. Men will turn from pride, presumption, and love of the world. They will deny self and take up the cross. Through them the love and magnanimity of the Lamb will be seen in contrast to the hate and malignancy of those who "make war with the lamb" (Rev. 17:14). And, at last, the objective of redemption will be achieved—the character of God will be perfectly restored in His people.

But the day of glory is not to come without a day of infamy. His disciples asked, "What shall be the sign of thy coming, and of the end of the world? And Jesus answered . . . , Take heed that no man deceive you. For many shall come in my name, saying, I am Christ; and shall deceive many." "For there shall arise false Christs, and false prophets, and shall shew great signs and wonders; insomuch that, if it were possible, they shall deceive the very elect" (Matt. 24:3-5, 24).

And what is our safety? Christ's counsel is clear: "Behold, I have told you before" (verse 25).

"Before the time for . . . [revival] shall come, . . . he [Satan] will endeavor to prevent it by introducing a counterfeit. In those churches which he can bring under his deceptive power he will make it appear that God's special blessing is poured out; there will be manifest what is thought to be great religious interest. Multitudes will exult that God is working marvelously for them, when the work is that of another spirit. Under a religious guise, Satan will seek to extend his influence over the Christian world." [25]

How, then, should Christians respond to the charismatic rattle at the church gates? In my neighborhood in surburban Washington, D. C., the prudent householder does not open the door to every knock. If it is night, he turns on the porch light and peers out. And at any time he calls out, "Who is there?" He does this even when he is expecting a friend, or when the postman is on the way with a gift package.

Can the prudent though expectant Christian do any less than to determine who is rattling the gate?

References

[1] George Otis, *High Adventure* (Old Tappan, New Jersey: Fleming H. Revell Co., 1971), p. 118. Copyright, Bible Voice Inc., Van Nuys, California.

[2] *Ibid.*, p. 126.

[3] Reprinted with permission from *Abundant Life,* July, 1968. Copyright Oral Roberts Evangelistic Association Inc., p. 18.

[4] *Ibid.*, pp. 13, 15.

[5] Religious News Service, Aug. 15, 1972, p. 16.

[6] James W. L. Hills, "The New Pentecostalism," *Eternity,* July, 1963, p. 18.

[7] James S. Tinney, "Black Origins of the Pentecostal Movement," *Christianity Today,* Oct. 8, 1971, pp. 4, 5.

[8] *The Nation,* Sept. 28, 1963, p. 173.

[9] Hills, *op. cit.*, p. 17.

[10] Hollenweger, *Enthusiastisches Christentum*, pp. 79 ff.; Damboriena, *Tongues As of Fire,* pp. 140-162.

[11] John T. Nichol, *Pentecostalism* (New York, 1966), p. 1, estimates 8 million; Damboriena, *Tongues As of Fire*, p. 142, numbers the worldwide pentecostal community at 12 to 14 million, four fifths of whom are outside the United States.

[12] William R. Read, *Avance Evangelico en la America Latina* (Buenos Aires: Casa Bautista de Publicaciones, 1970), p. 289.

[13] Alan Walker, *Breakthrough—Rediscovery of the Holy Spirit* (Nashville: Abingdon Press, 1964), p. 60.

[14] *Ibid.*, p. 60.

[15] Waldo A. Cesar, *Protestantismo e Imperialismo na America Latina* (Rio de Janeiro: Vozes, 1968), p. 105.

[16] Dr. David DuPlessis, founder and former secretary of the World Pentecostal Council in a speech at Minneapolis. Reported by Religious News Service, Sept. 17, 1969, p. 19.

[17] Tom Dorris, Washington *Evening Star and Daily News,* June 9, 1973, p. A-12.

[18] *National Catholic Reporter,* June 22, 1973, p. 10.

[19] James W. L. Hills, "The New Charismatics," *Eternity,* March, 1973, p. 33.

[20] "Christian Reality and Appearance," quoted in *Monday Morning,* a magazine for

Presbyterian Ministers, Nov. 17, 1969, p. 1.

    [21] Originally published in *New Covenant,* Ann Arbor, Michigan. Sept., 1971, p. 17. Reprinted with permission.

    [22] *World MAP Digest,* p. 21.

    [23] *Ibid.*

    [24] Ellen G. White, *The Great Controversy* (Mountain View, California: Pacific Press Publishing Association), p. 464.

    [25] *Ibid.*

2
The Challenge

Charismatic enthusiasts had given the Seventh-day Adventist Church gate a few tentative nudges through the years, without conspicuous success. But in the spring of 1972 the gate was rattled and predictions made of an impending "explosion" of spiritual dynamite among Adventists. It happened in Phoenix, Arizona. The occasion: A meeting of that city's chapter of the Full Gospel Business Men's Fellowship International, a Pentecostal front committed to sharing the gifts of the Spirit with the spiritually impoverished. The meeting began with praise to God for miracles and wonders and ended with a plan to bring the baptism of the Holy Spirit, with the accompanying gift of tongues, to the ministry of the Seventh-day Adventist Church.

Within a few minutes businessmen present pledged $2,-500 to the project. "That's what it takes to send these Seventh-day Adventist preachers—all the preachers in America and the world—the *Voice* magazine every month for a year," said the chairman, who had suggested the plan.* The *Voice,* published by the Fellowship, majors in miracles—accounts of healings, unknown tongues, prophetic revelations, all those phenomena characteristic of the charismatic movement. The Full Gospel Business Men's Fellowship, founded in 1953 by a group of Pentecostals, was living up to its activist—and ecumenical—image.

At this meeting the baptism with the Holy Spirit received special emphasis. Reported one participant:

"For two years I looked forward to this . . . wonderful experience of baptism of the Holy Spirit, and I couldn't find it in my own church. We didn't preach about it. We didn't want everything that God had for us—you know, . . . speaking in tongues. But I wanted what God wanted to give me. And I searched for this. God made me break down the barriers of denominationalism, and I went to other places, and eventually, on Easter Sunday, March 29, 1970, God poured out His Spirit into me and gave me the wonderful evidence He promised—'The Spirit gave them utterance,' and as the Spirit gave me utterance, I sang in the beautiful language of heaven."

Those present at the Phoenix chapter meeting did not go home with only a testimony about tongues. Before the meeting ended, several participants had addressed praise to God "as the Spirit gave them utterance." Captured by a tape recorder, the phrases have a rollicking rhythm reminiscent of a folk chant. I do not know how heaven would spell the words, and certainly not how heaven would translate them, but they sound like this:

Coopa shunda la-la-ba sigh-ah. . . . O coola ma-shunda, la munda caw sunda. . . .

Bracketing the words and interrupting them was repeated laughter. A minister in Sweden wrote me that he recently attended a meeting in which several thousand people raised their arms, vibrated their hands, and broke into what they called "holy laughter." It was, he said, an "unnerving experience." After listening to the Phoenix laughter a number of times

* All conversation is taken from a tape of the session.

while transcribing the tongues from a tape, I can sympathize with his reaction.

The Full Gospel session also had a prophetic message, delivered in a commanding, albeit ungrammatical, voice from the audience immediately following a prayer:

"Yea, my people, I say unto you today, that I'm in your midst. Yea, I am here to perform miracles. Yea, you have not seen nothin' yet. . . . This is only the beginning of what I shall do. This is the vision that I gave to [words garbled] when I spoke to Him who is all four corners of the earth, and this is spreading and it will spread more. . . . This is the day of salvation, this is the day of miracles, this is the day that you have never, never seen, and I am gathering my church together. My church, yea, all known nations, comin' into my church. The Holy Ghost is working. The Holy Ghost is sealing, sealing up the church. Those that will come in now will be sealed in this number. Jesus is coming soon. And I say, what you do, do quickly! I'm coming soon. I'm coming for a people who are ready, ready for my second coming. . . . All flesh shall receive the baptism. I say unto you, Arise, shine . . . open your eyes, look around, and you'll see greater and greater [wonders?]. . . . I shall pour out my Spirit. Gather yourselves together, for the great day of the Lord is here now, saith the Lord."

The tape recorder can be a cruel instrument. One is tempted to wonder what would be the reaction of those caught up in the emotion of the meeting were they to hear themselves later, in a less emotional setting. But one remembers, too, the mocking comment of some listeners on the day of Pentecost— "These fellows have drunk too much new wine!" (Acts 2:13, Phillips). (Not that the disciples sounded drunk. Just imagine your reaction if members of your family who were monolingual suddenly began to speak Chinese or Russian with great emotion.)

Peter's response ought not to be forgotten by a generation wedded to a humanistic religion:

" 'Fellow Jews, and all who are living now in Jerusalem, listen carefully to what I say while I explain to you what has happened! These men are not drunk as you suppose—it is after all only nine o'clock in the morning of this great feast day. No, this is something which was predicted by the prophet Joel,

> And it shall be in the last days, saith God,
> I will pour forth of my spirit upon all flesh:
> And your sons and your daughters shall prophesy,
> And your young men shall see visions,
> And your old men shall dream dreams:
> Yea and on my servants and on my handmaidens in those days
> I will pour forth of my Spirit; and they shall prophesy.
> And I will shew wonders in the heaven above,
> And signs on the earth beneath;
> Blood, and fire, and vapor of smoke:
> The sun shall be turned into darkness,
> And the moon into blood,
> Before the day of the Lord come,
> That great and notable *day:*
> And it shall be, that whosoever shall call on the name of the Lord shall be saved.

" 'Men of Israel,' " continued Peter, " 'I beg of you to listen to my words. Jesus of Nazareth was a man proved to you by God himself through the works of power, the miracles and the signs which God showed through him here amongst you—as you very well know. . . . There is no doubt that he died and was buried, and his grave is here among us to this day. But while he was alive he was a prophet. He knew that God had given him a most solemn promise that he would place one of his descendants upon his throne. He foresaw the resurrection of Christ, and it is this of which he is speaking. Christ was not deserted in death and his body was never destroyed. *Christ is the man Jesus, whom God raised up—a fact of which all of us are eyewitnesses!* He has been raised to the right hand of God; he has received from the Father and poured out upon us the promised Holy Spirit—*that* is what you now see and hear!' "

The reaction of the skeptical crowd to Peter's speech is instructive:

"When they heard this they were cut to the quick, and they cried to Peter and the other apostles, 'Men and fellow Jews, what shall we do now?'

"Peter told them, 'You must repent and every one of you must be baptized in the name of Jesus Christ, so that you may have your sins forgiven and receive the gift of the Holy Spirit. For this great promise is for you and your children—yes, and for all who are far away, for as many as the Lord our God shall call to himself!' . . .

"Then those who welcomed his message were baptized, and on that day alone about three thousand souls were added to the number of disciples" (Acts 2:14-41, Phillips).

One suspects that we "who are far away" ought not lightly to dismiss an experience mortised by divine inspiration into the very foundations of the church and its age-long witness.

Though the prophetic message given at the Riverside meeting lacks something in syntax, it does communicate a message sounded repeatedly in charismatic sessions: Jesus Christ is soon to return, and signs and wonders shall precede His appearing. Faith Healer Oral Roberts reports that more than three decades ago a message from God shaped his ministry into charismatic channels:

"I heard myself saying things I had never dreamed were possible for any man to say. The spirit of prophecy came on me and I began prophesying what God was going to do in the last days, how He was going to raise up men and give them His power to set humanity free from one end of the earth to the other, that He was going to pour out the nine gifts of the spirit to heal the sick body of the bride, and that Jesus Christ was coming soon. The words that flowed from my mouth were by the spirit of prophecy. I told the people that this last worldwide revival would be a revival of signs and wonders and that it would be characterized by a great wave of healing power coming from Heaven upon the sick bodies of mankind." [1]

On the occasion of the third appearance of Jesus Christ to

him, on May 9, 1968, Oral Roberts reports, he was commissioned to take the ministry of signs and wonders into the mainline Protestant churches:

"Wave after wave of God's power flowed over me. . . . Then a mantle of leadership from the Lord fell upon me, not upon me acting in myself but upon me as a servant and follower of Jesus Christ. . . .

"Then I knew for certain what I had held close inside me for these months, that the Spirit of the Lord was beginning to move over the earth in a way man had not experienced before. I knew for certain that the call I had received in 1947 to take His healing power to my generation would never be fulfilled unless I spent more time in the far countries of the earth. I knew too that there would be those people who would feel this, both those of Satan and those of God—including those in the full gospel churches, those in the historic churches and those who didn't belong to any denomination at all." [2]

Roberts, who left the Pentecostal ministry to become a Methodist, has described his reception by a Methodist bishop:

"When one of the bishops of the Methodist Church and I discussed my coming into an historical church with this ministry, I asked, 'Do you know who I am?'

"He said, 'I've heard you preach many 'times.'

" 'Do you know what I preach?'

"He said, 'I know it very well.'

" 'Do you know that I have the baptism with the Holy Ghost and speak in tongues every day of my life?' I asked.

"He said, 'Yes.'

" 'You know me, and you know that, and you still want me?' I asked.

" 'This is why we want you,' he said. 'We have got to have a renewal of the power of the Holy Spirit in our church.'

"Brother, this is the sound of the abundance of rain. This is the noise that we hear. Hallelujah! God is moving and opening the doors, and we who have the baptism with the Holy Ghost are going to have to come out from behind our denominational cloisters, our four walls, and share this with the hungry people throughout the world. . . ." [3]

"The Church of Jesus Christ, whatever name it goes by—Pentecostal, Nazarene, Presbyterian, Baptist, Methodist, Mennonite, Congregational, Catholic—is having a confrontation with the men and women of this age who are filled with the Holy Ghost and faith." [4]

As might be expected, in view of pentecostalism's historically divisive impact, denominational leaders exhibit signs of acute discomfort when tendered a charismatic greeting card. But the age of ecumenism is upon us, and "defenders of the doctrines and traditions" are cordial, if cautious. Recently, for example, the General Assembly of the United Presbyterian Church agreed that "neo-pentecostalism can make a valid contribution to the ecumenical church."

" 'We know,' " the report said, " 'that the misuse of mystical experience is an ever-present possibility, but that is no reason to preclude its appropriate use. . . . It is very possible that the Holy Spirit is preparing a renewal of the church in surprising ways and through unexpected channels.' " [5]

The Phoenix meeting, in addition to its stories of healings, emphasis on the baptism with the Holy Spirit, enthusiastic prayer, unknown tongues, and even a prophetic message, had unique features of special interest to Seventh-day Adventists. Already recorded is the raising of $2,500 to confront the Adventist ministry with the challenge of charismatic gifts. What I have not mentioned is this: the participant who reported on his baptism in the Spirit and speaking in tongues is a Seventh-day Adventist who, a year before, began to attend the Full Gospel group's meetings. It was he who reported that he had broken "down the barriers of denominationalism," and, as a consequence, on Easter Sunday, March 29, 1970, "sang in the beautiful language of heaven." It was his burden for bringing the baptism with the Holy Spirit and tongues to the Seventh-day Adventist Church that led to the decision to send the *Voice* to the Adventist ministry.*

---

* He tells his story in the January, 1973, *Voice.* A claim in that article—that the "former head of the ministerial department of our church" endorsed his experience—has been denied by the individual cited.

And there was more of special relevance to Adventists. Reported the chairman:

"Seventh-day Adventists . . . are talking about the Holy Spirit now more and more. One of their top leading (sic) pastors said, 'This is the answer, but somehow it's got to come and it's not going to come from the hierarchy; it's going to have to come from the grassroots. And our people are not quite ready, but they're almost ready.' "

"What would happen if all [Adventist ministers] started getting the *Voice* magazine every month?" he asked. "I guess there'd be an explosion and this auditorium would be too small to meet even all the Adventists."

"Brother ————," the chairman called, "we're going to have you stand here, and we're going to lay hands on [you], and touch [you] as though we're touching all the Seventh-day Adventist ministers.

"Here comes another [Adventist] brother. He's been praying for the baptism. He's all broken up. . . . Come up here, brother, and stand with ————.

"We want to reach the world of their church. Let's ask God, as we bless these men for what they've done, . . . that a revival will come to the Seventh-day Adventist Church."

There followed the prayer and the revelation from heaven and the laughter and tongues.

One suspects that much more is to follow. For Phoenix is only a touch of the charismatic hand that everywhere is reaching out to the Adventist Church, inviting its members to participate in the "revival," to thrill to the ministry of signs and wonders.

And the Adventist Church is responding. By study and prayer and fellowship with fellow Christians who feel they have a message to share with Adventists. And above all, by reexamination of writings God gave to the Seventh-day Adventist Church especially for its guidance in this confrontation.

Some seventy-five years ago, one on whom Adventists believe the prophetic gift rested, predicted that before Christ's return, "miracles will be wrought, the sick will be healed, and many undeniable wonders will be performed." [6]

Said the writer, Ellen G. White, "It is with an earnest longing that I look forward to the time when the events of the day of Pentecost shall be repeated with even greater power than on that occasion." [7]

And yet, when Adventists in Portland, Maine, began to speak in tongues in the mid-1800's—some fifty years before the rise of modern pentecostalism—she warned:

"Some of these persons have exercises which they call gifts and say that the Lord has placed them in the church. They have an unmeaning gibberish which they call the unknown tongue, which is unknown not only by man but by the Lord and all heaven." "May God deliver His people from such gifts." [8]

So the charismatic confrontation raises many questions: Is it the initial sprinkles of the latter rain, which God's Word says will bring renewal and reformation to His people? Could it be the work of that great angel of Revelation 18:1 come down from heaven, having great power and lighting the earth with his glory? Or is it the false revival of signs and lying wonders that the Bible says will precede Christ's return?— "For there shall arise false Christs, and false prophets, and shall shew great signs and wonders; insomuch that, if it were possible, they shall deceive the very elect" (Matt. 24:24).

What of tongues? Is this gift in God's arsenal of modern weapons for the church? How does one distinguish between the true and the false? Is speaking in tongues evidence of the baptism of the Holy Spirit? Can one be baptized with the Holy Spirit and yet not speak in tongues? And what, really, is the baptism with the Holy Spirit? What is tongues? Are there two gifts of tongues, one a gift of speaking intelligible foreign languages, another the gift of ecstatic utterance—that is, a speaking of the language of heaven? And how should Adventists, laymen and clergy alike, respond to invitations to join charismatic groups?

I find among Seventh-day Adventists two growing convictions:

The charismatic movement and its ministry can be discerned in those stirring scenes of the end of time described by the revelator; and only complete surrender to the possession of the Holy Spirit will suffice to meet the challenge of this prophetic day.

It was with these convictions and the challenge of the Riverside meeting in mind that I headed recently for a charismatic meeting on the campus of Catholic University to find what six years of neo-pentecostal emphasis have brought to Roman Catholic charismatics.

References

[1] Oral Roberts, *Life Story*, Tulsa, Oklahoma, p. 93.

[2] *Abundant Life*, July, 1968, p. 18.

[3] *Ibid.*, p. 11.

[4] *Ibid.*, p. 13.

[5] Quoted in May 30, 1970, Washington *Evening Star*, p. A-7.

[6] Ellen G. White, *The Great Controversy*, p. 588.

[7] *The SDA Bible Commentary*, Ellen G. White Comments, on Acts 2:1-4, p. 1055 (Washington, D.C.: Review and Herald Publishing Association).

[8] Ellen G. White, *Testimonies for the Church* (Mountain View, California: Pacific Press Publishing Association), vol. 1, pp. 412, 419.

13

Catholic Pentecostals

For the past several years a group of Catholic charismatics have met weekly in Caldwell Hall on the campus of Catholic University, in Washington, D.C. After attending a recent session I summarized my impressions for a priest:

"Well," I said, "if these meetings had taken place ten years ago, and the Pope and I had attended one, one of us would have turned pale, crossed himself, and walked out. And I," I added, "do not cross myself."

Catholic University enjoys unique status among Catholic educational institutions in the United States. It is *the* pontifical institute, meaning that it receives its authority directly from the Holy See, and therefore it should reflect, to an extent other Catholic schools may not, the policies and attitudes of the Vatican. That it is in Washington, D.C., seems appropriate. According to one author, the land on which the capital stands once bore the name of Rome, the stream that flows through it was then the Tiber, and the owner of the domain was a man named Pope![1]

Prior to Vatican Council II, the meeting in Caldwell Hall —one of 17 each week in the Washington area—would not have been deemed appropriate at Catholic University, or elsewhere in Catholic institutions. Today hundreds of such sessions are being held across America and, on a lesser but expanding scale, throughout the world.

But let us not be detoured from the eight-thirty appointment at Catholic University. As we enter Caldwell Hall, we are confronted by a sign reading "Jesus in me loves you." A Mass precedes the session, and those who have participated are drifting in as we join the 250 seekers already seated in a large circle. They are of all ages, white and black, Oriental, priest and laity. The dozen nuns are dressed in habits ranging from pre-Vatican II black or white and long, to the modern charcoal and short. Some college-age girls wear slacks and even shorts. Several participants grip cans of Pepsi and Mountain Dew.

What goes on during the next two hours would startle many Catholics and Protestants alike. Visualize a rather quiet Pentecostal meeting, with much reading of Scripture from modern translations, spontaneous individual and group prayer——some in tongues reminiscent of a rapidly recited Latin chant; a sea of hands raised heavenward in a peculiarly poignant gesture of invitation and expectancy, intermittent testimonies and sermonettes, spontaneous homilies on faith and surrender and receiving the baptism of the Holy Spirit, confessions of sin and lack of faith, and singing of folk songs to the rhythmic clapping of hands. If you are acquainted with traditional Catholic services, you will understand why I figuratively pinched myself several times and whispered, "I must have the wrong address."

The meeting begins when a young priest, a layman, and a teen-age girl enter and take their places in the center of the circle. She carries the musical badge of evangelical youth witness—the ubiquitous guitar. We are urged to greet those near us, and I respond to the hearty introductions of Sister Evangelina from Florida, on a preaching mission to our needy city, and "Diana from District Heights."

The guitarist strikes a chord and we sing,
"I am the resurrection and the life. He who believes in me
will live a new life. . . ."

The leader—the layman—rises. We are about to be introduced to an indispensable ingredient of all successful charismatic sessions—the conditioning speech. The expectancy of
the people and thus the tone of the meeting is established in
these preliminary remarks. Turning slowly to address the
whole circle, the speaker tells us that we must expect miracles.
It is important, he says, that we lift our hearts to Christ, in
faith expecting.

"Tonight," he continues, "you may see and hear strange
things. You will hear people pray to God in tongues. You will
hear them sing to Him in tongues. The gift of prophecy will
come.

"Let's not be afraid to listen to God, to listen to what He is
saying to us. We will pray together out loud. Don't be embar-
rassed. The Lord will be speaking to us. Let us hear what the
Lord is telling us. Let's not be afraid of silence. God wants us
to turn our hearts to Him, to focus on Him, to know that He
loves us, that He hears us. . . . We will raise our arms to God
in reception, expecting blessings to come."

We pray, "Father, soften us. . . . Bring us not to once-a-
week but every-day surrender. . . ."

We sing, the lyrics modern as a folk festival, the music
reminiscent of a medieval cloister:
"All of my life, I will sing praise to my God. . . ."

We pray aloud, simultaneously, and now I hear the
tongues, musical and low resembling a subdued Latin chant. I
am surprised at the observable distinction between the tongues
I have heard many times in Protestant Pentecostal meetings. If
this style of tongues is characteristic of Catholic charismatics,
someone must do a book on tongues from a different, and neglected, perspective—the cultural.

Now people rise spontaneously to read Bible verses or testify. A middle-aged woman urges her concern for air pollution.

"All right," responds the leader, "let's take a few minutes to pray about air pollution.

"Lord of everything, of the atmosphere and the cosmos . . ."

Two speakers stand to press the case for social involvement. "We must be more issue-oriented," one insists. (Protestant Pentecostals often are accused of neglecting social concerns, paticularly in South America.) A woman in her middle thirties speaks in rebuttal:

"Only a change of heart can result in a changed world," she says quietly. "I wonder if the action the Lord wants us to take is not penitential."

The chairman suggests that we pray sentence prayers, and from everywhere they come:

"We come, fragmented in spirit, body, and soul, to the Lord of healing."

"Make us better witnesses."

"Grant us the gift of faith."

An elderly man reads from Isaiah: "They that wait upon the Lord shall renew their strength. They shall mount up with wings like eagles; they shall run and not be weary; they shall walk and not faint" (Isa. 40:31, Taylor). [Yes, this paraphrased version appears to be *the* favorite.]'

We sing again: "Fill the valleys and the cities with a new song . . ."

Then there is group prayer. Each petitions God quietly, concentrating on his or her need. I glance at Diana from District Heights. Her head is bowed, her arms lifted in a curiously childlike invitation—like the beggars on Asian streets, I think, imploring, "Fill my rice bowl, please, God!"

I seek words to describe the worshipers and settle on expectancy, praise, receptivity.

The teen-ager with the guitar is on her feet. She turns slowly, making a full circle as she reads from Matthew 26:36, R.S.V.: "Then Jesus went with them to a place called Gethsemane." She delivers a brief homily on His suffering for us, on His willingness to yield His will to the Father. "Let this

cup pass from me," she reads, "nevertheless, not as I will . . ."
I look at the raptured face of the young priest. In how
many meetings like this are priests listening to women expound on God's Word, I wonder.

It is nine-fifteen. We sing:
"Spirit of the living God, fall afresh on *us*. . . ." I join in:
"Melt us, mold us, fill us, use us . . ."

A housewife testifies. She speaks of the stripes of Christ,
suffered for us. A middle-aged black woman bears witness to
healing from shingles:

"The doctor painted a bleak picture. I had a blinding
headache. Even my cornea was threatened. . . . I went home
and prayed, 'Jesus, You earned my salvation. I believe.' By
Tuesday the swelling was gone.

"The trouble with us," she concludes, "us sitting here, we
don't believe what we've been taught. Tonight there should be
healings here."

Another woman, perhaps 35, dark hair framing her pale
face, rises. "I'm Pat," she says. "Bear with me, I'm shaky.
And I'm kind of conservative. I wanted to tell you that I had
been healed, but I was afraid I would sound like Kathryn
Kuhlman. Then I said, 'Lord, do You want me to say something?' . . . We're sick, all of us. One day it penetrated. Dear
God, it's true! We're always going to be searching, for God
alone is perfect. I feel I lack faith."

The leader speaks: "Let's pray for Sister Pat." And we all
do, in a quiet murmur of intercession, that her faith may be
strong.

At nine-fifty-three we hear the first prophetic utterance:
"My people, is anything too great for me? They that ask in
faith shall receive."

The leader, too, speaks paternally, prophetically: "My
children, I want your hearts totally. Give yourselves to me."

I have marveled at the many testimonies in the book *Catholic Pentecostals* [2] that stress justification by faith, and I hear
them here, too.

A young man speaks: "I have learned that God loves me,

really loves me, and this knowledge has broken my heart. He died for me. It is through His sacrifice that I live, and through the intercession of the Holy Spirit, through His power and grace, that I grow. I have cast myself upon Him."

"Can this be the church of my grandfather and of his father before him?" I ask myself. No wonder Catholic bishops are "mystified, cautious, and basically unhappy," as Benedictine Father Kilian McDonnell has reported.[3] I recall an article— "What I Want for the Catholic Pentecostal Movement"—by Bishop Stephen A. Leven, of San Angelo, Texas.

Though wanting the movement to continue, the bishop makes plain in what direction:

"I want the movement to remain Catholic. . . .

"Jesus Christ comes to us as the Son of Mary. No one accepts Christ as he comes to us by neglecting Mary; no one honors him by downgrading her. Jesus Christ says, 'Upon this rock I will build my church; and the gates of hell will not prevail against her.' No one can accept Jesus Christ wholly who says to him, 'No, Jesus, the Church you built became corrupt and fell away. . . .'

"Jesus promised in John 6 to give us his flesh to eat and his blood to drink. No one can wholly accept Jesus Christ and be satisfied with bread and wine or crackers and grape juice.

"Many persons in the Catholic pentecostal movement do accept Jesus wholly and completely in the Church he established. Some do not. . . even some priests seem bent on deliberately protestantizing Catholic people in the name of ecumenism. Should they be permitted to remain in the movement?"[4]

Soon after ten o'clock the meeting ends. We are invited to attend an aftermeeting in room 519, where a seven-week program of praying for the Holy Spirit is being conducted. It is then that I think of the Pope and wonder what his reaction would be. Yes, ten years ago he would have crossed himself and walked out. But a lot of things have changed in the past ten years, a lot of things.

The Catholic charismatic movement had its beginning in

the universities: Duquesne; Notre Dame, of South Bend; Michigan State; Iowa State, Holy Cross, of Worchester, Massachusetts. Contrary to the case in Protestant pentecostalism, it began with intellectuals—professors of theology, philosophy, physics, history; graduate students working on doctorates, undergraduates.

How does the charismatic experience come to the Catholic pentecostal? Here are the testimonies of three who found new life during the 1967 awakening.

Roger Alexander was attending Michigan State University when, one weekend in 1967, he went with friends to Notre Dame, hopeful of participating in the charismatic phenomena.

When his friends began to pray over him, says Roger, "a strange physical sensation started in my hands and feet and gradually spread over my whole body. It was like an electric current or as though the inside of my body was shaking against my skin. For the first time in my life I had a real understanding of the power of God. After this I sat for a short while and prayed, thanking God for the wonders He had shown me. Suddenly my lips began to tremble. . . . And as I knelt a strange series of sounds poured forth from my lips. I had no control over the sounds that I made, and yet I was filled with an intense happiness and peace such as I had never known before." [5]

David Mangan teaches mathematics and religion at St. Thomas High School in Braddock, Pennsylvania. In February, 1967, a student at Notre Dame, he went on a retreat with friends from Duquesne University. On Saturday afternoon, the 18th, after participating in study and prayer groups, he walked into the chapel and stood before the altar:

"The next thing I knew I was lying prostrate on the floor crying and feeling such ecstasy as I may never feel again. I cried harder than I ever cried in my life, but I did not shed one tear. All of a sudden Jesus Christ was so real and so present that I could feel him all around. I was overcome with such a feeling of love that I cannot begin to describe it."

Later, David returned to the chapel to pray. Soon he again

found himself lying on the floor on his back, with his arms outstretched in the shape of a cross.

He says he didn't get much sleep that night but the next morning he felt as rested and comforted as if he had slept all day. He enjoyed the overpowering realization that God loved him. Later, on the same day, he had another prayer session. "This time I was so joyful that all I could do was laugh as I lay on the floor. I was so joyful because the Lord really cared. He knew what I needed. Boy, did he ever give it to me! He literally knocked me flat!" [6]

James Cavnar, now employed in apostolic work at the Newman Center in Ann Arbor, experienced baptism in the Holy Spirit in March of his senior year at Notre Dame. The degree to which one's understanding of theology can condition his experience may be discerned in his report.

As a professor from Duquesne laid hands on him, James reports, he didn't look for any outward manifestation. He believed that the baptism in the Spirit was received in faith by asking the Father.

"He stood before me for a moment, and then, in Christ's name, cast out Satan. As soon as he said the words I knew that a demon had left. I felt myself physically shaken and smelled clearly and distinctly the smell of burning sulphur, a smell I know well from chemistry lab." [7] James took this as a sign that what had been oppressing him was the power of Satan and that God's power had broken the devil's oppression.

Hands were laid on James, and he felt himself drawn to the Scriptures. Prayer became a joy—he remembers sitting in the chapel for a half hour just laughing out of joy over the love of God.

What has been the reaction within the Catholic Church to the movement?

"Church authorities fear having to deal with a movement which knows no jurisdictional boundaries, which cannot be pre-programmed, pre-planned and pre-packaged or pre-structured," says Catholic Theologian Kilian McDonnell. [8]

Reaction "seems to be one of caution and somewhat un-

A young man stops playing the guitar and starts "speaking in tongues" during a charismatic renewal meeting at St. Columba Roman Catholic church in Hopewell Junction, N.Y.

happy," concluded the *Report of the Committee on Doctrine of the National Conference of Catholic Bishops,* submitted to the bishops at a meeting in Washington, D.C., November 14, 1969. Nevertheless, said the report:

"The movement should at this point not be inhibited but allowed to develop. Certain cautions, however, must be expressed. Proper supervision can be effectively exercised only if the bishops keep in mind their pastoral responsibility to oversee and guide this movement in the Church. We must be on guard that they avoid the mistakes of classic pentecostalism. It must be recognized that in our culture there is a tendency to substitute religious experience for religious doctrine."

The bishops' report points up several differences between Catholic pentecostalism and classic, or Protestant, pentecostalism, differences borne out by my own observations. However, despite the bishops' attempt to emphasize the unique Catholicity of the movement, there is a documentable tie between it and classic pentecostalism. Though the charismatic breakthrough for Catholics can be dated to 1966-1967, individual Catholics have taken part in meetings of the Full Gospel Business Men's Fellowship International since 1962. Catholic pentecostalism's first leaders received the baptism of the Holy Spirit at interdenominational meetings that were the product of Protestant pentecostal initiative. Many Catholic charismatics began their search for the baptism by reading pentecostal minister David Wilkerson's *The Cross and the Switchblade.* (See, for example, testimonies in *Catholic Pentecostals,* footnote 2.) "Some Catholics operate Teen Challenge centers under Assembly of God sponsorship," reports Edward E. Plowman.[9] A Catholic charismatic mission to bring the movement to Costa Rica and Peru included the president of the Full Gospel Chapter in West Virginia.[10] Veteran Protestant pentecostal leader David DuPlessis is a frequent speaker at charismatic conferences. The *National Catholic Reporter* speaks of the "movement's acknowledged ties to Protestant classic and neo-pentecostalism."[11]

Despite the interrelationship of Catholic and Protestant

pentecostalism there are, as the bishops claim, differences: Catholic meetings tend to be more subdued, prayers are less bombastic, songs and even tongues more generally resemble a Latin chant. Catholic meetings often begin with a Mass, and many Catholic pentecostals report increased devotion to the Mass as the first evidence of new vitality of discipleship. Ironically, Catholic pentecostals seem to emphasize Scripture in its broader dimensions more than do Protestant pentecostals. Whether the differences are grounded in culture as well as Scripture is difficult to document.[12]

It is not easy to evaluate the charismatic movement rationally. Emotion seems to pervade not only the movement but even discussions concerning it. I shall not depart from the usual, then, in suggesting an emotional rather than an intellectual point to keep in mind while assessing the movement, both in its Catholic and classic pentecostal manifestations. Though the point is emotional, I intend it to lead the reader to a more dispassionate appraisal than might otherwise be the case: *The charismatic movement owes its existence to churches that have failed their people.*

Too long have sterile creeds and frigid formalism substituted for the living Christ in His living church! Too long has a socio-political panacea failed to provide a paradise on earth! Men are at last remembering that Christ did not say, "Tarry ye in Jerusalem, until ye get permission from the church," but rather, "Tarry ye in . . . Jerusalem, until ye be endued with power from on high" (Luke 24:49). He did not say, "Ye shall receive power after that the church bestows it on you," but rather, "Ye shall receive power, after that the Holy Ghost is come upon you" (Acts 1:8).

If the Church is to be the catalyst of reformation, she must return to her first love and her first methods, and inscribe on her banners again, "Not by might, nor by power, but by my spirit, saith the Lord" (Zech. 4:6).

"The real ecumenical crisis today," writes Theologian Harvey Cox in *The Secular City,* "is not between [Roman] Catholics and Protestants but between traditional and experimental forms of church life. If church leaders do not recognize this, within a few decades we shall see a cleavage in the Church that will be comparable to the one that appeared in the sixteenth century." [13]

In every church are those "other sheep" of Christ, no longer content with the husks of religion, who with the prodigal son are saying, "How many hired servants of my father's have bread enough and to spare, and I perish with hunger!" (Luke 15:17). Every man who professes Christ should ask himself that searching question, "Do I know the reality of the Holy Spirit in my life?"

I shall never forget those anxious weeks early in my ministry when I concluded that I was destitute of the Holy Spirit, that I walked into the pulpit with confidence in words rather than in the Word. And the awful distress that shrouded my soul when I realized that I would be held accountable for the spiritual growth of my church. I shall never forget those days and nights of prayer and searching that led me at last through the loopholes of my profession into the presence of Deity. Until one early morning hour there burst from my lips—no, not a babble of unintelligible sounds, but a clear-cut testimony of confidence and triumph: Jesus Christ is the Lord of my life! I am accepted in Him!

Oh, that I had found Him sooner! Strangely, it was an early acquaintance with charismatic phenomena on the one hand and dogmatism and rationalism on the other that turned me away from the church and from Christ. But that is the story of the next chapter.

References

[1] Laurence J. Kenny, S. J., "America, Land of Destiny," *Catholic Historical Review*, Oct., 1926, pp. 42, 43.

[2] Kevin and Dorothy Ranaghan, *Catholic Pentecostals*, Paulist Press, Paramus, N.J.

[3] *Commonweal*, Nov. 8, 1968, p. 203.

[4] *New Covenant* magazine, Ann Arbor, Michigan, Nov., 1971, p. 25. Reprinted with permission.

[5] Roger Alexander, "The Holy Spirit at Michigan State," *Acts, Today's News of the Holy Spirit's Renewal*, Sept.-Oct., 1967, p. 23.

[6] Ranaghan, *op. cit.*, pp. 24-28.

[7] *Ibid.*, pp. 63-65.

[8] *National Catholic Reporter*, June 12, 1968.

[9] Edward E. Plowman, *Christianity Today*, July 16, 1971, p. 31.

[10] *New Covenant*, Nov., 1971, p. 1.

[11] *National Catholic Reporter*, June 23, 1972, p. 16.

[12] For a Catholic's comparison of classic pentecostal and Catholic pentecostal services, see John S. Phillipson, "Two Pentecostal Experiences," *America*, March 29, 1969, p. 360.

[13] Harvey Cox, *The Secular City* (New York: Macmillan Publishing Co., Inc., 1965, 1966), p. 139, revised edition.

4

A Tale of
Two Churches

I can see her yet, a stout woman of 55, graying hair pulled into a bun, dark eyes often filled with tears as she sought the baptism with the Holy Spirit. Night after night, as preaching missions came to the Pentecostal church near my home in a small western Oregon lumber community, she attended in hope of being elevated to First-Class Saint. For the line of demarcation between those who had received the baptism and those who had not, extended even to social status in our town. You either had it—"it" being the "baptism"—or you didn't, and tongues, in its most incomprehensible form, was the proof.

Her name was Mrs. Cassels* and her religion was her life, compensating for an unbelieving husband, and children already married. And because baptism with the Holy Spirit was graduation *magna cum laude* to the inner circle of discipleship, she pursued it with the persistence of knights seeking the Holy Grail. And she got it at last, by her own testimony, at three

_____
* All names in this narrative are pseudonyms.

one morning while praising God for His mercies. The next night her husband was with her in church, to tell in wondering tones of finding his wife playing the piano "in the Spirit" at 3:00 A.M., and "praising God in the language of the angels." From that day on one occasionally would see her slump to the floor during a praise service, from which position, in semiconscious state, she would shout ecstatically, while the brass orchestra blew their approval. If the service was especially inspirational—or emotional (the worshipers did not distinguish)—others might join her, though not always on the floor. One night two of my high school classmates, girls from Pentecostal homes, received the Spirit and for two hours danced among the chairs, eyes closed, arms upraised and vibrating, touching nothing, expressions of "glory," "Hallelujah," and other undecipherable phrases coming intermittently from their lips.

And there were stories of miracles and healings and sundry wonders. One night, it was said, tongues of flame as at Pentecost descended on the roof of the church in such dazzling splendor that the fire department from a nearby town rushed to the church, believing it to be on fire! This story was told during an "appeal," for which the doors were locked and all sinners forced to face up to the evangelist's description of their lost condition. That preacher was no Jonathan Edwards for eloquence, but I gained a long-abiding misconception—and dislike—that night of the song with the words, "Praise the Lamb for sinners slain."

The healings were disappointing—— I saw no stunted limbs grow to maturity, no visible tumors disappear (though countless unseen tumors and cancers were said to have been rebuked to shriveled impotence), no blind eyes see, no deaf hear. Lest I sound cynical let me add that I do believe in God's power and willingness to heal, and believe even that some petitioners at the altar of that little Pentecostal church may have been made whole. My prudence in endorsing healing has grown through the years, however, as I have investigated claims made in various healing magazines.

After Mrs. Cassels' baptism with the Spirit, Mrs. Newton sought it with renewed hope—and perhaps even a touch of desperation. I can recall her in the perfervid atmosphere of an afterservice, kneeling in a circle of praying friends who laid their hands on her head and shouted expressions ranging from "Hit her, Lord!" to "Hallelujah!" Tears witnessing to the intensity of her want, she prayed, her quiet words unheard beneath the bedlam of insistence surrounding her, until at last her lips began to quiver, her words ran together into indistinguishable phrases, which emerged in turn into a cacophony of clauses, and laughter and tears mingled as she received her long sought "gift."

And I, who had received no baptism, either of water or of the Spirit, watched and wondered. I went a few times to the community church, the only alternative in our town. The Boy Scout leader taught a dogmatically persuasive Sunday school lesson. There were no grays in his theology. The commandments stormed anathemas from fluorescing tables of stone. Souls were predestined to eternal bliss or eternal damnation. Weaknesses of the flesh were met with verses redolent with "dead men's bones" and "whited sepulchres." He was dogmatism personified.

But for all the Scout leader's dogmatism, community church services seemed colorless compared to the Pentecostal variety. The minister, a tweed-suit-and-pipe type nearing retirement, seldom showed either emotion or erudition. I found his sermons less persuasive than his sales technique when he peddled tickets to a local dance. His themes seemed to be taken more often from the *Reader's Digest* than the book of Acts. Healings, both he and the congregation seemed assured, were from doctors; tongues were for talking—intelligibly; and miracles? Ah, yes, miracles.

My visits to the community church ended the week I saw the minister in a community play production called "Murder at Midnight." Dressed in a cancan outfit, he and four other local men were kicking up their heels to the accompaniment of a Dixieland piano piece. For me, it was back to the Pentecostal church, though my visits became increasingly infrequent. Somehow, even in those naive pubescent years I found it difficult to swallow the "Full Gospel" approach to Christ. It seemed instead a distorted gospel, majoring on emotionalism, minoring on reason. The community church, on the other hand, seemed sterile, aseptic, as if some spiritual apothecarian had dispensed soothing soul syrup to the congregation, leaving not a cough of praise in the churchload. Was there not, I wondered, some middle ground between the community church's dogmatism and rationalism and the Pentecostal church's emotionalism? Some middle ground on which faith and reason could coexist compatibly? I discovered no such acreage in our town.

One winter a touring revivalist and his family spurred me momentarily to thoughts of commitment. Billed into the Pentecostal church as the "Musical Fox Family," they were easily the finest musical talent in our town since a barbershop quartet the year before. The six girls in the family made all the females I had known in grade and high school look like plain Janes. They all had curly hair, ranging from blonde to auburn, and their eyes sparked a leitmotiv to their lively songs. A man would have had to be made of cast iron *not* to go to the altar, which was just below where they played and sang. But unlike some others who walked there, I went motivated both by emotion and reason, the former impelling me to the altar at a spot just out of range of the trombone slides of the two oldest girls, the latter seeking evidence on which to make a decision between them. I settled at last on loving them both.

It was probably Charlie Bass whose testimonies finally drove me from the Pentecostal services and my religious impulses into hibernation through several wintry years of spiritual torpor. Charlie was the father of two boys who had grown up with me through grade school. About 50, he walked with a rolling gait, arms tucked into the top of bib overalls, well-aimed squirts of chewing tobacco marking his route. It was the chewing tobacco that did Charlie—and me—in. I don't recall the first time he arose during testimony service to pull a packet of chewing tobacco from his pocket and surrender it to the preacher while announcing, "Well, today I got the victory, Hallelujah!" But I do recall the many encores, all played to similar accompaniment: "Well, today I got the victory, praise the Lord!" The saints would shout their approval, Charlie would pass over his tobacco, and I would wonder whether there was, in fact, "power in the blood." I decided at last that there was not, not even in the "Full Gospel."

From a more mature perspective I don't scorn Charlie. I pity him. Through the years I have surrendered and surrendered and surrendered *my* "packets" of appetite and presumption and love of the world. With the apostle Paul I have lifted my tears to heaven to confess, "My own behavior baffles me. For I find myself not doing what I really want to do but doing what I really loathe. . . . I often find that I have the will to do good, but not the power. . . . My conscious mind wholeheartedly endorses the Law, yet I observe an entirely different principle at work in my nature. This is in continual conflict with my conscious attitude, and makes me an unwilling prisoner to the law of sin and death. . . . It is an agonizing situation, and who on earth can set me free from the clutches of my sinful nature?" (Rom. 7:15-24, Phillips).

I have found the answer: "I thank God there *is* a way out through Jesus Christ our Lord" (verse 25, Phillips). In His last recorded words, just prior to His ascension, Christ assured His disciples, "But ye shall receive power, after that the Holy Ghost is come upon you: and ye shall be witnesses unto me" (Acts 1:8). In my search for a middle ground of faith and reason between dogmatism and rationalism on the one hand, and emotionalism or experience on the other, my boyhood experiences in my hometown churches have been helpful. They have aided me in formulating my personal response to the appeal of the charismatic ministry. They have kept me from the rationalism that is often the reaction to spiritual overbalance, and the dogmatism invited by the vitiated verities of spineless preaching. Here are two conclusions that have grown through the years.

First, doctrine and experience must be kept in balance. To become totally doctrine oriented is to be a dogmatist: cold, demanding, uncharitable, living in the letter of the law rather than in the Spirit of the gospel. On the other hand, to become totally experience oriented is to become an enthusiast, blown here and there by every wind of emotion, giving allegiance to whichever spirit inspires the loudest shouts (forgetting that the Holy Spirit often communicates in a "still, small voice"), ever seeking a higher "high," ever increasingly addicted to feeling.

One recalls the devils who "believe and tremble," convinced of truth but devoid of the transforming experience, and at the other extreme, the people of Lystra, who, having the experience but erring doctrinally, were so excited by Paul and Barnabas that they sought to offer sacrifices to them as gods. As Theologian Bernard Ramm observes, "the devils need a transforming experience and the Lystrians needed a course in systematic theology; neither had correlated doctrine and experience properly." [1]

The very nature of our age tempts us to one extreme or the other. Eternal verities are eroding, moral codes are in flux, randomness has become the keynote of human existence. And so we seek absolutes, "Thou shalt nots." Like the children we still are, we retreat to the security of doctrinal playpens, closing ourselves about with bars of dogma, while we shout for law and order.

Or, confronted with the impersonality of our computer age, the rationality of our scientific methodology, and the sterility of religious institutions, we seek feeling. We have trod the asphalt of formalized creeds and found the way wearying to our feet. We yearn for the feel of grass, the scent of flowers, the loam-soft paths of childhood faith. Oh, to be free again, to sing again, to laugh again, to *feel* again.

Which way, then, to go? We seek the way of God and are bewildered by conflicting waymarks. There is an Episcopal high road; the tradition-bound, "long, long trail a'winding" of Roman Catholicism; the intersection-studded midway of

Methodism and Presbyterianism; the borderless beltway of Unitarianism, the adventurous byways of a score of sects. Theological diversity, denominational confusion. Churches that have lost the way. Theologians who cannot find it. Which way to go? Suddenly, piercing through our confusion comes an invitation to enter directly into the heart of spiritual reality, and, moreover, to have one's acceptance confirmed by speaking in tongues! Away with doctrinal nit-picking! Down with denominationalism! Enter in, brother, and speak with the tongue of angels! No wonder the charismatic movement is sweeping like a spiritual broom through the cobwebbed corners of ecclesiastical structures!

But doctrine and experience must be kept in balance. For though emotional experiences may be powerful and compelling, they may also be dangerously deceptive. And this brings me to the second scriptural principle I have discovered. Psychic phenomena—unknown tongues, miracles, healings—are no sure sign of God's working.

We need only turn to the Sermon on the Mount for confirmation. There Christ draws a tragic picture of disillusionment and dismay. Beginning with Matthew 7:13, we note Jesus speaking of two ways set before Christians: the "narrow gate," easily found, which leads to life; the "wide gate" and the "broad road" that lead to destruction. "There are many people going that way," He says. The warning follows: "Be on your guard against false religious teachers, who come to you dressed up as sheep but are really greedy wolves" (Phillips).

How can one distinguish between the true treachers and the false? By the miracles they perform? By the unknown tongues they speak? By the devils they cast out and the good works they do? By none of these. Says Jesus, "You can tell them by their fruit."

"Every good tree produces good fruit; but a bad tree produces bad fruit."

Thus on the clear testimony of Jesus Christ we are warned not to evaluate men or movements on the basis of charismatic manifestations. "It is not everyone who keeps saying to me

'Lord, Lord' who will enter the kingdom of Heaven," says Jesus, "but the man who actually does my Heavenly Father's will.

"In 'that day' many will say to me, 'Lord, Lord, didn't we preach in your name, didn't we cast out devils in your name, and do many great things in your name?' Then I shall tell them plainly: 'I have never known you. Go away from me; you have worked on the side of evil!' " (Matt. 7:13-23, Phillips).

Several points are worth pondering here. First, the false teachers are not operating from outside of the church, but from within. They are false *religious* teachers. Second, they are empowered to perform miracles. Third, they are sincerely deluded. They come to Christ in judgment and plead the case for what they have done in His name. Fourth, though they have professed His name, they have not done God's will. They have stood in meeting after meeting, crying, "Lord, Lord," raising hands in praise and healing. They have ordered demons to depart in Jesus' name. They have spoken unknown tongues. Healings have occurred. Seeming conversions have resulted from their preaching. But Jesus rejects them. They have not done His will.

Especially vulnerable to deception are two classes of Christians. First, those who no longer believe in the malignant ministry of fallen angels, and who therefore attribute all supernatural happenings to God. Second are those who live for miracles, those who see miracles behind every bush, burning or not. This type of Christian is dependent on feeling. They feel saved, they feel peace, they feel God's hand on them.

It is almost impossible to talk to such people about doctrine. Their experience transcends doctrine. "An experience is better than an argument," they say. To call their experience into question, to submit it to the strictures of Scripture seems to them almost blasphemous. Others may doubt. Others may feel the need to go to God's Word for guidance and correction. But they *know*, for they *feel*. As with the drug addict, they transcend reality.

But in reality, they are drugged. They have swallowed the

"sorceries" by which all nations shall be deceived (Rev. 18:23). The Greek word for sorcery *(pharmakeia)* is self-explanatory. It speaks of enchantment with drugs—an addictive potion! Spiritual LSD in a dosage that distorts reality! That sends you on an extrasensory trip. In the dramatic pen of Revelation 17, John pictures a harlot dressed in scarlet—fallen Christendom—holding out a golden cup, from which she bids men drink (verse 4). " 'Fallen, fallen is Babylon the great!' " says a voice from heaven. " 'She has become a haunt of devils {who give her, her power}, a prison for every unclean spirit. . . .

" 'Come out from her, O my people,' " pleads another voice from heaven, " 'lest you become accomplices in her sins and must share in her punishment' " (Rev. 18:2, 4, Phillips).

What solemn and fearful words! How treacherous are the drugs by which evil spirits capture the minds of men, until, addicted to emotion, they set aside the Word of God to follow feeling!

Encounter a spiritual enthusiast, whether in the Pentecostal Church, the Full Gospel Business Men's Fellowship, or the charismatic wing of Catholicism, and he will almost invariably argue as follows, says Bernard Ramm: "(1) I have had this tremendous experience; (2) I find experiences like this reported in the New Testament; (3) therefore my experience is true.

"The enthusiast errs at two points," Ramm continues. "First, he does not realize a major contradiction. If the process is from experience to truth, then I must accept as valid all experiences that people claim to have had. Yet these experiences are contradictory. I can't experience all experiences. A Babel of experience exists; and if we move from experience to truth, we must go through the whole gamut. So the argument 'from experience to truth' doesn't free me but paralyzes me, for I don't know whether to follow Mary Baker Eddy or Sister Macpherson.

"Second, although emotional experiences are emotionally powerful and compelling, they are dangerously deceptive. There is no certainty of truth in the profundity of experience.

Many people who have had a remarkable, profound experience have later found themselves terribly deceived. "As soon as the question of deception is raised, the argument from 'experience to truth' collapses." [2]

The answer to the enthusiast's dilemma, then, is the New Testament pattern—from truth to experience. *It is the truth that makes us free.* Free from transgressing the will of our Father. Free from deception. Free from sin. It is the truth that enables us to know the will of our Father: "If you continue in my word, you are truly my disciples, and you will know the truth, and the truth will make you free" (John 8:31, 32, R.S.V.). Paul extols the Romans for conforming to true doctrine: "But thanks be to God, that you who were once slaves of sin have become obedient from the heart to the standard of teaching to which you were committed" (Rom. 6:17, R.S.V.).

The Spirit that baptizes us with power is called the Spirit of truth (John 16:13), and He is sent to guide us into all truth. It follows that the sign of the Spirit-filled disciple is to search the Scriptures daily to see if these things are so (see Acts 17:11).

"Correct, valid Christian experience is therefore determined by the correct interpretation of Scripture and the best in Christian theology," says Ramm. "The New Testament Christian is the Christian who determines the form, the pattern, the structure of Christian experience from the study of the New Testament and then seeks to conform his life to that. He thus moves from truth to experience. This is not contradictory because truth cannot contradict itself. In this there is no deception, for truth can lead only to reality. Therefore I am on safe, solid, certain ground when I move from truth to experience, and conversely, I am on uncertain ground when I move from experience to truth." [3]

We dare not, then, endorse the charismatic movement and ministry because of its phenomena, or even because of its good works. The question is, Does it do the will of the Father? Lest we too quickly reply, "Yes, for it is transcending denominational barriers in answer to Christ's prayer 'That they all may be one, Father,' " let us observe that the Bible speaks of a *false* ecumenism, a false transcending of barriers built on the foundation of truth. In preparation for Armageddon "spirits of devils working miracles" go forth unto the kings of the earth and the whole world (Rev. 16:14). What is their mission? To further the prestige of that false ecumenical movement that has "one mind" and gives its "power and strength" to the beast (chap. 17:13). "These," wrote John—in words "which God gave unto him, to shew unto his servants things which must shortly come to pass" (chap. 1:1)—"shall make war with the Lamb" (chap. 17:14). Those who are involved in the deceptions of this false religio-political system do not have their names written "in the book of life" (verse 8).

Paul warns of the antichrist, who "takes his seat in the temple of God." He is "produced by the spirit of evil and armed with all the force, wonders and signs that falsehood can devise. To those involved in this dying world he will come with evil's undiluted power to deceive" (2 Thess. 2:8, 9, Phillips). And why are some men susceptible to deception? Because "they have refused to love the truth which could have saved them. God sends upon them, therefore, the full force of evil's delusion, so that they put their faith in an utter fraud and meet the inevitable judgement of all who have refused to believe the truth and who have made evil their playfellow" (verses 10-12, Phillips).

Feelings, physical phenomena, charismatic manifestations—these are no sure sign of God's working!

Notice, for example, the similarity of the experience of Roger Alexander, the student from Michigan State who went to Notre Dame University to participate in a charismatic session and that which comes in spirit possession, as described in the spiritist textbook *Genuine Mediumship*.

Here is a portion of Roger's description:

"As they began to pray over me, a strange physical sensation started in my hands and feet and gradually spread over my whole body. It was like an electric current or as though the inside of my body were shaking against my skin."

From *Genuine Mediumship:*

"In entering the trance condition, your hands and body may twitch and jerk as if you were being subjected to a series of galvanic shocks. When the spirit power comes, there is manifested a peculiar jerking, twitching or vibrating of the hands and arms, sometimes extending to the whole body. . . ."

"When the spirit enters, in the arms are felt peculiar tingling, prickling sensations like needles and pins, sometimes akin to a current of electricity passing through from head to foot." [4]

Oral Roberts describes his sensations when the Spirit comes upon him:

"I felt physical contact with God's presence in my right hand. It was a tingling sensation like an electrical current. . . . I felt a strange and glorious sensation like an electrical current flowing through my hand. It seemed as if ten thousand volts of electricity surged through my body." [5]

Ellen White nearly a century ago wrote words of warning to Seventh-day Adventists:

"[Satan's] agents still claim to cure diseases. They attribute their power to electricity, magnetism [as hypnotism was called in her day], or the so-called 'sympathetic remedies.' In truth they are but channels for Satan's electric currents. By this means, he casts his spell over the bodies and souls of men." [6]

This is not to say that Roger Alexander and Oral Roberts are demon possessed. It is to say that one cannot on the basis of physical phenomena and charismatic manifestations determine *who* is working through a man. The testing question is, Does he do the will of the Father?

I often think, with affection, of my neighbors who attended those two churches in my hometown. I'll ever be a better man because of the moral principles taught by my scoutmaster, dogmatic though he might have been. And I still observe, from a distance, the quiet witness of Mr. and Mrs. Bell, members of the Pentecostal church there. Through the years neither has spoken in tongues. But both bear a much more persuasive testimony of God's presence in their lives, the fruits of the Spirit. Physical manifestations—shouting, jumping, ecstatic utterances—can be counterfeited; love, joy, peace, long-suffering, gentleness, goodness, faith, meekness, and temperance cannot.

Whether Charlie Bass ever got the "victory" over chewing tobacco, I don't know. But he and the Bells and my scoutmaster and Mrs. Cassels and all the rest inspired later study, which brought me to certain conclusions, among which is this: There is little to choose between a dogmatism that withers spiritual plants seeking root and an emotionalism that causes them to spring to full bloom in a night, only to topple of their own immature overbalance. When confronted with either dogmatism or emotionalism, I remember my hometown churches and am thankful for their lessons.

References

[1] Bernard Ramm, "Let God Be Your Compass," *His* magazine, June, 1969, p. 6.
[2] *Ibid.*, p. 8.
[3] *Ibid.*
[4] Vishita, Bhakta, Swami, *Genuine Mediumship*, Chas. T. Powner, Publisher, Chicago, 1941, p. 37.
[5] Oral Roberts, *Life Story*, p. 110.
[6] Ellen G. White, *Testimonies for the Church*, vol. 5, p. 193.

15
The Biblical Gift of Tongues Was ____

What was the Biblical gift of tongues? Few questions bring more contradictory replies from both theologians and lay Christians. Local congregations and denominations have split over the issue. Some Christians hold that tongues was the God-bestowed ability to speak foreign languages. Others believe instead that it was the gift of ecstatic utterance, with there being further division about whether this utterance was the language of heaven or simply ecstatic nonsense. Further to complicate the matter, some believe that a real foreign language was spoken on the day of Pentecost but that ecstatic utterance was spoken later in the Corinthian church.

"The human tongue is physically small, but what tremendous effects it can boast of!" wrote the apostle James (James 3:5, Phillips). He had in mind something other than glossolalia, or "tongue talk," as the expression can be translated literally. But the expressive tongues of Corinth and Pentecost can boast of tremendous effects—effects that reach across the centuries to touch our age.

One reputable twentieth-century Bible translator and theologian found a question about the tongues of Corinth so perplexing that he confessed to changing the intent of two verses of Paul's account in 1 Corinthians 14, saying that they simply could not mean what they seemed to mean! They must be, he thought, either a slip of the pen on the part of Paul, or, more probably, a copyist's error.[1]

Even the United States Government has become involved with tongues. In July, 1964, the U.S. Department of Health, Education, and Welfare announced that it had assigned a Federal research grant for a special psychological and linguistic study of the phenomenon. Recipient was Lutheran Medical Center in Brooklyn, New York, which assigned a professional team made up of two psychologists, a psychiatrist, and a linguist to the study.[2] Their findings were inconclusive.

We could make a nice contribution, then, to both church and state by settling what the Biblical gift of tongues was. I can understand why scholarly publications such as commentaries waffle on the answer; but this book is not a commentary, and I have no psychological needs that can be fulfilled only by the demonstrated ability to chart the taste buds on Biblical tongues. Adventist theologians and editors write with assurance on the doctrine of the Sabbath, the state of the dead, and even the esoteric fixtures of the heavenly sanctuary. Does not the church climate seem ready for a decisive definition, a simple declarative statement, such as "The Biblical gift of tongues was ———"?

A great deal *can* be said with assurance about tongues. To begin with, Christ promised the disciples that after His ascension they should expect a fuller outpouring of the Holy Spirit to empower them to witness for Him not only throughout the world but throughout all ages. (See Luke 24:46-49; John 14-16; Acts 1:4-8.)

At Pentecost the promised outpouring was accompanied by an associated phenomenon: The power to speak in unlearned foreign languages. Paul places the gift of tongues in listings of spiritual gifts given to the church by the Holy

Spirit. (See, for example, Ephesians 4:8, 11-16.) He expresses the will of God by saying, "Now concerning spiritual gifts, brethren, I would not have you ignorant" (1 Cor. 12:1).

The incident at Pentecost can be defined declaratively. Those tongues were foreign languages. Here is how Ellen White describes it in *The Acts of the Apostles:*

" 'There were dwelling at Jerusalem Jews, devout men, out of every nation under heaven.' During the dispersion, the Jews had been scattered to almost every part of the inhabited world, and in their exile they had learned to speak various languages. Many of these Jews were on this occasion in Jerusalem, attending the religious festivals then in progress. Every known tongue was represented by those assembled. This diversity of languages would have been a great hindrance to the proclamation of the gospel; God therefore in a miraculous manner supplied the deficiency of the apostles. The Holy Spirit did for them that which they could not have accomplished in a lifetime. They could now proclaim the truths of the gospel abroad, speaking with accuracy the languages of those for whom they were laboring. This miraculous gift was a strong evidence to the world that their commission bore the signet of Heaven. From this time forth the language of the disciples was pure, simple, and accurate, whether they spoke in their native tongue or in a foreign language. . . . Those who understood the different languages testified to the accuracy with which these languages were used by the disciples." [3]

Recognizing the gift at Pentecost to be a divinely endowed facility in foreign languages, we may assume that the same is true of the tongues of Acts 10. There Peter says he and his companions became convinced that God accepted Gentiles, when Cornelius and his household received the same gift as received by the apostles—that is, in Jerusalem on Pentecost.

Acts 19 records an experience at Ephesus involving about twelve men who had been baptized "unto John's baptism" (see verse 3). When Paul brought them added light on Christ's mission and the work of the Holy Spirit, they were baptized "in the name of the Lord Jesus" (see verse 5). Paul then "laid his hands upon them, the Holy Spirit came on them; and they spake with tongues, and prophesied" (verse 6). Nothing in either the language or the context indicates that these tongues differed from those of Pentecost.

The gift, as Ellen White puts it, enabled them "to speak the languages of other nations and to prophesy. Thus they were qualified to labor as missionaries in Ephesus and its vicinity and also to go forth to proclaim the gospel in Asia Minor." [4]

The book of Acts thus provides solid evidence of a gift of tongues through which the recipient was enabled to speak, for the purpose of proclaiming the gospel, languages he had not learned. The gift was needed by the infant church. Christian colleges and seminaries were not graduating scores of missionary linguists to take the Word to the nations of Asia Minor and elsewhere.

It is in Corinth that our problem of understanding begins, and simple declarative sentences lose their charm. It is hard, indeed, to give the "trumpet a certain sound" when the score itself seems to call either for two different songs or for the same song in two different keys. *The Seventh-day Adventist Bible Commentary* outlines the two positions generally taken on tongues in the Corinthian church:

1. "That the manifestation is to be described in terms of the phenomenon of tongues on the day of Pentecost (Acts 2); that the language spoken under the influence of the gift was a foreign language, one that could be easily understood by a foreigner of that tongue; that by speaking in a foreign tongue in the church when no one understanding the language was present the Corinthians were perverting the function of the gift; and that it was this misuse of the gift that Paul rebuked.

2. "That the manifestation was different from that on the day of Pentecost; that the language was not one spoken by men, and that thus no man could understand unless there was present an interpreter who possessed the gift of the Spirit to understand the language (1 Cor. 12:10); that its function was to confirm the faith of new converts (1 Cor. 14:22; cf. Acts

10:44-46; 11:15) and to provide personal spiritual edification (1 Cor. 14:4); that it was the exercise, in public assemblies, of this gift, designed primarily for private, personal edification, that Paul rebuked in 1 Cor. 14. Other views," the *Commentary* notes, "combine elements of these two views." [5]

If you were to talk to defenders of position number 1 you would find that a number of persuasive arguments leave little doubt that *they* are correct. If you were to talk to defenders of position number 2 you would find that a number of persuasive arguments leave little doubt that *they* are correct! Such confidence should be worth exploring at a little greater depth. Put on your thinking cap, secure your air hose, and prepare for descent into the theological cross currents of contrasting views.

Let us look first at ten arguments presented by those who believe that the tongues of 1 Corinthians 14 were foreign languages:

1. Fundamental to understanding the Biblical gift of tongues are principles of hermeneutics (the methodology of interpreting Scripture). First, we ought not to base a practice or teaching on any one passage of Scripture, especially when that passage is in any degree unclear within itself. Second, an unclear passage is interpreted by a clear passage. In Acts 2 the gift of tongues clearly is a divinely bestowed foreign language. 1 Corinthians 14, a passage with obscure elements, therefore must be interpreted by Acts, not Acts by Corinthians. Further, Paul obviously is dealing with the misuse of tongues in 1 Corinthians 14. He is addressing himself to a local church problem, not writing a manual on the use, or theology, of tongues.

2. The book of Acts was written some six years after the Corinthian letter. Had the gift of Pentecost differed from that of Corinth, we could have expected the writer to distinguish between the gifts. Paul himself moved on to Ephesus after 18 months with the Corinthians. We have concluded that the gift at Ephesus was foreign language. Because he does not distinguish between the two gifts, it is not unreasonable to assume that they were the same. Had tongues been ecstatic utterance anywhere, we could expect also a record of controversy between the intelligible and unintelligible tongues factions, and Jewish attacks on Christians for adopting, in ecstatic utterances, a well-known mark of heathenism.

3. Every New Testament passage dealing with "speaking in tongues" (Mark 16:17; Acts 2:4; 10:46; 19:6; 1 Cor. 12-14) uses the Greek word glossa for "tongue." An investigation of the term glossa throughout the New Testament shows that, aside from the above passages, it is used only for (1) the tongue as an organ of speech (Mark 7:33, 35; Luke 1:64; 16:24; Acts 2:26; Rom. 3:13; 14:11; Phil. 2:11; James 1:26; 3:5-8; 1 Peter 3:10; 1 John 3:18; Rev. 16:10), which evidently is not what is meant by "speaking in tongues," and for (2) an intelligible human language (Acts 1:19; 2:8, 11; 21:40; 22:2; 26:14; Rev. 5:9; 7:9, etc.). (In Acts 2:3 it is used to describe a shape.) It is most remarkable that in the known Greek texts outside the New Testament, even those that refer to pagan ecstatic experiences, there is no known instance in which the word glossa or "tongue" means ecstatic utterance or gibberish. Though in Greek usage glossa does, rarely, refer to "an obsolete or foreign word," this still is far different from ecstatic utterance. How could glossa mean ecstatic utterance, if this term is never so employed in the known texts that relate pagan experiences of ecstasy? Since Paul in 1 Corinthians 12-14 speaks of "tongues" by using the term glossa as his co-missionary Luke did in Acts when referring to speaking in "tongues," namely as known foreign languages (Acts 2:6, 8, 11), it is safe to conclude that Paul must have had the same thing in mind, especially since other Greek words were used in pagan texts for persons who spoke in a state of ecstasy, which Paul could have employed if he had had ecstatic utterance in mind.

4. Both the meager testimony of the early church fathers and the later testimony of the Reformers interpret the tongues of 1 Corinthians as languages. Only with the advent of theologians who did not believe God was able miraculously to provide knowledge of a foreign language, and the emergence of the modern tongues movement have some interpreters sought

scriptural validation for ecstatic utterances.

5. God works through man's intelligence and places a premium upon intelligible communication; thus for Him to inspire an unintelligible utterance through the Holy Spirit would be incompatible with His own nature. (See, for example, Isa. 1:18; Rom. 12:1; 1 Peter 1:13.) The tongues of Pentecost were intelligible languages given for the intelligent purpose of communicating the gospel.

6. 1 Corinthians 14 itself indicates that the gift was intelligible but being used wrongly. First, we are told that a man who speaks in tongues edifies himself. A man cannot be edified without comprehension. The speaker must, therefore, be conscious of what he is saying, though listeners may not be. Second, Paul refers to the "tongues" of ancient Assyria and Babylon (see verse 21, margin; Isa. 28:11, 12), the historical allusion establishing that his subject is real languages. Third, verse 22—"Wherefore tongues are for a sign, not to them that believe, but to them that believe not"—shows that these tongues are real languages, to be used to bring unbelievers to the truth. Paul cautions the Corinthians that they are not to use the gift unless the unbeliever knows the language, for they would think "ye are mad."

7. If we assume that 1 Corinthians 14 is speaking of ecstatic utterances, we are confronted with irreconcilable contradictions. For example, Paul's assurance that tongues are for nonbelievers (verse 22) becomes incompatible with what he has said previously. One translator, J. B. Phillips, here switches the negative and the positive, and adds a footnote admitting that he has departed from the Greek text! An interpretation that calls for altering the Greek text should not commend itself to Bible-respecting Christians.

8. The background of the Corinthians suggests the idea that pride in speaking foreign languages may have been their problem. The chief city of Greece in everything but education and a seaport, Corinth, thronged with visitors from many lands. Foreign tongues were common in its streets, and it is likely that many of its citizens, especially of the higher classes, were multilingual. Ability to converse in other tongues was a status symbol. It probably made the Corinthians feel less inferior to the large Roman colony there.

The Corinthian Christians were largely Gentiles and mostly lower class. The combination of class consciousness, their pagan background, and the all-too-human desire for status may have led them to abuse the gift of languages by using it in church meetings rather than among those to whom they should have been witnessing.

9. Paul's statement that the "manifestation of the Spirit is given to every man to profit for the common good" (1 Cor. 12:7), rules out using a gift for personal pleasure; since ecstatic utterance cannot profit others when used outside the church, where Paul implies the gift really belongs, ecstatic utterance cannot be a gift of the Spirit.

10. Even the casual reader will discern that Paul is censuring and correcting the Corinthian church for misusing a gift, rather than describing a new form of tongues differing from that bestowed in Jerusalem at the beginning. Consistent with this understanding is the spiritual condition of the Corinthian church: Believers were squabbling with each other, filled with envy and spiritual pride; indulging immorality and heresies, misusing the Lord's Supper, disregarding decorum—in general, acting like unreasoning children. Paul's primary concern is not with what the Holy Spirit has bestowed on the church, but with the way the Corinthians are abusing it. At Pentecost the gift of tongues was used correctly, to reach non-Christians with the message of Christ; at Corinth the same gift was used incorrectly, for personal worship and personal stature in the church service, where it could be understood only by a few or none, and hence could benefit no one but the speaker.

Does the case for tongues as a foreign language convince you? Then it might be well to read no further. I have sat in a courtroom and, after hearing one side of a case, wondered how any sane person could doubt the defendant's guilt, only to wonder, after hearing the other side, why the defendant ever was brought into court on such flimsy evidence. If you do agree that fairness demands hearing both sides, proceed—and with an open mind, please. (But not *too* open, lest evidence of merit trickle out before making an impression.)

To other equally able Bible students, tongues in the Corinthian church quite obviously could not be the gift mentioned in Acts 2, 10, and 19. They also begin with a statement of hermeneutics:

The first step toward an accurate understanding of 1 Corinthians 14 is to listen attentively to what Paul actually says —to understand each word according to the sense he intended it to convey; to determine the meaning of each statement in relation to its own immediate context, the chapter as a whole, and chapters 12 and 13 (Paul's introduction to chapter 14); and to trace the logical development of his argument. We must accord him fair opportunity to serve as his own interpreter before we conclude that what he wrote is not intelligible in its own right and turn elsewhere in Scripture for what we suppose to be a clearer explanation. As we thus permit Paul himself to tell us what he meant by what he wrote we should refrain from introducing conjectures of our own about the situation in the church at Corinth, or about what we imagine Paul or the Holy Spirit would or would not do. All such conjectures tend to read uninspired opinions into the inspired Word, and thereby contaminate it.

As a matter of fact no statement in 1 Corinthians 14 favors foreign languages over ecstatic speech.* Many statements would support either equally well. But certain categorical statements, taken as they read and in context, do favor the latter. These statements are six:

1. Paul's repeated emphasis on the superiority of the gift of prophecy and the inferiority of the gift of tongues (verses 1-5, 23-25, 39). Peter's sermon at Pentecost was prophetic in content and foreign language in form. The foreign-language tongues of Acts 2 were of utmost importance to the infant church; under the circumstances they were essential to the

---

* The expression is used here for lack of a better one. The reader will take care, however, to reserve judgment as to whether its use in this chapter equates with the modern phenomenon that goes by the same name.

proclamation of the gospel. If the tongues of 1 Corinthians 14 are, indeed, the same as those of Acts 2, why would Paul so severely depreciate them in contrast with the prophetic gift— placing them even below "helps"? Only if the tongues of 1 Corinthians 14 are of a different kind than those of Acts 2 does this difference in value make sense.

2. Repeated and unqualified statements that the "one who speaks in a tongue speaks not to men but to God" (verse 2), that he "edifies himself" (verse 4) while "the other man is not edified" (verse 17), and that he may "keep silence in church and speak to himself and to God" (verse 28). Understood at their face value and in context, these statements would be irrelevant and would have to be understood in an accommodated sense if the gift, here, consists of the ability to speak in foreign languages. In what way would a man be edified by speaking to himself in a language he did not understand? Furthermore, the foreign-languages tongues of Acts 2 were evangelistic in their objective. What evangelistic purpose could be served by a Corinthian Christian speaking to himself and to God in a foreign language he did not understand? Only if the tongues are ecstatic speech do these forthright statements, as they actually read, and in context, make sense. To dispose of them by the a priori judgment that what Paul really meant was that the tongues speaker speaks to himself and to God only because no one else understands him, is to read into Scripture something that is not already there.

3. Repeated statements, illustrations, and hypothetical situations emphasizing the fact that no one understands the tongues speaker (verses 2-12, 16-19, 23, 27, 28). Paul does not qualify any of these statements with an explanation or even a suggestion that the situation would have been different if representatives of certain foreign-language groups had been present in the church at Corinth. This suggestion also reads into the text something that is not there. His statements, as they read and in context, make sense only if the Corinthian tongues were something other than foreign languages.

4. The repeated and emphatic distinction between

pneuma *(spirit)* and nous *(mind)*, and between *unintelligible speech originating in the* pneuma *and intelligible speech originating in the* mous *(verses 3, 14-16, 19). Paul plainly states that the tongues speech to which he refers originates in the* pneuma *and not in the* nous, *which he says is "unfruitful" (unproductive) during tongues speech. Nothing in the text or context suggests Paul meant other than what he says.*

5. The musical-instrument illustrations (verses 7, 8) are directly apropos to language of the spirit but not foreign languages. In these illustrations unintelligibility resided in the instruments, not in the hearers. If the tongues thus illustrated were foreign languages, unintelligibility would reside in the receptor, not in the source of the sound. But if the tongues are language of the spirit the difficulty would reside in the source of the sound, and the illustrations would thus correspond exactly with the situation they were given to illustrate.

6. The statement concerning "many different languages in the world," in verses 10, 11, is clearly an illustration because Paul draws a lesson from it in verse 12. If the tongues of the chapter are, indeed, foreign languages, why would Paul illustrate foreign languages by foreign languages? That would be tautological. On the other hand, foreign languages might appropriately be used to illustrate ecstatic utterance.

Having ascertained as accurately as possible what Paul actually says in 1 Corinthians 14, let us inquire if other passages of Scripture can provide additional light on the subject. The only other passage that speaks specifically of the nature of the gift of tongues—Acts 2, which records the manifestation of the gift at Pentecost—explicitly identifies the tongues on that occasion as foreign languages. Can we conclude from this that the manifestation of the gift referred to in 1 Corinthians 14 was, likewise, foreign languages? A comparison of the two passages reveals certain similarities:

a. Both deal with a genuine gift of tongues, not a counterfeit.

b. Both use the same Greek words for "speak" and "tongues."

    c. Both refer to tongues as a sign to convince unbelievers of the presence and operation of the Holy Spirit. This sign value was effective in Acts, ineffective in Corinthians.

    d. In both, unbelievers react unfavorably—in Acts, in spite of the fact that they understand; in Corinthians, because they do not understand.

    e. Both mention the conversion of unbelievers—actual, in Acts; hypothetical in Corinthians.

    f. Both mention the prophetic gift as well as the gift of tongues.

    The differences between Acts 2 and 1 Corinthians 14 may be summarized as follows:

	Corinth (1 Corinthians 14)	Pentecost (Acts 2)
1. The speakers:	Laymen	The apostles
2. The hearers:	Primarily church members	Primarily unbelievers
3. Form:	Prayer, song, thanksgiving	Preaching
4. Function:	Devotional—pastoral	Evangelistic
5. Addressed to:	God	Men
6. Audibility:	Audible or inaudible	Audible
7. As languages:	Not referred to as such	Specifically said to be
8. Interpretation:	Required, to edify	Not required, to edify
9. Comprehension:	Hearers did not understand	Hearers understood
10. Content:	Devotional (song, prayer, gratitude)	Prophetic
11. As prophecy:	Distinct from	Equivalent to
12. Objective:	To express gratitude to God	To convert unbelievers
13. Result:	Unbelievers alienated	Unbelievers converted
14. Edification:	No	Yes
15. Sign value:	Ineffective	Effective
16. Importance:	Minor	Major

    Significant similarities without significant dissimilarities would be impressive evidence for the probability that the Corinthian tongues were, like those at Pentecost, foreign languages. But the much more numerous and fundamentally significant dissimilarities noted above preclude arguing that the tongues of 1 Corinthians 14 must be foreign languages because those of Acts 2 were foreign languages. Obviously, here, the usual rule that a clear passage (in this case, Acts 2) can be used to interpret an unclear passage (1 Corinthians 14), does not apply. Two of these dissimilarities argue decisively against identifying the tongues of 1 Corinthians 14 as foreign languages:

(1) The gift of tongues as Paul presents it in 1 Corinthians 14 is not a form of communication between man and man, but between man and God; the gift of prophecy is superior to the gift of tongues in that prophecy is a primary means for communicating divine truth among men, and for this reason it is to be earnestly desired. In Acts 2 the two gifts function as one; in 1 Corinthians they function independently of each other. In Acts 2 the gift of tongues is prophetic, in 1 Corinthians it is not. Only when the inarticulate syllables of tongues speech (as in 1 Corinthians 14) are interpreted, or explained, in intelligible language can tongues speech become the first step in a process for communicating spiritual truth between one person and another, and thus edify the hearer as well as the speaker. Even so, the tongue speech of 1 Corinthians 14 does not qualify as prophecy, as in Acts 2.

(2) The tongues speaking of which Paul writes in 1 Corinthians 14 had to be interpreted before it could edify the hearers, whereas the tongues of Acts 2 needed no interpretation (Acts 2:6). Those who heard the apostles speak on the day of Pentecost not only understood; they believed and were baptized that very day—three thousand of them—without an interpreter (Acts 2:6-8, 41). In striking contrast the tongues speaking in the church at Corinth could only convince unbelievers who chanced to be present that the believers were "mad" (1 Cor. 14:23). It required interpretation* before it could benefit anyone other than the speaker (verses 2, 6-11, cf. 17).

* Some argue a distinction between interpretation and translation, in both Greek and Hebrew. According to their view, a translator renders a foreign language into another language; an interpreter simply interprets the meaning of something. In interpreting tongues he tells their meaning; he does not translate from one language to another. Unfortunately for this theory, the linguistic distinction between interpretation and translation is not absolute; the words can have both meanings. If you are interested in the technicalities, see Appendix A.

5

The gift of tongues was manifested in the apostolic church under a variety of circumstances, no two of which were precisely alike, and it served a variety of purposes. There was no fixed pattern with respect to who spoke in tongues, their status with respect to baptism, the content of what was spoken, the immediate purpose of the gift, or the results. For these reasons the phenomena of one occasion cannot be considered normative for what took place on another occasion; the tongues of Acts 2 are not necessarily analogous with those of 1 Corinthians 14, and the nature of the gift could well have varied along with all of the other variables.

That the language of the spirit had, in fact, earned a legitimate place, along with foreign languages, as a valid manifestation of the gift, is evident from the above analysis of 1 Corinthians 14. As we have seen, a number of Paul's statements in that chapter must be explained away or interpreted in an accommodated sense if the Corinthian tongues were foreign languages. Such is not the case if the Corinthian tongues were ecstatic utterance; each and every statement can be taken precisely as it stands. Furthermore, since Paul makes no distinction between the Corinthian tongues and the genuine gift of which he approves, it is reasonable to conclude that the two were identical. The form of the gift is the same throughout the chapter, irrespective of whether reference is to the genuine gift of which Paul approves, or to the gift as manifested at Corinth, or to a hypothetical situation.

Accordingly, the error at Corinth consisted in wrong use of what was, in and of itself, genuine. The contrast in 1 Corinthians 14 is never between a true gift and a spurious gift, but between a right and a wrong use of a genuine gift. At no point does Paul criticize or condemn the Corinthian tongues per se, but only the way in which they were exercised. Paul approves a private exercise of the gift; he disapproves of a public use unless the tongues are translated—in order to edify the hearers as well as the speaker.

Bible scholars on the charismatic side of the courtroom conclude, then, that the tongues of 1 Corinthians 14 consisted of utterances in which individual believers vocalized deep feelings of gratitude for the blessings of salvation and love for their Lord in prayer, song, and thanksgiving. These utterances originated with the subconscious pneuma, *or inner being, without passing through the* nous *into conscious articulate expression. In effect, they consisted of subconscious, audible meditation on the goodness of God, and Paul accepted them as evidence of the inner response of the speaker to the operation of the Holy Spirit upon his heart. The problem at Corinth arose when this personal devotional exercise was introduced into public religious gatherings and tended to dominate them. It was valid for the speaker and edified him; it was not intelligible to the hearers and did not edify them—nor did it even have sign value. It was, nevertheless, a valid testimony to the experience of the speaker, and, if interpreted for the benefit of the hearers, given a minor role in the service and conducted in an orderly fashion, Paul had no objection to its public use. It was permitted; it was not encouraged.*

So there you have them, the two positions most generally taken on the tongues of Acts 2 and 1 Corinthians 14. The respective arguments might be expanded, emphasis applied differently, and further points introduced; but in essence the hardcore positions of the respective sides reduce to the above.

Is there, then, nothing more to be discovered about the Biblical gift of tongues? Must our simple declarative sentence, "The Biblical gift of tongues was ———," be left blank? And if it must, are we therefore left without criteria to identify the modern manifestations of tongues as Biblical or non-Biblical? In the face of neo-pentecostalism's rattling of the Adventist gate, its penetration of some 100 other denominations, its insistence that the baptism of the Holy Spirit is certified only by the gift of tongues and the miraculous manifestations that testify to a supernatural presence in the movement, the answers we must give are of no little significance.

To the first question, What was the Biblical gift of tongues? I wish I could answer simply, It was the divinely bestowed gift of foreign languages. The theology of tongues is so much more tidy, and understandable, when pigeonholed under one gift rather than under two. And if language was the gift, the manifestations of our day can be rebuked with even greater ease, as we shall see in the next chapter.

But despite the factors that predispose me to look longingly to language for the answer, too many verses of chapter 14 have to be explained at too great length for me to feel comfortable with that answer. On the other hand, I feel uncomfortable also with the ecstatic gibberish of today's tongues movement, for reasons I shall make clear.

I have not found a linguistic analysis of chapter 14 to be particularly helpful. (It does make some seemingly simple answers appear even more simple!) I have a friend, a Greek scholar, who tells me that for years he taught that chapter 14 was best explained on the basis of misused foreign languages; after a careful—and, it is presumed, scholarly—linguistic analysis, he changed his position, and now is teaching that chapter 14 is best explained on the basis of ecstatic utterance. I would be more impressed if I did not have another friend, a Greek scholar, who tells me that for years he taught that chapter 14 was best explained on the basis of ecstatic utterance; after a careful—and, it is to be presumed, scholarly—linguistic analysis, he changed his position, and now is teaching . . . yes, you guessed the answer: misused foreign languages!

In my less restrained moments and, I suppose, contrary to sound exegesis, I have simply tried to place myself in Paul's place and have asked, What would I have said, had the problem been misused foreign languages in Corinth? I can tell you how I would have concluded chapter 14: "Look, you Corinthian Christians were given this gift not to astound your fellow Christians with your Spirit-bestowed erudition, but to preach the gospel. Go to it! If you have been given the ability to speak Egyptian, head for Alexandria. If you can speak Chinese, let not another man of Cathay die before you hit the road." But no, Paul says simply, "Forbid not to speak in tongues"—and he makes that concession after having reduced the gift to one of the least bestowed by the Holy Spirit. If you must use tongues in the church, he adds, be sure that what you say is interpreted.

To be fair, one possibility would make my suggested conclusion irrational, even if the Corinthians were abusing the gift of foreign languages: if they were misusing the gift *only in the church,* while using it in its God-ordained manner without. Though Paul has written many things "hard to be understood," as Peter lamented, he shows no evidence of irrationality; the answer, therefore, must be that the Corinthians were using foreign languages for their intended purpose outside the church, or that the problem in Corinth was something else entirely. In either case, Paul has an answer that speaks to us across the centuries: When confronted with a difficult church problem, one that threatens the unity of the church, meet it in the context of the superiority of love.

Confessing that we (I use "we" here in pious confidence that there are other honest souls!) do not know precisely what tongues was in the Corinthian church is far from saying that we are left without criteria by which to identify modern tongues as Biblical or non-Biblical. The counsel Paul gives to the Corinthians goes a long way toward invalidating most of what today passes for tongues. Other principles of Scripture combine to make us wholesomely suspicious not only of modern tongues but of the modern tongues movement. For it is not without significance, I believe, that tongues today spring from polluted theological wells. Before finishing this book you will find that no Biblical basis exists for asserting that tongues are *the* evidence of the baptism of the Holy Spirit, as classical pentecostalism teaches. Also un-Biblical is the holiness theology of sanctification that points to a second work of grace. And the pentecostal movement itself has a history of opposition to the law of God; it has rejoiced in release from divinely imposed inhibitions, exalted feeling above reason and experience above Scripture. Further, it utilizes grossly unscriptural methods of inducing speaking in tongues, which in its modern manifestation is not a language, either of men or of angels, as we shall see. All the above add up to persuasive reasons for questioning both the modern tongues phenomenon and the movement for which it speaks, even without having learned for a certainty just what happened in Corinth.

Whatever their problem, the Corinthian church was precious to Paul, who had established it during his second missionary journey (Acts 18:1-18). For 18 months he had labored, leaving a church that quickly succumbed to numerous moral and spiritual problems, about which he learned from the household of Chloe (1 Cor. 1:11), a letter the church wrote him (chap. 7:1), and personal visits by some Corinthian believers (chap. 16:17). From Ephesus, during his third journey, Paul wrote to correct the situation.

That the Corinthian Christians were confused not only about tongues but about spiritual gifts in general is evident from Paul's counsel to them: "About gifts of the spirit, there are some things of which I do not wish you to remain ignorant" (1 Cor. 12:1, N.E.B.). With tender concern for his spiritual children, Paul affirms that gifts of the Spirit are bestowed to edify the body of Christ. He speaks of the unity of the body and of the importance of the members to the body and to one another. Then comes the deeply sensitive and perceptive chapter on love, which assumes greater significance when read in the context of the misuse of tongues. The apostle exalts the supremacy of love, delicately suggests the need for spiritual maturity, and lays down rules for decency and order in corporate worship.

To correct the misconceptions of the Corinthian church, Paul exalts the gifts related closely to natural talents, while placing tongues, one of the miraculous manifestations, near the bottom of the list—(1) wisdom, (2) knowledge, (3) faith, (4) healing, (5) miracles, (6) prophecy, (7) discerning of spirits, (8) tongues, (9) interpretation (1 Cor. 12:8-10).

Again, in verses 28-30, he enumerates gifts, tongues again trailing—(1) apostles, (2) prophets, (3) teachers, (4) miracles, (5) healing, (6) helps, (7) governments, (8) tongues, (9) interpretation. Other lists bring the total gifts to sixteen or more.

Are all in the church to expect a gift?—a question of significance in light of Pentecostal insistence that all who have been baptized by the Holy Spirit will speak in tongues. Says Paul:

"In each of us the Spirit is manifested in one particular way, for some useful purpose. [In passing, don't miss that "useful purpose"; it is one useful test that can be brought to bear on modern tongues.] One man, through the Spirit, has the gift of speech, while another, by the power of the same Spirit, can put the deepest knowledge into words. Another, by the same Spirit, is granted faith; another, by the one Spirit, gifts of healing, and another miraculous powers; another has the gift of prophecy, and another ability to distinguish true spirits from false; yet another has the gift of ecstatic utterance of different kinds [the Greek reads only "tongues"; "ecstatic" is supplied here, as is "unknown" in the K.J.V.], and another the ability to interpret it. But all these gifts are the work of one and the same Spirit, distributing them *separately to each individual at will*" (1 Cor. 12:7-11, N.E.B.).

The apostle drives the point home, as if he had anticipated the pentecostal error:

"Are all apostles? all prophets? all teachers? Do all work miracles? Have all gifts of healing? Do all speak in tongues of ecstasy? Can all interpret them?" (verses 29, 30, N.E.B.) Paul's conclusion is obvious: No! "The higher gifts [which do not include tongues] are those you should aim at," he concludes (verse 31, N.E.B.).

Because not everyone receives the same gift, all of which, collectively, are as necessary to the whole church as organs are to the whole man, all church members must share their gifts, without any member either despising or envying another with a different gift. One has no more reason to take spiritual pride in expounding God's Word than in speaking in tongues—if one ever were justified in taking pride in spiritual gifts. Unity of the church must take priority over the exercise of any gift, the apostle stresses. In fact, the gifts are to be used to promote the unity of the church (see Eph. 4:11-14), which fact should haunt members who have fragmented congregations with their insistence that all must speak in tongues, if they are baptized by the Holy Spirit.

Any gift, though good in itself, can be abused, the apostle seems to tell us; any doctrine can be emphasized out of proportion to its place in the gospel. Teachings of secondary importance can be elevated to testing truths, and Christians who do not subscribe to the favored emphasis can be stigmatized as second-class saints. Such has happened to tongues, with a number of denominations finding in this gift not only their credentials as instruments of God but also their very reason for being. What they call the "full gospel" is shown by Paul to be a distorted gospel, twisted out of shape by misplaced emphasis on gifts. Paul chides the Corinthians for their pride in tongues. He sees spiritual vanity destroying the purpose of any charisma. He questions whether tongues is in reality the sign of a deep religious experience—as in our day it is often assumed to be—or a mature spiritual life, or a morally responsible church. "Do not be children in your thinking" (1 Cor. 14:20, R.S.V.) he tells them. "My brothers, don't be like excitable children but use your intelligence" (Phillips). What a rebuke to a church that considered itself elitist because of spiritual gifts! Not charismatic gifts but true piety—lives producing the fruit of the Spirit—is yet the most persuasive evidence of discipleship.

There is something that means even more than having a gift, Paul emphasizes: Having love. Returning to a prior theme in his letter (chap. 8:1), he speaks of a "better way." No gifts from God, no deeds for Christ, not even martyrdom for His sake, are of value without love. A member of the church who could speak in tongues (a little gift, 1 Cor. 13:1-3), or prophesy (a big gift, Gal. 5:22), was counted as nothing, if he lacked love. Says the apostle, "Though I speak with the tongues of men and of angels. . . . And though I have the gift of prophecy, and understand all mysteries, and all knowledge; and though I have all faith, so that I could remove mountains, and have not charity [love], I am nothing" (chap. 13:1, 2)— zero, utterly without value in the body of Christ. Tongues, prophecy, knowledge—all gifts—would pass away, but love would last forever. "Make love your aim," he says, "and earnestly desire the spiritual gifts, especially that you may prophesy" (1 Cor. 14:1, R.S.V.). He thus in one sentence both summarizes his counsel on love and introduces his counsel on the use of tongues in the Corinthian church.

The primary concern of Paul in 1 Corinthians 14 is the use the Corinthians are making of tongues *in the church*. His testing question is, Does this use of tongues build up the church? Nothing the church does, he makes plain, is to violate the principles of love and church unity; nor is divine and church authority to be flouted. To understand these points is to understand a great deal about the tongues problem of Paul's day and about the tongues problem in our own day; and to follow this counsel is to settle the tongues problem, whatever it was in Corinth, whatever it is today. For when love rules the life, when unity of the body of Christ is one's first concern, when divine and church authority are respected, tongues, whether the physical organ or the gift, whether foreign language or language of the soul, are tamed.

What can we conclude from 1 Corinthians 14? The Ad Hoc Committee on the Charismatic Movement, a group set up in 1972 by the officers of the General Conference of Seventh-day Adventists, reported in February, 1973, an "overview" on which some 24 Adventist New Testament Bible scholars and other specialists in the charismatic were agreed. Few Adventists would digress from their consensus:

"1 Corinthians 14:1-5. Those in the church who made love their aim would be led to re-evaluate spiritual gifts, especially the use that was made of tongues in Corinth; and this re-evaluation based on the matter of usefulness for the church would cause them to elevate prophecy and put tongues in its proper and respective place. Though not denying the edification of the individual, the edification of the church was the dominating principle.

"1 Corinthians 14:6-12. Paul counseled: In the use of tongues or prophecy (as spiritual gifts) in the congregation,

The Ad Hoc Committee on the Charismatic
Movement met under the chairmanship of N. R. Dower,
secretary of the Ministerial Department,
General Conference of Seventh-day Adventists.

PHOTOS BY THE AUTHOR

Two of the committee members, Fred Veltman
of Pacific Union College and V. Norskov Olsen of
Loma Linda University.

aim at edifying the church. In relation to corporate worship, any utterance is useless for the upbuilding of the church unless it is meaningful. Strive to excel in building up the church.

"*1 Corinthians 14:13-19.* Corporate worship has a horizontal as well as a vertical dimension—we meet with others in the worship of God because of this fact. We need to enlighten, to encourage and strengthen one another. And this social side of worship was neglected by the tongues-speaker, who thought only of himself. In corporate worship, edification was to be dependent upon understanding. The intelligible aspect of public worship was stressed to the point of exclusion of the unintelligible—this called for the use of the mind in this meaningful worship.

"*1 Corinthians 14:20-25.* Paul now made an appeal to the Corinthians to be mature in thinking. Just as prophecy had a sign value for the believer, so tongues had sign value for the unbeliever. What impression would be made, Paul asked, if all were to speak in tongues at the same time in the church and a nonbeliever were to come into the congregation? The principle enunciated was that there could be no conversion of an individual or building up of the church unless there were first intelligible communication.

"*1 Corinthians 14:26-33.* The guidelines for the use of both prophecy and tongues in the assembly were summed up in the principle of the edification of the church. If any were to speak in a tongue, this was to be done in turn and, at most, by three; and it was to be followed by 'interpretation' (translation). [Here the report had the following footnote: In the absence of interpretation, the tongues-speaker was to be silent (verse 28).] Two or three prophets were also permitted to speak, again in turn, while the others remained silent and weighed what was said. For God is not the author of confusion, Paul argued, but of peace and order.

"*1 Corinthians 14:34-36.* Women were, in some way not explained to us, involved in the misuse of tongues in the Corinthian church. This text must not be construed to mean that women must not speak in church, as Paul had already recognized such a practice in chapter 11, verse 5.

"1 Corinthians 14:37, 38. Paul's instruction regarding the use of tongues was to be accepted with the same authority as the words of Christ.

"1 Corinthians 14:39, 40. 'So, my brethren, earnestly desire to prophesy, and do not forbid speaking in tongues; but all things should be done decently and in order' (R.S.V.). Paul here added to the concept of edification of the church the concept that all things were to be done decently and in order.

"In this way Paul rounded out his counsel regarding the problem of tongues in the Corinthian church.

"Summary of General Principles

"From our study we have particularly learned:

"1. In Acts, tongues (i.e., speaking in previously unlearned but known languages) was a means of communicating the gospel and a sign to those unbelievers who accepted the gospel that God was active in Christ's disciples. It was thus a means of building up the church by adding new believers.

"2. In Acts, the majority of narratives recording the outpouring of the Holy Spirit contain no mention of a corresponding manifestation of speaking in tongues.

"3. Maturity, self-control and self-discipline should be exercised in the use of gifts.

"4. Order and decency must be maintained in the exercise of spiritual gifts.

"5. Spiritual gifts must enhance the unity of the church.

"6. Spiritual gifts should edify the church, not just one's self.

"7. One person may have more than one gift.

"8. Many persons may have the same gift.

"9. Love surpasses all spiritual gifts.

"10. All should desire spiritual gifts, and especially the greater gifts.

"11. In the church, speaking in tongues should not only be intelligible but also intelligent in content; thus there is an emphasis not only on clarity of words but also on significance of thought.

"12. Speaking in tongues is under the control of the individual.

"13. Speaking in tongues is only one of the gifts.

"14. Personal experience, spiritual gifts, and the results of these gifts must be tested by the Word of God.

"15. If one has a true gift of the Spirit, he will also manifest the fruit of the Spirit—especially love." [6]

Of course we are left with questions. But since when has mature faith, on which not only Paul but all Scripture places such a premium, demanded answers to everything?

References
[1] J. B. Phillips, *The New Testament in Modern English,* p. 373.
[2] Religious News Service, July 17, 1964, p. 13.
[3] Ellen G. White, *The Acts of the Apostles* (Mountain View, California: Pacific Press Publishing Association), pp. 39, 40.
[4] *Ibid.,* p. 283.
[5] *The SDA Bible Commentary,* additional note on 1 Corinthians 14, p. 795.
[6] The report was accepted by the officers of the General Conference on Feb. 14, 1973.

16
Silly Syllables or Inspired Utterance?

One evening in their French-style mansion in Hollywood, Pat Boone's wife, Shirley, was praying in tongues, a "gift" that had been given her some days previously.

Pat interrupted her. " 'Shirley, can you say that again?'

" 'What, Pat?'

" 'Were you praying in tongues, honey?'

"Shirley answered, 'Yes, I was, did you hear me?'

" 'Please try to say it again—what you just said.' Then Shirley started again and Pat stopped her.

" 'Say it slower, honey.' She slowed down and prayed with the Spirit again and then again.

" 'Shirley—do you know what you're saying?' For all of his four years in high school Pat had selected Latin for his language credits. God had seen to it. Pat knew his wife never spoke nor understood a single word of Latin, but now Shirley was praising the Lord of Heaven in beautiful, flawless *Latin*—magnifying God!" [1]

The incident happened at a critical time in Pat Boone's career, which was floundering. His good-guy image just didn't fit the sexy-movie mold. Television network shows were looking elsewhere. His finances were shaky. And to top all, his church was suggesting he take his membership elsewhere, for his activities with charismatic groups did not fit its concept of discipleship. Rather than yield to discouragement, Pat looked for God's hand in the circumstances.

"Listen, George," he said to a friend, George Otis, on the telephone, "I think I may be ready. Could we get together somewhere to study about the Holy Spirit?"

They could and did, at George's home. George had already received the baptism of the Holy Spirit and had spoken in tongues. After a period of Bible study that night, Pat asked God to baptize him with the Holy Spirit and to give him a new prayer language. He waited. Nothing happened.

Says Otis: "Maybe forty seconds had gone by when a thought came to me—an unusual one. Was it coming from that still small voice? I waited and prayed, trying to test it in my heart. It persisted, so I got up and walked to his chair. I said quietly with one hand on his shoulder, 'Pat, why don't you raise your hands and just sing to Jesus—but not in English?' Never had I thought about anyone *singing* with the Spirit as I had prayed with others before for the baptism.

"Immediately it started! No one ever heard this singer pour out such a song! The melody was intricate, exquisite, soaring, and then fluttering down and around. The words were distinct, and they seemed to fit perfectly with the melody. It went on and on, and now he was quietly walking with his hands lifted. Back and forth across the room. How I would like to be able to play that song back again! I know it pierced the ceiling shooting heavenward to bring fragrance and delight to his Heavenly Father. There was a sense of praise, adoration, worship, of magnifying God. The deep of his spirit was calling to the deep in God's great heart!" [2]

Praying in Latin . . . singing in tongues . . . tongues at a Catholic charismatic meeting and the Phoenix meeting of the Full Gospel Business Men's Fellowship International. . . .

"Coopa shunda la-la-ba sigh-ah. . . . O coola ma-shunda, la munda caw sunda . . ."

Foreign language? The language of heaven? Babbling or gibberish? Most pentecostals would answer that tongues is one of the first two, either a foreign language unknown to the speaker or the language by which the Holy Spirit communicates with the Father and the Son and, it is to be supposed, the angels. Writes Dr. Howard M. Ervin, dean and professor of Old Testament at the Graduate School of Theology, Oral Roberts University, Tulsa, Oklahoma:

"When we speak our native tongue, we speak the words that are in our minds, words that in choice, inflection, nuance, and color manifest our personalities. When we speak in 'tongues, as the Holy Spirit gives utterance,' we speak those words that are in the mind of the Spirit, words that manifest his personality unfettered by the censorship of the human ego. These words are, therefore, an exquisitely personal self-manifestation of the Holy Spirit." [3]

It matters a great deal, Dr. Ervin believes, that tongues be language.

"The biblical writers understood these utterances to be bona fide languages. At Pentecost believers spoke the 'dialects' of the assembled multitude (Acts 2:6). The Corinthians spoke 'families of languages' (1 Cor. 12:10), expressly defined as 'the languages of men and of angels' (1 Cor. 13:1). The 'other tongues' at Pentecost were unknown to the speakers but intelligible to those who spoke those particular dialects (Acts 2:11). In the assembly at Corinth, the tongues, whether of men or angels, were unintelligible until interpreted by their Divine Author (1 Cor. 14:13, 27)." [4]

Adds Dr. Ervin:

" 'Babbling' is indefensible in any context, whether private devotions or corporate worship. If tongues are merely 'ecstatic babbling,' they are totally irrelevant to Christian worship. There can then be no legitimate concern for their regulation and use in the congregation." [5] Dr. Ervin's conviction is unequivocal: Tongues must be a language. Are they?

Many modern tongues speakers believe so. Eighty-three per cent of glossolalists who responded to a questionnaire by an internationally known linguist believed they were speaking in a foreign tongue.[6] Publications of the movement seek to document instances of speech in an identified language. Says an article in the January, 1973, *New Covenant:*

"The many testimonies to identified tongues that we have received span the world. They have been living languages as well as languages no people has spoken for centuries. Sometimes the whole message in tongues was in a specific language: sometimes there was a sentence or two in the midst of a message, as though for the one or two people there who would be able to recognize it. The Spirit of God is not limited in his power to time, place, or culture: his work is to draw the entire world under the Lordship of Jesus."[7]

Among the testimonies recounted in the *New Covenant* are the following:

★ An Irish priest who had been a missionary in Nigeria was walking back to the dormitory at the Maryhill School in Cochabamba, Bolivia, one night in January, 1971. In the darkness he heard a priest from the United States pacing the patio, praying in the gift of tongues he had received earlier that evening. He was praying in perfect Yoruba, a language of Nigeria, as the priest from there was able to recognize.[8]

★ Ray Bringham and other American neo-pentecostal leaders were present at an ecumenical conference to introduce Spanish Catholics to the charismatic renewal. When Father Roman Carter, a Dominican priest stationed in Avila, heard Ray praying in Portuguese, a language that Father Carter knew but Ray did not, Father Carter decided to be baptized in the Spirit.[9]

★ Maria von Trapp of the Trapp Family Singers, is a missionary in New Guinea. Home on leave, she reported to *New Covenant* on her baptism in the Holy Spirit:

"For me it was a rather quiet experience with no strong emotional effects. Over a period of time I gradually began to feel much closer to the Lord. Speaking in tongues really helped in this, although at first I thought that I just had a few silly syllables and was not confident it really was from the Lord. But one night when I was babysitting . . . a stream of Chinese sounding syllables began to come and convince me that it was from the Lord." [10]

★ A Filipino sister was visiting a prayer group in Canada. In the middle of a long message in another tongue, she heard a sentence in her own language meaning "Build up the Church."

★ A priest who had spent ten years in Uganda, working with Teso-speaking people, heard a Canadian woman repeat a number of times a phrase in Teso meaning "Thank you for what you do." The incident resolved doubts and hesitations he had had.

★ A man doing research on African literature was staying with a Swedish-American, who always began prayer in tongues with the same phrase. The researcher came to know the phrase by heart, inflection and rhythm as well as sounds. Then he came upon it in his studies—the identical words, inflection and rhythm—in a classic Zulu epic poem of the early nineteenth century, describing a great warrior-king. Its meaning: "He who can strike a blow, but no man can attack." [11]

★ In one Michigan prayer meeting a young woman gave a message in tongues, and a pentecostal minister interpreted. A listener testified that the interpretation was nearly a word-for-word translation of the message, which was in the Greek-Aramaic dialect spoken in Palestine in the first century. "Several instances of classical Hebrew excerpts from the psalms praising the Lord for his goodness or calling his people to trust in him were recognized as such and the interpretations verified by persons present who had a good knowledge of Hebrew." [12]

In a book on the Indonesian revival of 1966-1967, Mel Tari, a former youth evangelist on Timor, tells of the Spirit falling on his home church congregation:

The woman in front of Mel was "an illiterate person and didn't even know our official Indonesian language that is used all over our country. She knew only her tribal language, which is Timorese. Naturally she didn't know any English. At that time, however, I knew a little English because I had studied it in school. And this lady began to pray out loud in beautiful perfect English.

" 'Oh, Jesus, I love You,' she said. 'Oh, I want to take the cross and follow You. Oh, I love You, Jesus,' and she just went on and on worshiping the Lord. . . .

"Then a man on the other side of the church began to pray in German. He stood there, and the words of worship and praise to the Lord were just beautiful. After that, people started to stand all over the church, worshiping the Lord in different languages.

"Heaven came down that night, and it was wonderful. Some were speaking in French. Some were praising God in different tribal languages. And one lady kept saying, 'Shalom, Shalom,' even though she had no idea she was speaking Hebrew." [13]

"Alos ben-e-maw ca-shata. Belongo be-sigha ca-shunda absirda. Maw lingo paterna o-lana paw-saw-da . . ."

Hundreds of alleged incidents of actual languages could be cited, and, as we noted, a leading tongues theologian, Dr. Howard Ervin, says that it matters very much that tongues actually be languages. Are we ready, then, to conclude that modern tongues speaking meets Dr. Ervin's test of authenticity?

Hardly. During the past few years hundreds of tapes of alleged languages spoken in tongues have been studied by linguists, among them such internationally known experts as Dr. William J. Samarin, professor of anthropology and linguistics at the University of Toronto; Dr. William Welmers, professor of African Languages at UCLA; Dr. Eugene Nida, of the American Bible Society. *In not one case has the taped sample proved to be a foreign language or even a language at all!*

Says Dr. Samarin in *Tongues of Men and Angels:* "There is no mystery about glossolalia. They always turn out to be the same thing, strings of syllables, made up of sounds taken from among all those that the speaker knows, put together more or less haphazardly but which nevertheless emerge as word-like and sentence-like units because of realistic, language-like rhythm and melody. Glossolalia is indeed like language in some ways, but this is only because the speaker (unconsciously) wants it to be like language. Yet in spite of superficial similarities, glossolalia is fundamentally *not* language. All specimens of glossolalia that have ever been studied have produced no features that would even suggest that they reflect some kind of communicative system." [14] *

Professor Samarin's research is based on studies of tongues used in pentecostal meetings in Europe and North America, among people from different social classes and speaking different languages. His book includes scores of samples taken from tapes and elsewhere. "In construction as well as function," he says, "glossas are fundamentally different from languages." [15]

But what of the classical Latin of Shirley Boone?

"It is extremely doubtful that . . . alleged xenoglossia [speech in a real, but unlearned, human language] are real," Samarin maintains. "Any time one attempts to verify them he finds that the stories have been greatly distorted or that the 'witnesses' turn out to be incompetent or unreliable from a linguistic point of view.† . . .

"A case of xenoglossia could be proven real only if, on the

---

* The alliteration and repetition that give tongues their rhythmic quality come through clearly in samples cited by George Barton Cutten in *Speaking in Tongues:*
"Prou pray praddy"
"Pa palassate pa pau pu pe"
"Heli terratte taw"
"Terrei te te-te-te"
"Vole virte vum"
"Elee lete leele luto"
"Sine sirge singe"
"Imba imba imba"
(George Barton Cutten, *Speaking in Tongues* [New Haven: Yale University Press, 1927], p. 174 ff.)

† Professor Samarin cites examples. See pages 103-128 of his book. He disagrees with Sherrill's book *They Speak With Other Tongues,* frequently cited by laymen, as having proved the contrary. All Sherrill did, according to Samarin, was to play some tape recordings to a group of people to see if they could identify any languages in the texts. He reports: ". . . although no language known to these men was recorded, they had frequently identified language *patterns* on the tapes." Professor Samarin finds glossas to be different in both construction and function from real languages.

one hand, it were demonstrated that the speaker could not possibly have learned the language in any normal way and, on the other hand, that the language spoken was incontestably a real one. Fulfilling these requirements is difficult, hence the number of cases of xenoglossia is negligible or nil, depending on how much credibility one attributes to the investigations." [16]

Other linguistic scholars concur with Samarin's view. William Welmers, professor of African Languages at UCLA, places modern tongues speakers in two categories: Those who "believe they are speaking in some real, existing human language," and those who believe they speak in a "real human language that no longer exists"—or, possibly, in one that does not yet exist. He does not rule out the possibility that such incidents did occur in the Corinthian church:

"Perhaps some of the Corinthian believers spoke in, let us say, the then current form of Egyptian; in Corinth, it might have been impossible to find a person who could interpret on the basis of this normal competence. That would almost surely be true if one of the believers spoke the first-century form of Chinese, and it would have to be true if he spoke ancient Sumerian, which was a dead language by that time. In such cases, however, someone with the competence of a number of modern linguists would quite quickly have been able to identify the language. *It can confidently be said that no such identification has been made, or is possible, in the case of contemporary glossolalic utterance.*" (Italics added.) [17]

How can linguists be so sure? After all, they have not heard every language in the world. "True," concedes Dr. Welmers, "but among the Christian linguists who have been asked to listen to tape recorded samples of contemporary glossolalia, experience in several hundred of the world's three to four thousand languages is brought to bear on the subject, and this experience involves virtually every group of related languages in the world, though we may have missed a very few small groups in the interior of South America or New Guinea. Although I myself have studied only a small number of utterances, others have studied scores or even hundreds. If these utterances are in real human languages, certainly by this time at least a few of them would have cropped up here and there which were identifiable by one of us. . . . To date, no linguist has identified any glossolalic utterance as any real human language, whether existing today, in the past, or in the future." [18]

But what of Dr. Ervin's belief that tongues are words "in the mind of the Spirit, words that manifest his personality unfettered by the censorship of the human ego"? Words, therefore, that are "an exquisitely personal self-manifestation of the Holy Spirit"?

Dr. Welmers is unimpressed.

"Even a 'heavenly language,' if it is translatable, must show something of the characteristics of language as we know it. God is not irrational, and human language exists simply because we are created in God's image." [19] Comparing a glossolalic utterance with its interpretation, Dr. Welmers found only "irrationality." [20]

A federally financed report on tongues* noted: "There was no similarity in the interpretation of the various 'interpreters.' One interpreter said the tongues-speaker was praying for the health of his children; another interpreter would report the same speech to be an expression of gratitude to God for a recently successful church fund-raising effort. The most common interpretations were general statements that the speaker was thanking and praising God for many blessings." [21]

On another count also, Dr. Welmers faults the idea that tongues is a heavenly language: Its poverty in the characteristics that make a language rich. Samples invariably reveal syllable structure and sequences more elementary and restricted than in English. "I would," he says, "certainly expect far more—more by way of variety, originality, and interest—from a 'heavenly language'; and one can readily find much more in any earthly language." [22]

Eugene Nida, a world-renowned expert on linguistics,

* See chapter 5, p. 54.

studied a recording of alleged glossolalia and concluded certain elements of true language are missing.

"The types of inventory and distributions would indicate clearly that this recording bears no resemblance to any actual language which has ever been treated by linguistics. . . . If then, it is not a human language, what is it? One can only say that it is a form of 'ecstatic speech.' . . . On the basis of what I have learned about this type of phenomena of 'tongues' in other parts of the world, apparently there is the same tendency to employ one's own inventory of sounds, in nonsense combinations, but with simulated 'foreign' features. At least in West Africa and Latin America, the types of glossolalia employed seemed to fit into this description." [23]

Stuart Bergsma reports: "Mosiman studied many such supposed cases and found not one to be authentic. Robert L. Dean, a contemporary psychologist, comes to the same conclusion." [24]

Says Father Kilian McDonnell, a Catholic theologian and scientist who has studied the charismatic movement for four years with a team of anthropologists:

"Pentecostals claim that competent linguists have recognized languages spoken in meetings, but most scientists would lay this recognition to psychological factors." [25]

In more than twenty years of investigating the tongues movement I have never heard tongues that appeared to be other than a collection of manufactured words drawn from the speaker's reservoir of sounds. Once one gets the hang of it, tongues of the manufactured variety are not difficult to produce. For example, the preceding sample—*Alos ben-e-maw cashata. Belongo be-sigha ca-shunda absirda. Maw lingo paterna o-lana paw-saw-da*—is my own creation, spoken while writing this chapter. If my status among Adventists depended on my speaking in such tongues, I am quite sure I could develop an impressive patter with a minimum of practice. Of course, I do not believe that what I have produced either was motivated by the Holy Spirit or is similar to what the disciples spoke at Pentecost. I do believe, however, that it is intrinsically the same product as that called tongues within both classic pentecostalism and the neo-pentecostal movement.

It is interesting and perhaps quite significant that most modern tongues speakers exercise their "gift" only after instruction—instruction, as I have personally observed, often given in the context of dominating psychological pressure. I find it difficult, if not impossible, to conceive of Dr. Ervin's concept of true tongues resulting from any of the following three examples of instructions. The fact that virtually all tongues speakers either are "coached" or have heard others speak in tongues is in itself ground for suspicion that we are not dealing with the language of angels.

Larry Christenson, an American Lutheran minister and tongues enthusiast, gives the following directions on how to speak in tongues:

"In order to speak in tongues you have to quit praying in English. . . . You simply lapse into silence and resolve to speak not a syllable of any language you have ever heard. Your thoughts are focused on Christ, and then you simply lift up your voice and speak out confidently, in the faith that the Lord will take the sound you give him, and shape it into a language. You take no thought of what you are saying: as far as you are concerned, it is just a series of sounds. The first sounds will sound strange and unnatural to your ear, and they may be halting and inarticulate (have you ever heard a baby learning to talk?)." [26]

A "Praise Sheet" circulated by a pentecostal group, the Rainbow Revival, gave the following directions to those "seeking the baptism of the Holy Ghost":

"The Baptism of the Holy Ghost is usually received while praising the Lord over and over. The Chart . . . is to show you how to do this. Repeat the words of praise in the first space over and over for two or three minutes, then repeat the words in the second space the same length of time, thus continuing on, allowing about two or three minutes for each space.

"While praising the Lord in this way, you should speak about two or three times faster than you ordinarily talk. Stop when you start to get tired, and you can commence again later on when you are rested.

"Some Christians will find that after they have continued to repeat these words of praise real fast, they will commence to stammer, but they should continue on as this usually takes place just before the Holy Ghost starts to speak thru *[sic]* them in unknown tongues. They should keep right on for several minutes, speaking in tongues until the Holy Ghost is speaking thru them in a clear language, which will be the evidence to them that they have been baptized with the Holy Ghost!" [27]

Harold Bredesen, pastor of First Reformed Church, Mount Vernon, New York, and a pentecostal enthusiast, instructed tongues seekers at Yale:

"(1) To think visually and concretely, rather than abstractedly: for example, try to visualize Jesus as a person; (2) consciously to yield their voices and organs of speech to the Holy Spirit; (3) to repeat certain elementary sounds which he told them, such as 'bah-bah-bah,' or something similar. He then laid his hands on the head of each seeker, praying for him, and the seeker did actually speak in tongues." [28]

Decom belumba! Which is to say, One doesn't have to go to Yale to duplicate that achievement! Acquaintance with a Yale traditional, "The Whiffenpoof Song," might help, however, for it contains the line, "We are poor little lambs who have lost our way, baa, baa, baa." Such instructions make one wonder whether the modern "gift" is not of pagan, rather than Christian, origin, and whether it was not intended for pagan *children.** Perhaps, in the context of tongues, we have not adequately explored the significance of Paul's words in 1 Corinthians 13:11: "When I was a child, I spake as a child, I understood as a child, I thought as a child: but when I became a man, I put away childish things."

* Perhaps the saddest commentary on the Yale outburst was pronounced by one of the participants. Reports Stanley D. Walters ["Speaking in Tongues," *Youth in Action*, May, 1964, p. 10]: "Of the students involved, some later became unsure that the outbreak was a genuine work of the Spirit. I talked to one who had spoken in tongues when Mr. Bredesen first visited the campus, could do so later whenever he wished and on his own initiative *did so in my presence*, yet doubted that it was a work of the Spirit. A devout Christian, he was genuinely perplexed."

The apostle also urged the Corinthians to "pray with the understanding" as well as "the Spirit" (chap. 14:15). The modern tongues seeker, to the contrary, is urged to put aside his understanding, to take no thought of what he is saying, to repeat words for a period of time at two to three times the speed with which he normally speaks, to repeat elementary sounds—procedures that are used, in part, by hypnotists, by spiritists in preparing for possession by a spirit entity, and by totalitarian brainwashers!

And what is the result when one then speaks in tongues? The same as when one yields the will at last to the friendly brainwasher: there is a sense of euphoria, of relief, peace, relaxation. It feels good! Dr. Welmers reported the same psychological reaction after reading aloud a glossolalic utterance he had been listening to for hours. His explanation has significant implications:

"In free vocalizing, one lets his vocal organs move from syllable to syllable with a minimun of conscious control—much as some people do with their entire bodies in a sort of random dancing. One may indeed, as many have claimed, be thinking of something entirely different while so 'speaking.' In such circumstances, one gets the impression that he is *not responsible* for something he is doing. Actually, of course, we *are* responsible to God for what we do, and as Christians we know it. If we could only feel for once that we were *not* responsible, wouldn't we all feel absolutely great? From this point of view, the modern experience of 'speaking in tongues' may be not only something *other than* the work of the Holy Spirit, but may be *contrary to* it. The Holy Spirit should be making us feel responsible to God, not irresponsible." [29]

Repeatedly in his letter to the Corinthians Paul emphasizes both responsible worship and communication. He ranks prophecy above tongues because it communicates truth—a message from God, teaching about the Christian life, a knowledge about spiritual things. As with flutes, harp, and bugle, tongues are useful only when their sounds can be distinguished, otherwise they have no purpose. "You might just as well be addressing an empty room" (1 Cor. 14:9, Phillips). You "will be speaking into the air" (R.S.V.).

That tongues do not produce communication (as verified in 1 Corinthians 14) is of serious consequence for the spiritual unity of the believers, and another reason the gift is inferior to prophecy. He urges the Corinthians to seek those gifts that build up the church, making it evident that tongues is not in this category.

The apostle's choice is unmistakable. In the congregation, he says, he would rather speak five words with his mind—that is, intelligible words—than 10,000 words in an unintelligible tongue. Unintelligible prayer, he says, "is no help to the other man" (verse 18, N.E.B.).

Paul then appeals to the Corinthians to be mature in thinking. Though tongues had sign value for the unbeliever, Paul emphasizes that if such a one were to come into the congregation and hear a babble of voices, he would think them mad. No individual could be converted, no church built up, unless there were first intelligible communication. In their childish and emotional concept of Christianity the Corinthians may have hoped to impress the pagan world with phenomena similar to those of the mystery religions of the day. Paul reminded the Corinthians that Christianity's mystery was a revealed mystery, not a secret.

Paul speaks of spiritual gifts from the perspective of principles undergirding responsible religious experience. His evaluation is damaging to speaking in tongues, even when it is used in communion with God in prayer. Says he: "If I use such language in my prayer, the Spirit in me prays, but my intellect lies fallow" (1 Cor. 14:14, N.E.B.). The original language places two spiritual agents in opposition to each other, the *pneuma,* the spirit, and the *noos,* the mind.

A former professor at the University of Chicago, Carl G. Tuland, makes an observation on this point that seems important whether tongues is a foreign language or ecstatic utterance. (As is evident in his observation, he believes the latter):

"Now, man's emotional life (his spirit) as well as his intellect (his mind) can operate independently of God's guidance, if man chooses to do so. His surrender can be unilateral, of either emotions or mind, and it can be complete, comprising the whole man. Upon these decisions depends ultimately the type of a Christian's religious experience. A man, therefore, who prays in a tongue, makes his human emotions receptive for an ecstatic religious experience. However, his mind—understanding, intellect, moral judgment—is inactive. This in reality results in a subconscious religious experience, and human emotions become the basis for individual belief. Paul contrasts the emotional and intellectual factors in religion in subsequent passages. Although a man's emotions are moved by the Spirit, when he prays in ecstasy, it is without active moral participation. There is no intelligent discernment, no intellectual assent of his mind. This distinction made by the Apostle touches upon the most important point: praying with tongues is in reality an inferior type of religious experience as compared with a conscious relationship of the Spirit-filled mind with God, man, and truth.

"In spite of these arguments," Tuland continues, "the Apostle is careful enough not to discard the gift entirely, nor does he condemn its manifestations, but merely its excessive, uncontrolled use in the churches, and the exaggerated spiritual importance attributed to it. He strives for soundness of religion in the individual and in the church, but how can this be achieved when every soul is mastered by his emotions and not by spiritual intelligence?" [30]

One must suspect that not only good theology but valid psychological truths lie behind Paul's counsel to pray with the understanding as well as the Spirit, and behind Christ's caution against " 'babbling on like the heathen' " (Matt. 6:7, N.E.B.). Was Christ telling us not only that we need not repeat pleas endlessly to be heard by Him but that mindlessly repeated clichés unfit the mind for the working of the Holy Spirit? indeed, constitute a welcome mat for the devil? What *did* happen in those heathen rites, where mindlessly repeated prayers throbbed hypnotically into the believers' ears? Did the former heathen practices of members of the Corinthian church have anything to do with their misuse of spiritual gifts?

Both in the first century B.C. and earlier the heathen used ecstatic speech in worshiping their gods. "Prophets and mystics of Assyria, Egypt, and Greece reportedly spoke in foreign tongues during states of ecstasy and uttered unintelligible phrases said to be revelations from the gods." [31]

The "Report of Wenamon," written about 1100 B.C. from Byblos, on the coast of Syro-Palestine, often is cited as containing the most ancient account of ecstatic speech. Reporting the experience of a youthful worshiper of Amon, who was possessed by a god, the account says, "Now when he sacrificed to his gods . . . the god seized one of his noble youths, making him frenzied, so that he said: 'Bring [the god] hither! Bring the messenger of Amon who hath him. Send him and let him go.' " [32]

A candid look at the paragraph, however, fails to reveal the alleged ecstatic utterance. The result of the frenzy is *intelligible* speech—"Bring [the god] hither! Bring the messenger of Amon who hath him. Send him and let him go." Were modern "ecstatic tongues" so intelligible, one suspects they would lose their attraction—as this quotation should for those seeking ancient evidences of ecstatic speech.

Plato (427-347 B.C.) reveals knowledge of religious ecstatic speech. In the *Phaedrus* he wrote of families engaged in holy prayers, rites, and inspired utterances. [33] In the *Ion* he compared poets, inspired men, to the Corybanthian revelers who became ecstatic in both utterance and action and to the Bacchic maidens of the Dionysian cult. [34] "No one," he argued, "attains real, effective, inspired divination when he is in possession of his mind, but only as his power of intelligence is fettered in sleep or upset either by disease or some divine frenzy." [35] Those listening to the diviner needed an interpreter or a prophet to expound his dark sayings.

In the *Aeneid*, Virgil (70-19 B.C.) described the Sibylline priestess on the isle of Delos, whose ecstatic state and speech originated in a haunted cave, where drafts and winds made weird sounds and music. When unified in spirit with the god Apollo, she spoke in tongues, sometimes understood and sometimes incoherent.[36]

Chrysostom, a noted church father, described the pythoness in this way:

"This same Pythoness then is said, being a female, to sit at times upon the tripod of Apollo astride, and thus the evil spirit ascending from beneath and entering the lower part of her body, fills the woman with madness and she with dishevelled hair begins to play the bacchanal and to foam at the mouth, and thus being in a frenzy to utter the words of her madness."[37]

The Graeco-Roman world, too, had its mystery religions, among them the Osiris cult, which originated in Egypt; the Mithra cult of Persia, and the Eleusinian, Dionysian, and Orphic cults which started in Thrace, Macedonia, and Greece. Little evidence exists for glossolalia among these cults, but the following reasons have been argued for its likelihood: (1) The whole system of beliefs, initiatory rites, and religious practices centered in spirit possession; (2), the Christian terms for glossolalia *(pneuma* and *lalein glōssais)* come from the Greek vernacular, which existed long before the New Testament was written; (3) in the account of *De Dea Syria,* Lucian of Samosata (A.D. 120-198) described a case of glossolalia uttered by the itinerant devotees of the Syrian goddess Juno.[38]

Gerhard Kittell found comparable phenomena in the divinatory practice of the Delphic Phrygia, the Bacides, and the Sibyls.[39] "Oracles of the great 'lord' at the Shrine of Delphi, as Heraclitus put it, were revelations of the god's will through ecstasy, not through sensible words. So were the Sibyl's unintelligible cries. A priest or priestess, seized by sudden trances of the spirit, uttered mystic sayings which were held to be all the more divine as they were least rational or articulate. Philo in Alexandria had taken over the Greek notion, arguing that such ecstasy, when the mind or conscious reason was superceded, was the highest reach of the human soul in its quest for God."[40]

Such pagan concepts survive even today. Members of the saffron-robed Hare Krishna movement report an ecstatic experience through repetitiously chanting the name of their god.

"When you chant the Holy Name of God," says one member of the sect, "you feel and experience a certain kind of ecstasy. Happiness because it's re-establishing your relationship with God and you're in a spiritual realm. When you see us dancing on the streets we're dancing because we're constantly happy. The spreading of the Holy Name of God through our chants—Hare Krishna, Hare Krishna, Krishna Krishna, Hare Hare, Hare Rama, Hare Rama, Rama Rama, Hare Hare—and distributing literature is our service to God." [41]

Yogi Maharishi Mahesh has taught the Beatles the way to " 'serenity, joyfulness, and the expansion of consciousness' by the constant repetition of one word—*which must be meaningless!*" [42]

Not a few centuries lie between Yogi Maharishi Mahesh's instruction and the heathen belief that mystic sayings were all the more divine as they were least rational and articulate; between the instruction of Larry Christensen, Harold Bredesen, and the Rainbow Revivalists on the one hand, and Plato's suggestion that one seeking inspired divination must lose possession of his mind, on the other. But when we compare them philosophically and theologically they seem more kin than alien. And we find it not so difficult after all to make the transition from twentieth century glossolalia to the unknown tongues of the Corinthian church. We may not know just what their tongues were, but their misuse seemed to involve a tuning out of rational faculties and a tuning in of emotions, until what came through was a strange blending of ripened heathenism and immature Christianity. We might not be surprised should we discover that they were superimposing pagan glossolalic practices onto Christian worship services.

In fact, some commentators believe that Paul was hinting at this very problem in 1 Corinthians 12:2:

"You know how, in the days when you were still pagan, you were swept off to those dumb heathen gods, however you happened to be led. For this reason I must impress upon you that no one who says 'A curse on Jesus!' can be speaking under the influence of the Spirit of God. And no one can say 'Jesus is Lord!' except under the influence of the Holy Spirit" (N.E.B.). The commentators who see pagan influence in Corinthian practice theorize that blasphemies inadvertently had been spoken in "ecstatic utterance," thus bringing Paul's rebuke on their emotional—and vocal—excesses. Whatever the facts, Paul is emphasizing that in Christian worship one cannot evade responsibility for what he says. Under "dumb heathen gods" one was assumed to be the more divine for his irrationality, but an irrational attack on Jesus could not be attributed to the Holy Spirit. It was evidence instead of the survival of heathen influence.

If the Corinthian believers were using ecstatic speech rather than foreign languages in their new worship of Jehovah, I can believe that Paul considered their pagan background in rebuking them so gently for excesses and in setting rational restrictions on their practices. I suspect, however, that we are on safest ground in not seeking an explanation of the tongues of 1 Corinthians 14 in pagan practices. In the first place we simply do not have enough evidence about what went on in pagan religions. The source material in this chapter, skimpy as it is, constitutes the bulk of what is available. The temptation is to make it say more than we can be sure of, to fit the concept of ecstatic tongues misuse, by which we would like to explain 1 Corinthians 14. Apart from the shaky methodology involved in such a procedure, we lack enough information to do so. And whatever the gift of tongues is in 1 Corinthians 14, it is a *genuine* gift. Misused, yes, but genuine. To seek its origin in pagan practices seems an affront to the Holy Spirit.

We need not, however, absolve the Corinthians from letting their pagan backgrounds influence their perspective on spiritual gifts. As Edward Schweitzer observes:

"In Corinth a conception of the Spirit of God was predominant, which mixed up Holy Spirit and enthusiasm. To the Corinthians an utterance seemed to be the more godly the more miraculous it appeared. Thus glossolalia was the highest degree of spiritual maturity, just because it showed itself depending on the mysterious power which could not be identified with any natural faculty of man." [43]

One has only to observe the emphasis in pentecostal ranks of our day to confirm how human it is to equate spiritual maturity with spiritual phenomena!

Though we cannot be dogmatic about precisely the nature of the gift of tongues in the Corinthian church, we can be quite sure of one thing: They were not gibberish. A look at incidents of tongues speaking in the New Testament church lends no encouragement to the idea that Bible Christians spoke gibberish as a gift of the Holy Spirit. As we already have observed, at Pentecost and throughout the Book of Acts tongues is a divinely endowed foreign language. Paul's emphasis on understanding and maturity in the Corinthian letter leaves little room to assume approval of a divinely endowed gibberish. With Dr. Ervin I would agree that "babbling is indefensible in any context, whether private devotions or corporate worship." There can be no "legitimate concern" for regulation and use of gibberish in the congregation.

And here is where concern about modern tongues must be stated without stuttering. With the possible exception of an infinitesimal sample, they are not a language, either of men or of angels. They range from primitive nonsense to sophisticated gibberish. They conform to no scriptural example, whether in Acts 2 or 1 Corinthians 14. Often they are induced by methods that not only have no precedent in Scripture but are contrary both to scriptural principles and mature thinking. Their source would seem more closely allied to pagan irrational utterances than to the Word, who placed such a premium upon accurate and intelligible communication that He Himself came down where He could be known and read of all men. Not once in all the Scripture is there record of gibberish coming from the lips of Him who is our example in all things.

What do these conclusions say to us about Pat Boone, who sings ecstatic stanzas under alleged Spirit influence; his wife, reported to have prayed in classical Latin; and all the thousands of others who are praying and talking in an unknown tongue?

First of all, the sincerity of most tongues speakers is not in question. The source of their experience is. Second, if they are in fact speaking in a foreign language, a number of Christian linguists are waiting to testify in their behalf. Says Dr. Welmers:

"If I should ever hear in such an utterance a language I recognize, or something that sounds strikingly like something in a group of languages with which I am acquainted, I will make it known immediately and unmistakably. If any such utterance displays more of the structure of language than any I have heard, I will do nothing to conceal that fact, and will indeed point out precisely where the similarities lie." [44]

Despite the examples of tongues in intelligible foreign languages given in this chapter, let me repeat: Not one of the hundreds of samples of tongues submitted to linguists has proved to be a foreign language—or even a language at all. One must, in charity, remember how often under deep emotional stress, we hear what we want to hear and that with no intention of varnishing facts.

The disciples were given the gift of foreign languages to meet a specific need. One wonders why God would give the gift of speaking in classical Latin, long a dead language, spoken by no nation. Or why the Holy Spirit would inspire repetition of a classic Zulu epic poem of the early nineteenth century. Not even the assumption that the Corinthians had the gift of ecstatic utterance would seem to explain these incidents. In fact, one searches all the Scripture in vain for their precedent, and not finding it there is left to wonder whether the answer to these incidents must not be found instead in one of the following explanations: (1) self-stimulated; (2) psychologically or hypnotically induced; (3) a counterfeit gift, supernaturally aided.

With Dr. Welmers we must conclude:

"All available evidence, as investigated by a number of responsible Christian linguists (at least one of whom rather expected the opposite results, and none of whom can fairly be accused of approaching the subject with a closed mind), indicates that contemporary glossolalic utterances do not meet the Biblical or linguistic criteria for being recognized as valid spiritual experiences in accord with Scripture." [45]

References

[1] George Otis, *High Adventure*, p. 146.

[2] *Ibid.*, pp. 148, 149.

[3] Howard M. Ervin, "As the Spirit Gives Utterance," *Christianity Today*, April 11, 1969, p. 10 (626). Copyright 1969 by *Christianity Today*; reprinted by permission.

[4] *Ibid.*, p. 7.

[5] *Ibid.*, p. 10.

[6] William J. Samarin, *Tongues of Men and Angels* (New York: The Macmillan Company, 1972), p. 227.

[7] "Identified Tongues," *New Covenant Magazine*, Ann Arbor, Michigan, January, 1973, p. 20. Reprinted by permission.

[8] *New Covenant Magazine*, November, 1971, p. 6. Reprinted by permission.

[9] *Ibid.*, p. 15.

[10] *Ibid.*, pp. 16, 17.

[11] *Ibid.*, January, 1973, p. 20.

[12] *Ibid.*, pp. 20, 28.

[13] Mel Tari as told to Cliff Dudley, *Like a Mighty Wind*, copyright 1971 by Creation House, 499 Gunderson Drive, Carol Stream, Ill. 60515, pp. 26, 27.

[14] Samarin, p. 227.

[15] *Ibid.*, p. 124.

[16] *Ibid.*, p. 112.

[17] William E. Welmers, "The Baptism, Power, Gifts, and Fruit of the Holy Spirit," an unpublished manuscript, p. 19.

[18] *Ibid.*, p. 20.

[19] *Ibid.*, p. 22.

[20] *Ibid.*, p. 23.

[21] Religious News Service, July 17, 1964, p. 13.

[22] Welmers, *op. cit.*, p. 23.

[23] Cited by V. Raymond Edman, "Divine or Devilish?" *Christian Herald*, May, 1964, p. 16. Copyright 1964 by Christian Herald Association, Inc.

[24] Stuart Bergsma, "Speaking With Tongues," *Torch and Trumpet*, XIV, November, 1964, p. 9.

[25] Kilian McDonnell, "Catholic Pentecostalism: problems in evaluation," *Theology Digest*, XIX, No. 1, Spring, 1971, p. 47.

[26] Cited by John Miles, "Tongues," *Voice* XLIV, February, 1965, p. 6.

[27] Plunkett Rainbow Revival, 2158 Redcliff St., Los Angeles, California 90039.

[28] *Ibid.*

[29] Welmers, *op. cit.*, p. 28.

[30] Carl G. Tuland, "Speaking With Tongues, a philological and text-analytical study," an unpublished manuscript, p. 14.

[31] E. Mansell Pattison and Robert L. Casey, "Glossolalia: A Contemporary Mystical Experience," *International Psychiatry Clinics* (Boston: Little, Brown and Company, 1969), vol. 5 no. 4, pp. 133-148.

[32] George A. Barton, *Archaeology and the Bible* (Philadelphia: American Sunday School Union, 1917), p. 353.

[33] Plato, "Dialogues of Plato," trans. Benjamin Jowett, vol. VII of *Great Books of the Western World*, ed. R. M. Hutchins (Chicago: Encyclopaedia Britannica, Inc., 1952), sec. 244.

[34] *Ibid.*, secs. 533, 534.

[35] Moffatt, *New Testament Commentary*, p. 212.

[36] Virgil, *Aeneid,* trans. James Rhoades, vol. XIII of *Great Books of the Western World,* ed. R. M. Hutchins, Book VI.

[37] Chrysostom, "Homilies on First Corinthians," trans. T. W. Chambers, vol. XII of the *Nicene and Post-Nicene Fathers,* ed. Philip Schaff, First series (New York: The Christian Literature Company, 1889), Hom. 29.2.

[38] Ira J. Martin III, *Glossolalia in the Apostolic Church* (Berea, Kentucky: Berea College Press, 1960), p. 80. Cited by Robert G. Gromacki, *The Modern Tongues Movement* (Philadelphia: Presbyterian and Reformed Publishing Company, 1967), p. 8.

[39] Gerhard Kittell, *Theological Dictionary of the New Testament,* trans. Geoffrey W. Bromiley (Grand Rapids: W. B. Eerdmans Publishing Company, 1946), vol. I, p. 722.

[40] Moffatt, on 1 Corinthians 14, p. 214.

[41] Religious News Service photo caption, ER-NO-2A-73-TT.

[42] Nelson Palmer, "The Baptism in the Holy Spirit and Speaking in Tongues," an unpublished manuscript, p. 36, quoting the Melbourne (Australia) *Herald,* Saturday, Sept. 2, 1967.

[43] Edward Schweitzer, "The Service of Worship," *Interpretation,* XIII (October, 1959), p. 403.

[44] Welmers, *op. cit.,* p. 28.

[45] *Ibid.,* p. 29.

17

Tongues in the Adventist Church

He refused to tell my secretary why he wanted to see me, but because the unknown can add spice to the daily menu, I suggested that she show him in. "He doesn't look dangerous or anything," she reassured me.

And he didn't. He had mild blue eyes, a thinning patch of sun-faded hair, and a generous nose set above a nervous, now-you-see-it, now-you-don't, smile. A salesman for a stationery company, he was dressed in a brown suit, white shirt, and nondescript tie.

We exchanged a few banalities about business and the weather before he turned the conversation to current religious developments, beginning with ecumenism and ending with tongues. What did I think about tongues, he wanted to know. Well, tongues are for talking, was my noncommittal reply.

"I've been speaking in tongues now for almost six years," he said. "Got the gift at a Pentecostal meeting in Indianapolis. I'm still an Adventist, however, and I believe the time has come to bring the gift to the Seventh-day Adventist Church.

After all, we teach the perpetuity of spiritual gifts, don't we?"

We do. We spent a few minutes on a few verses. When Christ ascended to His Father after His death and resurrection, He "gave gifts unto men" (Eph. 4:8). The gifts were given for "the perfecting of the saints, for the work of the ministry, for the edifying of the body of Christ" (verse 12). In his Corinthian letter, Paul thanks God that His people are to "come behind in no gift, waiting for the coming of our Lord Jesus Christ" (1 Cor. 1:7).

"Don't we believe that the spirit of prophecy is still manifest in the church?" he asked. He knew the answer as well as I: Yes. In Acts 2:17, 18, Luke repeats the words of Joel 2:28-32: "And it shall come to pass in the last days, saith God, I will pour out of my Spirit upon all flesh: and your sons and your daughter shall prophesy, and your young men shall see visions, and your old men shall dream dreams: and on my servants and on my handmaidens I will pour out in those days of my Spirit; and they shall prophesy."

And, of course, Adventists have long linked Revelation 12:17 and Revelation 19:10 to demonstrate that God's remnant people who live on earth at the time of His second coming will have two marks: fidelity to the commandments of God, and the spirit of prophecy, the latter of which Adventists believe has been manifested through Ellen G. White.

Leaning over my desk and looking at me intently, my visitor repeated, "I have a burden to bring the gift of tongues to the Adventist Church."

"You and a dozen others," I replied, "including the Full Gospel Business Men's Fellowship International. The trouble is, you are a little late. The gift of tongues, or something very similar, appeared among Adventist believers over a hundred years ago—even before the modern pentecostal tongues movement had its beginning in 1901. In fact, a purported message in tongues had influence, for a time, with early Sabbathkeeping Adventists as to when to begin and to end the Sabbath. And the ordination of an Adventist pioneer was also purportedly confirmed by a message in tongues. But, as one might anticipate, not all the tongues were genuine. Adventists had to go to the Word of God for answers to some perplexing questions. And the answers they found," I said, "pretty well explain why there has not been more tongues speaking in the Adventist Church."

My visitor left at last, still believing Adventists are missing something. And with that conclusion I am agreed. But there are things in life—including certain so-called "gifts"—one is better off without. But let the experience of our pioneers speak for itself.

One of the first two tongues incidents occurred in 1848, when believers still were divided about what hour the Sabbath began. In a letter of July 2, 1848, written from Berlin, Connecticut, James White, husband of Ellen G. White and later president of the General Conference, describes what happened:

"There has been some division as to the time of beginning the Sabbath. Some commenced at sundown. Most, however, at 6 P.M. A week ago Sabbath we made this a subject of prayer. The Holy Ghost came down, Brother Chamberlain was filled with the power. In this state he cried out in an unknown tongue. The interpretation followed which was this: 'Give me the chalk, Give me the chalk.'

"Well, thought I, if there is none in the house then I shall doubt this, but in a moment a brother took down a good piece of chalk. Brother Chamberlain took it and in the power he drew this figure on the floor.

This represents Jesus' words, 'Are there not twelve hours in the day?' This figure represents the day or the last half of the day. Daylight is half gone when the sun is south or half way from each horizon, at 12 o'clock. Now go each way six hours and you will get the twelve-hour day. At any time a [sic] year the day ends at 6 P.M. Here is where the Sabbath begins at 6

P.M. Satan would get us from this time. But let us stand fast in the Sabbath as God has given it to us and Brother Bates." [1]

Here, indeed, is an amazing early experience in which either a *false tongue or a false interpretation confirmed a false time to begin the Sabbath.* It was only after six years of further study and prayer that our Adventist forefathers yielded this conviction—confirmed by a seemingly supernatural incident—to the evidence of Scripture: the Sabbath begins at sundown (see Lev. 23:32, Mark 1:32). No wonder Adventists have developed a healthy emphasis on trying the spirits and subordinating experience to truth!

Chamberlain was involved also in another early tongues episode, in either 1847 or 1848. At a meeting in North Paris, Maine, Brother Richard Ralph spoke in an unknown tongue. Chamberlain interpreted the message, saying it was directed to Brother J. N. Andrews, and that it directed him to prepare for the gospel ministry. The incident was witnessed by Mrs. S. Howland, Mrs. Frances Howland Lunt, Mrs. Rebecka Howland Winslow, and N. N. Lunt, all of whom were present, and later signed their names to an account. [2]

Richard Ralph spoke in tongues again in 1849, in Centerport, New York, where a weekend conference of Sabbathkeeping Adventists was being held in the home of William Harris. [3]

An S. H. Rhodes, who had preached the Advent message prior to 1844, had become depressed and left human society, living as a hermit for three years, 30 miles from the nearest settlement. Visits to encourage him to become again a spiritual leader in the movement had ended in failure.

Early in November, 1849, Hiram Edson, who had failed to change Rhodes's mind on two earlier occasions, decided to make one more effort. After traveling 14 miles, however, he turned around and went home, under the deep impression that his journey was premature. Ten days later, at a conference of believers, he spoke of his burden for Rhodes and suggested that Ralph go with him in another attempt to change his mind. Mrs. White told Brother Ralph that she thought

Brother Edson's sympathy and desires had led him to be unduly hopeful. She advised him to be sure that the call was from the Lord before accompanying him on another mission that she feared would be as fruitless as former ones had been.

Sunday evening, November 18, a group of believers, including Mrs. White, met for special prayer for guidance in this matter. Wrote Hiram Edson:

"Bro. Ralph asked the Lord, in secret, to pour out His Spirit upon us if it was His will that we should go after Bro. Rhodes. The Spirit was poured out, and it settled upon us, so that the place was awful, and glorious. While I was inquiring of the Lord if He had sent His servant so far to go with me to hunt up Bro. Rhodes, that moment Bro. Ralph broke out in a new tongue, unknown to us all. Then came the interpretation [evidently given by Ralph]—'Yes to go with thee.' I then saw the reason why the Lord did not want me to go after Bro. Rhodes when I started ten days before; for it was His will that Bro. Ralph should go with me." [4]

On Monday morning, during another prayer session, Mrs. White received a vision:

"The Angel pointed to the earth, where I saw Bro. Rhodes in thick darkness; but he still bore the image of Jesus. I saw that it was the will of God that Brn. Edson and Ralph should go after him. . . . The Angel pointed me to the snare of Satan that bound him; and I saw that he thought that there was no hope, no mercy for him; and it would be of no use for him to try. I saw that Brn. Edson and Ralph should make him believe there was hope, and mercy for him, and tear him away, then he would come among the flock; and that Angels would attend them on their journey." [5]

This vision was notable not only for its content, but because it was contrary to Mrs. White's earlier expressed personal skepticism of the benefit of visiting Rhodes.

The men immediately started on their mission, as Edson wrote, "in full faith that God had taken Brother Rhodes' case into His own hands, and that He would come with us."

Finding Rhodes, they told him that they "had come in the

name of the Lord to get him to go with us to see the brethren, and go with us into the Kingdom. God displayed his convincing power, and Bro. Ralph spoke in a new tongue, and gave the interpretation in power, and in the demonstration of the Holy Ghost." [6]

The visit and the accompanying charisma impressed Rhodes. He reconsecrated himself to teaching the Sabbath truth and worked loyally until his death in 1897. In an account of the experience, Adventist Pioneer J. N. Loughborough says, "I never heard him [Ralph] speak in tongues. I think there were only about two other instances . . . that the gift was manifest through him, and then only when some critical point was under consideration." [7]

The Lord early revealed to Ellen White the dangers inherent in the exercise of tongues. In 1850 she wrote:

"I saw that the exercises were in great danger of being adulterated, . . . former opinion and knowledge governing in a measure their exercise, therefore implicit confidence could not be placed in these exercises. . . .

"I saw that we should strive at all times to be free from unhealthy and unnecessary excitement. I saw that there was great danger of leaving the word of God and . . . trusting in exercises. . . . I saw danger ahead." [8]

We know little about an incident in 1851. A Sister Shimper reported from East Bethel, Vermont, that "the gift of tongues, and solemn manifestations of the presence and power of God" had occurred at the ordination of G. W. Morse. [9]

J. N. Loughborough is the source for still another tongues experience, which took place in Vergennes, Michigan, in 1853. A "tall woman," he says, in the midst of "a harangue on holiness," "broke out in what she called tongues."

Loughborough recorded her speech as: " 'Kenne kenni, kenne kenno, kenne kenne, kenne kennioe,' and the same combined in other order." [10]

The Sunday following the Vergennes meeting the woman spoke in a neighborhood schoolhouse—another "harangue on the subject of holiness," wrote Loughborough.

The woman claimed that she talked in the Indian tongue, and that the Lord was preparing her to be a missionary to the Highland Garlic tribe, which had a reservation on the Flat River, near Vergennes. Said Loughborough:

"While she was talking in the schoolhouse, one of these Indians came up to the door with his gun on his shoulder, going off on a hunt. Some of the boys who sat near the door went out and told him to come in, that the woman would talk in his language. So he took his seat near the door, leaning his gun against the wall. As she saw him take his seat, she broke out in her 'Kenne kenni,' et cetera. The Indian stared at her, jumped up, and grabbing his gun, rushed out of the house with a 'Whoop!' and said, 'Very bad Injun that! Very bad Injun that!' The boys followed him and inquired, 'What she say?' He said, 'Nothing; she talk no Injun.' "

The woman's stepson challenged her to accompany him to the house of a man who interpreted for the Indians, who could test her tongues. She assented, says Loughborough, "and he took her over, and said to the interpreter, 'Here is a woman who says she talks in your language. She will talk, and I want you to tell me what she says.'

"So she rattled off her gibberish, which she called tongues.

"He then said to the interpreter, 'What did she say?'

"The interpreter replied, 'She did not say one word of our language.'

"She then asked, 'May I pray in your language?'

" 'Yes,' he said, 'pray all you please.'

"So she kneeled down and rattled off some more of her so-called tongues. The young man inquired what she said. The reply was, 'She has not uttered a word of my language.' She replied, 'I talk Injun, anyway.'

"The interpreter said, 'Madam, I have been interpreter for 17 different tribes of Indians, and you have not uttered a single Indian word.' "

Said Loughborough: "Of course that put an end to her influence in Vergennes." [11]

In the same account Loughborough quotes Mrs. White as

saying, during a talk at Vergennes:

"That tall woman, who came in and sat down by the door a few moments ago, claims to be very holy. She also claims to have the gift of tongues. The words she rattles off are mere gibberish. She does not talk any language. If every nation on earth heard her, none of them would understand a thing, for she does not talk any language. . . ."

In 1863 the Adventist Church had its last major confrontation with spurious tongues and other counterfeits of the gifts of the Spirit. It happened in Portland, Maine. What went on can be imagined from counsel sent the Portland church by Mrs. E. G. White. The similarity to numerous charismatic meetings of our day is obvious from her account.

"The only remedy for the East is through discipline and organization. A spirit of fanaticism has ruled a certain class of Sabbathkeepers there. . . . Some of these persons have exercises which they call gifts and say that the Lord has placed them in the church. They have an unmeaning gibberish which they call the unknown tongue, which is unknown not only by man but by the Lord and all heaven. Such gifts are manufactured by men and women, aided by the great deceiver. Fanaticism, false excitement, false talking in tongues, and noisy exercises have been considered gifts which God has placed in the church. Some have been deceived here. The fruits of all this have not been good. 'Ye shall know them by their fruits.' . . .

"Some . . . have much to say upon the gifts and are often especially exercised. They give themselves up to wild, excitable feelings and make unintelligible sounds which they call the gift of tongues, and a certain class seem to be charmed with these strange manifestations. A strange spirit rules with this class, which would bear down and run over anyone who would reprove them. God's Spirit is not in the work and does not attend such workmen. They have another spirit." [12]

She expressed her concern both for the divisive character of the manifestation and the impression it would make on "unbelievers":

"Some rejoice and exult that they have the gifts, which

others have not. May God deliver His people from such gifts. What do these gifts do for them? Are they through the exercise of these gifts, brought into the unity of the faith? And do they convince the unbeliever that God is with them of a truth? When these discordant ones, holding their different views, come together and there is considerable excitement and the unknown tongue, they let their light so shine that unbelievers would say: These people are not sane; they are carried away with a false excitement, and we know that they do not have the truth." [13]

The "thorough discipline and organization" Ellen White called for in meeting such fanaticism was interpreted as even disfellowshipment for those involved. Of a group of Sabbath-keepers near Tyrone, Michigan, "who profess to have much of the Holy Spirit" but are influenced by a spirit that is decidedly unholy," James White wrote: "The cause here has been in great danger through fanaticism, coming from the above named class; but if a straightforward course is taken, and those who still hold on to their false impressions and strange exercises are disfellowshiped by the brethren, the unholy leaven will be entirely purged out." [14]

Other more recent incidents seem to have been used of God to communicate His Word, though they do not correspond in all respects to the Biblical gift of tongues. [See Appendix C.] Assuming the authenticity of some if not all the reports, one is left with the conviction that man does not write the rules by which the Holy Spirit works. But neither does one ignore the criteria by which charismatic phenomena are to be tested.

A succinct listing of "divinely given guidelines" to determine whether charismatic manifestations are from God appeared in the *Review and Herald* during June and July of 1972. [15] Written by the editor, Kenneth H. Wood, the three editorials were "to provide information and some guidelines" in answering the question, "How should Seventh-day Adventists relate to the neo-pentecostal movement?"

Wood listed ten guidelines, the first five of which documented Christ's promise of the Holy Spirit to His followers, the manifestations of both genuine and counterfeit outpourings of the Spirit before the Second Advent, and that the miracles and signs and wonders of the last days would not necessarily be of divine origin nor prove genuine discipleship.

Wood was concerned that some Christians "will label as fanaticism even the genuine baptism of the Holy Spirit." He quoted Ellen White:

"The baptism of the Holy Ghost as on the day of Pentecost will lead to a revival of true religion and to the performance of many wonderful works. Heavenly intelligences will come among us, and men will speak as they are moved upon by the Holy Spirit of God. But should the Lord work upon men as He did on and after the day of Pentecost, many who now claim to believe the truth would know so very little of the operation of the Holy Spirit that they would cry, 'Beware of fanaticism.' " [16]

How does one determine whether a spirit is of God? Wood gave three tests: Whether the spirit (1) acknowledges "that Jesus Christ is come in the flesh" (1 John 4:2), (2) relates properly to God's law and revelation (Isa. 8:20), and (3) bears the right fruit. He stressed that the Holy Spirit "is given to those who obey, not to those who ignore, reject, or oppose God's law," citing Acts 5:32 in support: "And we are his witnesses of these things; and so is also the Holy Ghost, *whom God hath given to them that obey him.*" (Italics Wood's.)

Turning specifically to tongues, Wood asserted that there is both a genuine gift and a false gift. The genuine, for which he cited Acts 2:1-13, "enabled the apostles . . . to break the language barrier in preaching the gospel." Passing no judgment upon 1 Corinthians 14, Wood simply linked the false gift with the "unmeaning gibberish" that had appeared among Adventists in Portland, Maine. Like all other gifts of the Spirit, the gift of tongues is "bestowed at the discretion of the Spirit, not of the individual. It is only one of several gifts, no more unique than other gifts, and, like the others, is given selectively, not to all (see 1 Cor. 12:28-31)."

Wood wrapped up his criteria with three short observations on tongues: *"c.* Love is greater than either the gift of tongues or the gift of prophecy (1 Cor. 13:1, 2). *d.* To prophesy (say something spiritually edifying) is more desirable than to speak in tongues (1 Cor. 14:1-5, 9). *e. Order must prevail* (verses 33, 40)." (Italics are his. See Appendix B for entire editorial.)

Though he left open the question of whether genuine tongues are always, as at Pentecost, a foreign language, Wood's use of Ellen White's comments on "unmeaning gibberish" would seem to imply his nonacceptance of ecstatic speech, at least in public when uninterpreted (if gibberish can ever be interpreted) and likely in private worship as well. Is his view typical of what most Adventists believe?

A search of Adventist literature on charismatic phenomena will reveal that the church has never promoted ecstatic tongues speaking, nor has it linked tongues speaking with the baptism of the Holy Spirit, baptism, or conversion. Whenever Ellen White has written favorably of glossolalia, either in its Bible setting, in Adventist history, or in its eschatalogical manifestations, she has had in mind an intelligible foreign language, not previously learned by the speaker, through which the gospel of Jesus Christ has been or would be proclaimed in a manner not otherwise possible. Whenever she has written unfavorably of glossolalia, she has had in mind speech meaningless both to speaker and listener. Such tongues, she has written, are "manufactured by men and women, aided by the great deceiver." [17]

A study of glossolalia by psychiatrists E. Mansell Pattison and Robert L. Casey supports the idea of human manufacture. The two conducted studies on a small group of volunteers, studying their speech both in normal and glossolalic conversation. Their conclusion: "Glossolalia is a learned phenomenon and can be reproduced by naïve experimental subjects, either by imitation or upon request to 'make up a strange language.' " Glossolalia, they said, "lacks sememic or semantic structure, which differentiates it from true language," [18] the conclusion also of William J. Samarin and other linguists.[19]

Pattison reports that several glossolalics he studied told him that "one of their favorite pastimes was creating new words for their glossolalic vocabulary." [20]

John L. Sherrill, author of *They Speak With Other Tongues*, admits that he "often did mouth nonsense syllables in an effort to start the flow of prayer-in-tongues. But sometimes," he said, "the easy, effortless flow never came. I'd be left listening to the sound of my own foolishness. It was obvious to me that the Holy Spirit was no part of these noises: the ridiculousness of it would sweep over me, and from there it was not far to wondering if the Holy Spirit had ever been a part of tongues." [21]

Even such a tongues enthusiast as David Wilkerson, author of *The Cross and the Switchblade*, warns of false tongues, which he reports finding increasingly among the Jesus movement.[22]

Why do people manufacture tongues?

A psychiatrist in Berkeley, California, Paul Morentz, found six dominant personality traits among glossolalists of mainline churches: "(1) Hostility to authority, (2) the wish to compensate for feelings of inadequacy, (3) the wish to rationalize feelings of isolation, (4) the wish to dominate, (5) strong feelings of dependency and suggestibility, and (6) wish for certainty." [23]

These finding have been disputed by other psychiatrists, and it does not appear that one can accurately conclude anything other than that one cannot accurately conclude anything. Theologians as well as scientists have permitted presuppositions to distort their studies.[24]

Whatever the motivations of the tongues advocate, he will not find "unmeaning gibberish," however it is packaged, an appreciated "gift" within the Adventist Church. Particularly will it be received with suspicion when it is linked with the baptism of the Holy Spirit. As we will find in another chapter, tongues and the baptism are usually not traveling companions.

References

[1] James White, letter written July 2, 1848, from Berlin, Connecticut.

[2] Document File 311 of the White Estate.

[3] See J. N. Loughborough letter to M. E. Kern, Sept. 26, 1916 [Document File 311], and "Tongues in Early S.D.A. History," by A. L. White, *Review and Herald,* March 5, 1973.

[4] Hiram Edson in *Present Truth* (Middletown, Connecticut), Dec., 1849, p. 35.

[5] *Ibid.*

[6] *Ibid.*

[7] Letter to M. E. Kern, Sept. 26, 1915. [Document File 311.]

[8] Letter to *Review and Herald* (Saratoga Springs, New York), written July 30, 1851, and published Aug. 19, 1851, p. 15.

[9] Manuscript 11, 1850. Quoted by A. L. White, *Review and Herald,* March 23, 1973.

[10] See *Pacific Union Recorder,* Dec. 23, 1909, and J. N. Loughborough in *Review and Herald,* June 10, 1884, pp. 378, 379.

[11] *Pacific Union Recorder,* Dec. 30, 1909 (see also J. N. Loughborough, in *Review and Herald,* June 10, 1884).

[12] Ellen G. White, *Testimonies for the Church,* vol. 1, pp. 411-414.

[13] *Ibid.,* pp. 418, 419.

[14] James White, "Western Tour," *Review and Herald,* June 9, 1853, p. 12. Report of conference in Tyrone, Michigan.

[15] Kenneth H. Wood, "The Charismatic Movement," *Review and Herald* (Washington, D.C.: Review and Herald Publishing Association), June 22, 1972, p. 2; "Testing the Spirits," June 29, 1972, p. 2; "None Need Be Deceived," July 6, 1972, p. 2.

[16] Ellen G. White, *Selected Messages,* book 2, p. 57. (See also Ellen G. White, *Gospel Workers,* pp. 170, 171.)

[17] ———, *Testimonies for the Church,* vol. 1, p. 412.

[18] E. Mansell Pattison, M.D., and Robert L. Casey, "Glossolalia: A Contemporary Mystical Experience," *International Psychiatry Clinics,* vol. 5, no. 4, p. 142.

[19] See chapter 6.

[20] E. Mansell Pattison, M.D., "Behavioral Science Research on the Nature of Glossolalia," *Journal of the American Scientific Affiliation,* Sept., 1968, p. 81.

[21] John L. Sherrill, *They Speak With Other Tongues* (New York: Pyramid Books, copyright 1964, pp. 127, 128). Used with permission of McGraw-Hill Book Company.

[22] David Wilkerson, *Jesus Person Maturity Manual* (Glendale, California: Regal Book Division of G/L Publishers, 1971).

[23] *International Psychiatry Clinics,* p. 139.

[24] See, for examples, L. P. Gerlach and V. H. Hine, *The Charismatic Revival: Processes of Recruitment, Conversion and Behavioral Change in a Modern Religious Movement.* Unpublished paper, University of Minnesota, 1966.

18
A Strange Song

The forty-seventh annual camp meeting of the Ohio Conference, held on the Mansfield fairgrounds, had everything Adventists have come to expect. Visiting speakers recounted inspiring stories of mission advance and challenged the crowds—up to 632 on Sabbath—to further sacrifice. At early-morning devotionals and evening evangelistic meetings, congregations sang the old hymns with old-time Adventist fervor—"Power in the Blood," "From Greenland's Icy Mountains," "The Coming King Is at the Door." Prayer bands met daily to remember the sick, missionaries, colporteurs, and the work in Ohio. And many were the prayers in that 1908 gathering that the Holy Spirit would add power to the witness of God's remnant church.

Then, as unexpectedly as the storm that had divided and gone around the camp, leaving only the collapsed straw tent as evidence of what might have been, came a break in the routine. Ringing out in a woman's voice that penetrated the recesses of the fairgrounds came a prophetic utterance in song:

"He is coming; He is coming;
"Get ready; Get ready: . . .
"Receive ye the Holy Ghost."

Again and again, as people came hurrying from their tents, the singer, a woman in her mid-thirties, repeated her sober message in song. With tears streaming down her cheeks she assured her audience that the words were "dictated by the Spirit." [1]

The listeners were not so sure. Even in 1908 Adventists believed in testing so-called divine utterances, heavenly tongues, and charismatic rattlings. An ensuing discussion, in which the woman's husband and others of their family and friends joined, did little to build confidence. The discussion soon grew into disorder, police were called, and the visitors landed in jail. A lengthy boldface heading in the next day's Mansfield *Daily Shield*[2] reveals something of the issues of that hectic Friday afternoon:

"Gift of tongues causes trouble. Mackin claims to be master of Chinese jargon, which he says came to him from God while his mother became an expert in Yiddish as the result of a vision. Dissension at camp meeting results in the arrest of Mackin, wife and daughter, and two lady companions—they hold services behind prison bars and seem quite proud of distinction." *

History might have left the Mackins in jail, and Adventist historians to question the judgment of the camp meeting officials who reacted so inhospitably to them and their friends. But the Mackins assured themselves of further notoriety, and us of a revealing record, by taking their claims to Ellen G. White. And so we meet them again, on a crisp Thursday morning in November, at her home in Elmshaven, California. The account of their conversation and subsequent events brings further insight to the church as it contemplates its re-

---

* According to the article, Mackin claimed to have received the gift of tongues a week before his appearance on the campground. "After a little meditation," wrote the reporter, "Mackin gave an exposition of the gift he claims to have received. It sounded like Chinese."

Though Mackin said he had been an Adventist for 16 years, K. C. Russell reported in the *Advent Review and Sabbath Herald* of September 10, 1908, that the Mackins and their company "had formerly been connected with our people."

sponse to the modern tongues movement, and therefore deserves careful study.

When Mrs. White came downstairs from her study that November 12, 1908, she had never met the Mackins, nor had she heard of their experience at the Mansfield camp meeting. They were there, the well-dressed couple told her, to discuss an unusual experience that had come to them during the 1905 Week of Prayer in their Findlay, Ohio, church.

Here is the account, recorded stenographically by Clarence Crisler, one of Mrs. White's secretaries. Also present was her son W. C. White, who had set up the meeting with the Mackins, after conferring with them the day before.[3]

RALPH MACKIN: "In the Week of Prayer reading for that year, every article was directed to the people to seek for the Holy Spirit. We set aside in our little church three days for fasting and prayer, and we fasted and prayed for three days—that is, not constantly together, but we felt the need of a deeper work and felt the necessity of coming into possession of more of the Spirit of God. We began to study from that time on the work of the Holy Spirit. . . .

"The message that the Lord gave me particularly was to follow the life of the apostles. In the first place, in Matthew 18:1-3, when the apostles came to the Saviour, we read:

" 'At the same time came the disciples unto Jesus saying, Who is the greatest in the kingdom of heaven? And Jesus called a little child unto him, and set him in the midst of them, and said, Verily I say unto you, Except ye be converted, and become as little children, ye shall not enter into the kingdom of heaven.'

"Now, I teach that . . . the thing we are to do is to seek Jesus for the power of conversion. That is, if we accept the Sabbath truth, the state of the dead, and all those things—I may accept those things, and advocate and teach them, and yet lose heaven, and *am not a converted man, unless I have sought Jesus for His converting power.*

"In the next place, I turn to John 17, and read the prayer that Jesus offered before His crucifixion. There He prayed for sanctification. 'Sanctify them through thy truth: thy word is truth.'

"Then I turn to Luke 24, to show when they came into possession of that blessing termed sanctification—the apostles—and the experience of their lives; and I read from verse 45 and onward to the end of the chapter:

" 'Then opened he their understanding, that they might understand the scriptures, and said unto them, Thus it is written, and thus it behoved Christ to suffer, and to rise from the dead the third day: and that repentance and remission of sins should be preached in his name among all nations, beginning at Jerusalem. And ye are witnesses of these things. And, behold, I send the promise of my Father upon you: but tarry ye in the city of Jerusalem, until ye be endued with power from on high. And he led them out as far as to Bethany, and he lifted up his hands, and blessed them. And it came to pass, while he blessed them, he was parted from them, and carried up into heaven. And they worshipped him, and returned to Jerusalem with great joy: and were continually in the temple, praising and blessing God. Amen.'

"Now I teach that this blessing is the blessing of sanctification that they received, that He bestowed upon them; and when we seek God—if we are a sinner, until we are converted; if we are converted, then we put up the prayer for the power of sanctification to live clean, wholesome lives. *Not* that it is the work of an instant; *not* 'once sanctified, always sanctified'; that is not true. But we should so firmly and eagerly put up our petition that we receive the blessing. It has the same physiological effect on us—oh, we just want to praise Jesus, and it makes us so loving and gentle and kind. But we notice that the disciples were not ready yet to go out with that blessing to do work for the Master. He told them to tarry until they were endued with power from on high. Then we put up our petition and hold right on by faith, and that which encouraged us to do this was the chapter entitled 'The Shaking Time' in *Early Writings*—we hung right on by faith, until great drops of sweat stood on our brow. Believing that the same power that the disciples had was for us today, we were encouraged to hold on.

"When that promised blessing came on us, as we put up our petitions to God, we had the same experience as recorded here in Acts 2 in regard to the apostles. When that promised power came upon us we spake in other tongues as the Spirit gave us utterance.

"In Toledo, when we were bearing our message on the street, a man who was a Polish Catholic stood on the street when Mrs. Mackin was speaking; and as the Spirit of God came upon her, and spoke to them through her in another language that she could not understand, this Polish gentleman exclaimed, 'I know what that lady is speaking. She is speaking in my own tongue of a calamity which is soon to be visited on this city.'

"In other instances, when one comes into this blessing of speaking with tongues, the Lord may give me the same tongue, and we may hold a conversation in the language that the Spirit of God may have given us utterance in. Even three or four may take part in the conversation, and yet it is a foreign tongue to them, and one waits on the other until the other is through; and it is all in order. This is the experience we received, according to the promised blessing.

"And then, in accordance with that, Acts 10, Peter's experience in the home of Cornelius corroborates it; and then Acts 19; and from the study of the Word, in our experience, and the persecution, and everything that has come with it, we have found, so far as we are able to discern, our experience corroborates [sic] with the experience of the early apostles as recorded in the Word.

"One instance: We were shut up in the jail at Clyde, Ohio. . . ."

ELLEN G. WHITE: "How long ago?"

MACKIN: "Six or eight weeks ago. In Clyde there lives a very devoted family that we knew there, and that is a credit to our people. The little children—there are four of them—are all taught to pray every evening and morning; and it is very interesting to see the family at the hour of worship.

"Now, we went there, and they hung on for this blessing that we had received; and they put up their petition for this blessing, and came into possession of this blessing; and as the Spirit came upon them, some of them wept, and among others that wept was a little girl ten or eleven years old. Well, the grandma came into the room, and she saw the little girl weeping, and she thought I had a mesmeric influence over the child. But a few weeks later the same Spirit came upon the child when we were in the city of Toledo, and gave the message; and so they had evidence that it was not the result of any control that I might have over the child. When I came back to the town, nearly four weeks later, one of the relatives had me arrested for having this mesmeric power, as they term it.

"The trial was set, and I simply produced the evidence from the Word of God that we were living in the last days, and, according to Acts 2, in the last days the Lord had promised to pour out the Spirit of God upon all flesh, and the boys and girls were to prophesy.

"And by the way, it was through this little girl—the Spirit of God coming upon this child—that we were directed to go to Toledo when we did. When under the influence of the Spirit, she pointed her finger directly at me, and then toward Toledo, and through the Spirit of prophecy she says, 'You go to Toledo'; and since this accorded with Acts 2: 'Your sons and your daughters shall prophesy'; and knowing the family—putting the test to the life—we dared not hesitate to go.

"We were told at the same time that we would be put in prison in Toledo. That came to pass, and we had the evidence that we were directed by the Spirit because that which had been prophesied came to pass. We bore our message in the city, and they came and locked us up. . . .

"If we are in a delusion, we are honestly there. But if this is from the Spirit of God, we want to follow it. . . .

"This Spirit tells us to search the Word; tells us to be earnest; and tells us to be careful about our diet; tells us exactly what you have said.

"Now, my wife, the Spirit operates through her, and we believe that this is the gift of prophecy that is to be poured out onto all flesh. This Spirit leads us into kindness and purity of life, and we can't understand it—why—only that as the Word of God has said, that these experiences come as the result of receiving the blessing of the Spirit of God.

"They circulate all manner of evil reports about us, which are wholly untrue. We are surprised when we hear them; there is not a syllable of truth in them. But it accords with just what the Word says. The first people to shut us up were the Adventists, at the Ohio camp meeting."

ELLEN G. WHITE: "What party? There are many Adventists."

MACKIN: "The Seventh-day Adventists. The year before that, we were not in possession of this blessing fully, but we had come into possession of sufficient of the Spirit of God that we would love to get people into our tent and pray with them —just as in volume 8, you remember, it says:—

" 'The time has come for a thorough reformation to take place. When this reformation begins, the spirit of prayer will actuate every believer and will banish from the church the spirit of discord and strife. Those who have not been living in Christian fellowship will draw close to one another. One member working in right lines will lead other members to unite with him in making intercession for the revelation of the Holy Spirit. There will be no confusion, because all will be in harmony with the mind of the Spirit.'—*Testimonies to the Church*, vol. 8, p. 251.

"Through this blessing, and our interest in the people, we assisted 26 people to go to the camp meeting who otherwise could not have gone—where they might get strength. This work went on until this last year.

"Before we went onto the campground—we did not go until Friday—my wife and two other ladies (my mother, and another lady, Sister Edwards, a sister-in-law to the president of the conference)—before we went upon the campground this last year, they three were seeking the Lord. I had gone downtown on an errand; and the Spirit of God told her (Mrs. Mackin) to go on the campground, and there sing; and there He would tell her what to sing.

"And she wept just like a child, and just seemed like she could not stand it because that the Lord showed her the condition of our people—soon the plagues would fall, and they were unready. There was no meeting in progress, and the Spirit of the Lord came upon her as she went onto the campground, and (turning to Mrs. Mackin) you may tell her what words you sang."

MRS. MACKIN: "The Lord put this burden upon me. I could not stand it. I wanted to tell it so bad, and sing that song so bad. And I could not get rid of it till I would do it. 'Oh, pray,' says I to Sister Edwards; and so I stood on the campground, and I sang just what the Lord gave me. The Lord—this is what I sang:—

"He is coming; He is coming;
Get ready; Get ready."

"And then that statement in *Early Writings* [p. 71]—

" 'How many I saw coming up to the falling of the plagues without a shelter. Receive ye the Holy Ghost.' These are the words I sang. I sang them over and over again. They could hear it all over the campground, and they came together; but before that, the Lord showed me how they would wring their hands as the plagues were falling. The Lord can show anything in just a moment, better than He could tell it to us. And so He showed me how they would wring their hands, and that put on me a greater burden than ever. Well, that is when they arrested us.

"I asked one of the ministers, on the witness stand—he was a man from Pennsylvania—'Would you consider that singing sufficient to disturb a camp meeting?' He said, 'I never heard such singing in my life. It just thrilled me through and through.' This is what everybody says. It is in a most beautiful tone of voice, and it just seems to lift us from off the earth. It is when the singing is extemporaneous—dictated by the Spirit—that it is the most wonderful.

"If you have any light for us . . ."

ELLEN G. WHITE: "I do not know that I have anything special that I could say. There will be things that will transpire at the very close of this earth's history, it has been presented to me, similar to some of the things that you have represented; but I cannot say anything on these points now."

MACKIN: "Is there any question, Brother White, or anything now?"

W. C. WHITE: "I do not know as there is anything more than to pray that the Lord will give Mother some word, and then take time for matters to develop. It is better, in presenting anything to her, to present the subject briefly and clearly, and then perhaps have another interview with her later on."

MACKIN: "We are fasting and praying. If we are in a delusion, we want to know it, just as much as if we were in the right."

MRS. MACKIN: "Our brethren certainly think that we are in a delusion."

ELLEN G. WHITE: "What place was this that you speak of, where this singing was?"

MACKIN: "Mansfield, Ohio, at the camp meeting."

ELLEN G. WHITE: "Our people—Sabbathkeeping people?"

MACKIN: "Yes, our own people."

W. C. WHITE: "Was that verse that Mrs. Mackin sang last night extemporaneous or a known hymn?" [At the prayer meeting in the sanitarium chapel Brother Mackin had given his testimony in the praise service and was followed by Mrs. Mackin, who sang.]

MRS. MACKIN: "Oh, that was one of our published hymns. It is in the new *Christ in Song*."

MACKIN: "From hearing that you could scarcely gain an idea of her singing when the words are given to her by the Holy Spirit. The most wonderful thing is when she sings 'Glory!' She says when she sings it she seems to be in the presence of Jesus, with the angels. She repeats the word 'Glory!'

over and over again. She has been tested with the piano, and musicians say it is a freak—the lowness and highness with which she does it. She cannot do it only as she prays in the Spirit and special power comes upon her."

MRS. MACKIN: "We don't have this power, only as we seek Jesus."

MACKIN: "The Lord has given us power, Sister White, to cast out demons. Many people are possessed with demons. I remember a statement you wrote a few years ago that many were possessed with demons as verily as they were in the days of Christ. When we are in a meeting, and these demons are in a meeting, they may cause people to do queer things. I noticed in the Bible when Jesus was in the Temple that demons at once came out. 'Hold thy peace, and come out of him.' The Lord instructs us to lay the people down, lest the demons throw them when they come out. We found in the beginning that when we begin to rebuke these demons they oftentimes close the eyes of these people, and will sometimes cause them to bark like a dog, and stick out their tongue; but as we continue to rebuke them, why, the eyes open and they become calm, and the demons——

"Now it is through the gift of the Spirit that the Lord tells us when the demons are gone, that they are all gone. One lady in particular had six demons, and she said she just felt them when they came out—it just seemed to pull her in every part of the body.

"But our brethren say that they can't be in the last days; but we find that it coincides with just what the Saviour said in the last chapter of Mark, in that great commission: 'And these signs shall follow them that believe; In my name shall they cast out devils; they shall speak with new tongues;' and so on."

MRS. MACKIN: "We did not get this all at once, either."

MACKIN: "Read the remaining verses of Mark: 'And these signs shall follow them that believe; In my name shall they cast out devils; they shall speak with new tongues; they shall take up serpents; and if they drink any deadly thing, it shall not hurt them; they shall lay hands on the sick, and they shall recover. So then after the Lord had spoken unto them, he was received up into heaven, and sat on the right hand of God. And they went forth, and preached everywhere, the Lord working with them, and confirming the word with signs following. Amen.' Our experience, so far as we are able to discern, corroborates [sic] with the Bible. Here is something that I would like to read [here Mackin read extracts, including the following, from an article in the April 11, 1899, *Review and Herald,* by Sister White, entitled "The Newcastle Camp Meeting"]:

" 'During the night of the first Sabbath of the Newcastle meeting, I seemed to be in meeting, presenting the necessity and importance of our receiving the Spirit. This was the burden of my labor—the opening of our hearts to the Holy Spirit.'

"In connection with the receiving of power from on high there is a question, it seems to me, just as pertinent now as in the days of the apostles—What is the evidence? If we receive it, will it not have the same physiological effect on us as it did back there? It can be expected that we shall speak as the Spirit gives us utterance."

ELLEN G. WHITE: "In the future we shall have special tokens of the influence of the Spirit of God—especially at times when our enemies are the strongest against us. The time will come when we shall see some strange things; but just in what way—whether similar to some of the experiences of the disciples after they received the Holy Spirit following the ascension of Christ—I cannot say."

MACKIN: "We will continually pray to the Lord about this, and ask Him to give you light in regard to it. So I leave you our address, and if you have anything for us after this, we shall be glad to receive it."

W. C. WHITE: "You will probably spend a few days here, will you not?"

MACKIN: "If the Holy Spirit tells us that our work is done now, we will go; if He tells us to tarry, we will tarry. It leads us. As I have presented this message to different congregations the Spirit of God has witnessed to it, and many weep, and they say, 'Oh, we need power, we need help, and this is the power promised, and let us seek God.' "

MRS. MACKIN: "The real test is love—1 Corinthians 13."

MACKIN: "Satan wants to hinder this work. We are sealed by the Holy Spirit of Promise. I present it from *Early Writings* when the angels are about to loose the four winds, Jesus gazes in pity on the remnant, and with uplifted hands cries, 'My blood, Father, My blood, My blood, My blood!' He repeats it four times; for His people are still unsealed. He commissions an angel to fly swiftly to the four angels holding the four winds, with the message, 'Hold! Hold! Hold! Hold! until the servants of God are sealed in their foreheads.' And as I bring these things before the congregation it is the most earnest and devoted ones that it seems to affect, mostly."

At this point, Mrs. White began to recount incidents from her experience with fanaticism in the early days of the Adventist Movement, continuing to speak for nearly thirty minutes. She mentioned believers' indulging in strange bodily exercises, acting largely on the basis of impressions, seeking humility by creeping upon the floor, dancing and singing—with repeated shouts of "glory"—and jumping with uplifted hands while praising God, for as long as a half hour. She referred also to believers who thought it wrong to work, and others who believed the righteous dead had been raised.

She had been called by God to rebuke such fanaticism, she said, because it brought the cause of God into disrepute, turned the minds of unbelievers from the living Word to the doings of men, and hindered the proclamation of the message. The strength of the church, she said, lay in the power that accompanies a clear presentation of the Word. The law of God is to be exalted and the features of the three angels' messages (Rev. 14:6-12) plainly outlined so that all men might hear the truth and decide whether to obey God or man. The Holy Spirit, she emphasized, works in a way that commends itself to the good judgment of people.

As Mrs. White continued to speak of her early experiences

with fanaticism, Mackin broke in:

MACKIN: "If we would now have the spirit of prayer, and this power would come upon my wife, would you be able to discern whether this was of the Lord or not?"

ELLEN G. WHITE: "I could not tell you anything about it. But I am telling you these experiences in order that you may know what we have passed through. We tried in every way possible to rid the church of this evil. We declared in the name of the Lord God of Israel that God does not work through His children in a way that brings the truth into disrepute, and that unnecessarily creates deep-seated prejudice and bitter opposition. In our work we must take a straightforward course and seek to reach the people where they are."

MACKIN: "I remember reading very much of this in volume I of *Testimonies for the Church*—your experience in rebuking fanaticism, and of the cause in the East when they set the time, in 1855, I believe."

ELLEN G. WHITE: "Some would dance up and down, singing, 'Glory, glory, glory, glory, glory.' Sometimes I would sit still until they got through, and then I would rise and say: This is not the way the Lord works. He does not make impressions in this way. We must direct the minds of the people to the Word as the foundation of our faith.

"I was but a mere child at that time; and yet I had to bear my testimony repeatedly against these strange workings. And ever since that time I have sought to be very, very careful lest something of this sort should come in again among our people. Any manifestation of fanaticism takes the mind away from the evidence of truth—the Word itself.

"You might take a consistent course, but those who would be influenced by you might take a very inconsistent course, and as a result we should very soon have our hands full of something that would make it almost impossible to give unbelievers the right impression of our message and work. We must go to the people with the solid Word of God; and when they receive that Word, the Holy Spirit may come, but it always comes, as I have stated before, in a way that commends itself to the judgment of the people. In our speaking, our singing, and in all our spiritual exercises, we are to reveal that calmness and dignity and godly fear that actuates every true child of God.

"There is constant danger of allowing something to come into our midst that we may regard as the working of the Holy Spirit, but that in reality is the fruit of a spirit of fanaticism. So long as we allow the enemy of truth to lead us into a wrong way we cannot hope to reach the honest in heart with the third angel's message. We are to be sanctified through obedience to the truth.

"I am afraid of anything that would have a tendency to turn the mind away from the solid evidences of the truth as revealed in God's Word. I am afraid of it; I am afraid of it. We must bring our minds within the bounds of reason, lest the enemy so come in as to set everything in a disorderly way. There are persons of an excitable temperament who are easily led into fanaticism; and should we allow anything to come into our churches that would lead such persons into error we would soon see these errors carried to extreme lengths; and then because of the course of these disorderly elements a stigma would rest upon the whole body of Seventh-day Adventists.

"I have been studying how to get some of these early experiences into print again, so that more of our people may be informed; for I have long known that fanaticism will be manifest again, in different ways. We are to strengthen our position by dwelling on the Word, and by avoiding all oddities and strange exercisings that some would be very quick to catch up and practice. If we were to allow confusion to come into our ranks, we could not bind off our work as we should. We are trying to bind it off now, in every way possible.

"I thought I must relate these things to you."

MACKIN: "Well, now, that which you have stated does not correspond with our experience. We have been very cautious in this matter, and we find that the experience through which we have passed, and which we have endeavored to outline briefly to you this morning, tallies exactly with the experience of God's servants of old as given in the Word."

ELLEN G. WHITE: "During the years of Christ's ministry on earth godly women assisted in the work that the Saviour and His disciples were carrying forward. If those who were opposing this work could have found anything out of the regular order in the conduct of these women, it would have closed the work at once. But while women were laboring with Christ and the apostles, the entire work was conducted on so high a plane as to be above the shadow of a suspicion. No occasion for any accusation could be found. The minds of all were directed to the Scriptures rather than to individuals. The truth was proclaimed intelligently, and so plainly that all could understand.

"Now I am afraid to have anything of a fanatical nature brought in among our people. There are many, many who must be sanctified; but they are to be sanctified through obedience to the message of truth. I am writing on this subject today. In this message there is a beautiful consistency that appeals to the judgment. We cannot allow excitable elements among us to display themselves in a way that would destroy our influence with those whom we wish to reach with the truth. It took us years to outlive the unfavorable impression that unbelievers gained of Adventists through their knowledge of the strange and wicked workings of fanatical elements among us during the early years of our existence as a separate people."

MACKIN: "Well, now, this that you are giving us, would this be considered testimony under the Spirit, or is it simply counsel—of relating your experience?"

ELLEN G. WHITE: "I am giving you history."

MACKIN: "But you do not say that that applies to our case now, until you have further light on it?"

ELLEN G. WHITE: "I could not say; but it appears to be along that line, as I am afraid of it. It appears to be along that line that I have met again and again."

W. C. WHITE: "It is now twelve o'clock. Would you not like to rest before dinner?"

ELLEN G. WHITE: "Well, I could not let you go before I had said what I have said. I would say: Be guarded. Do not let anything appear that savors of fanaticism, and that others would act out. There are some who are eager to make a show, and they will act out whatever you may do—whether it be of the same tenor or not. I have been very careful not to stir up anything like strangeness among our people."

MACKIN: "But it is true that when the Holy Spirit does come, as is stated in your works, that many will turn against it, and declare that it is fanaticism?"

ELLEN G. WHITE: "Of course they will; and for this reason we ought to be very guarded. It is through the *Word*—not feeling, not excitement—that we want to influence the people to obey the truth. On the platform of God's Word we can stand with safety. The living Word is replete with evidence, and a wonderful power accompanies its proclamation in our world."

MACKIN: "Well, we must not tire you."

MRS. MACKIN: "Praise the Lord!"

ELLEN G. WHITE (rising, and shaking hands): "I want the Spirit of the Lord to be with you, and you, and me. We are to be just like God's little children. The power of His grace must not be misunderstood. We must have it in all meekness and humility and lowliness of mind, that God may make the impression Himself upon the minds of the people. I hope the Lord will bless you and give you a solid foundation, which foundation is the Word of the living God." [3]

The interview ended, the Mackins departed—but not yet into silence. Despite Ellen White's cautions about fanaticism, they wrote to the Clyde, Ohio, church that they had something good to report on their return home. W. C. White had a different slant, reporting to Elder A. G. Daniells, president of the General Conference, that the Mackins seemed to be "very nice-spirited people, but their experience is somewhat peculiar." In a subsequent report to S. N. Haskell, president of the California Conference, he said the Mackins "cannot with justice refer to their visit . . . as an encouragement in their claims to a special mission and work." [4]

Mrs. White herself wrote Haskell that the experience of the Mackins "seemed to be a facsimile of that which we were called to meet and correct in our early experience." [5]

She added:

"Toward the close of our interview Brother Mackin proposed that we unite in prayer, with the thought that possibly while in prayer his wife would be exercised as they had described to me, and that then I might be able to discern whether this was of the Lord or not. To this I could not consent, because I have been instructed that when one offers to exhibit these peculiar manifestations, this is a decided evidence that it is not the work of God." [6]

On December 11, 1908, the Mackins at last received the attention they had coveted—though not the confirmation of their experience they had sought. On that date Ellen White wrote them a letter that got right to the point:

"Mr. and Mrs. Ralph Mackin:

"Dear Brother and Sister: Recently, in visions of the night, there were opened before me some matters that I must communicate to you. I have been shown that you are making some sad mistakes. In your study of the Scriptures and of the Testimonies, you have come to wrong conclusions. The Lord's work would be greatly misunderstood if you should continue to labor as you have begun. You place a false interpretation upon the Word of God, and upon the printed Testimonies; and then you seek to carry on a strange work in accordance with your conception of their meaning. You suppose that all you do is for the glory of God, but you are deceiving yourselves and deceiving others.

"Your wife, in speech, in song, and in strange exhibitions that are not in accordance with the genuine work of the Holy Spirit, is helping to bring in a phase of fanaticism that would do great injury to the cause of God, if allowed any place in our churches.

"You have even supposed that power is given you to cast out devils. Through your influence over the human mind men and women are led to believe that they are possessed of devils, and that the Lord has appointed you as His agents for casting out these evil spirits.*

"I have been shown that just such phases of error as I was compelled to meet among Advent believers after the passing of the time in 1844, will be repeated in these last days. In our early experience, I had to go from place to place and bear message after message to disappointed companies of believers. The evidences accompanying my messages were so great that the honest in heart received as truth the words that were spoken. The power of God was revealed in a marked manner, and men and women were freed from the baleful influence of fanaticism and disorder, and were brought into the unity of the faith.

"My brother and sister, I have a message for you: you are starting on a false supposition. There is much of self woven into your exhibitions. Satan will come in with bewitching power, through these exhibitions. It is high time that you call a halt. If God had given you a special message for His people, you would walk and work in all humility—not as if you were on the stage of a theater, but in the meekness of a follower of the lowly Jesus of Nazareth. You would carry an influence altogether different from that which you have been carrying. You would be anchored on the Rock, Christ Jesus.

"My dear young friends, your souls are precious in the sight of Heaven. Christ has bought you with His own precious blood, and I do not want you to be indulging a false hope, and working in false lines. You are certainly on a false track now, and I beg of you, for your souls' sake, to imperil no longer the cause of truth for these last days. For your own souls' sake, consider that the manner in which you are working is not the way God's cause is to be advanced. The sincere desire to do others good will lead the Christian worker to put away all thought of bringing into the message of present truth any

---

* In a letter written the same day "To Our Brethren in California," Ellen White wrote: "The work of declaring persons possessed of the devil, and then praying with them and pretending to cast out the evil spirits, is fanaticism which will bring into disrepute any church which sanctions such work."—*Pacific Union Recorder,* December 31, 1908. (Republished in *Selected Messages,* book 2, pp. 46, 47.)

strange teachings leading men and women into fanaticism. At this period of the world's history, we must exercise the greatest of care in this respect.

"Some of the phases of experience through which you are passing, not only endanger your own souls, but the souls of many others; because you appeal to the precious words of Christ as recorded in the Scriptures, and to the Testimonies, to vouch for the genuineness of your message. In supposing that the precious Word, which is verity and truth, and the Testimonies that the Lord has given for His people, are your authority, you are deceived. You are moved by wrong impulses, and are bracing up yourselves with declarations that mislead. You attempt to make the truth of God sustain false sentiments and incorrect actions that are inconsistent and fanatical. This makes tenfold, yes, twentyfold harder the work of the church in acquainting the people with the truths of the third angel's message." [7]

So, at last, the Mackins disappear from Adventist Church history. We know nothing more of them. Whatever influence they had disappeared after the foregoing letter, and another, referred to on page 130, were published. But the fanaticism that called forth the counsels remains to challenge the church. And the counsels yet remain to bear their inspired witness:

"You will be exposed to the fallacies of satanic agencies. Fearful waves of fanaticism will come. But God will deliver the people who will earnestly seek the Lord, and consecrate themselves to His service." [8]

"Such experiences will come to us from time to time. Let us give no place to strange exercisings, which really take the mind away from the deep movings of the Holy Spirit. God's work is ever characterized by calmness and dignity. We cannot afford to sanction anything that would bring in confusion and weaken our zeal in regard to the great work that God has given us to do in the world to prepare for the second coming of Christ." [9]

References

[1] *Review and Herald*, Aug. 10, 1972, p. 8.

[2] Mansfield, Ohio, *Daily Shield*, Aug. 22, 1908.

[3] The entire Mackin interview, appearing in three successive issues of the *Review and Herald* (Aug. 10, 17, and 24, 1972), was recorded in Manuscript 115, 1908.

[4] *Review and Herald*, Aug. 24, 1972, pp. 7, 8.

[5] *Ibid.*, p. 7.

[6] *Ibid.*, pp. 7, 8.

[7] *Ibid.*, pp. 8, 9.

[8] Ellen G. White, *Selected Messages*, book 2, p. 47.

[9] Ellen G. White, letter 338, 1908. (Published in *Selected Messages*, book 2, p. 42.)

19

"Shout, Shout, We're Gaining Ground"

I do believe without a doubt
The Christian has a right to shout[1]

asserted a chorus in a Methodist songbook of 1800. And shout they did, those Methodists of a century and more ago. Their uninhibited exuberance is memorialized in a song called "The Methodist," published in Stith Mead's Methodist songbook of 1807, *Hymns and Spiritual Songs.* [2]

> The *World*, the *Devil*, and *Tom Paine*
> Have try'd their force, but all in vain.
> They can't prevail, the reason is,
> The Lord defends the Methodist.
> They pray, they sing, they preach the best,
> And do the Devil most molest.
> If Satan has his vicious way,
> He'd kill and damn them all today.
> They are despised by Satan's train,
> Because they shout and preach so plain.
> I'm bound to march in endless bliss,
> And die a shouting Methodist.

And they did quite literally die shouting. "An aged person," says Winthrop S. Hudson,[3] "would rejoice at being still able 'to shout,' and a death would be recorded: 'She went off shouting.' " [4]

Alexander Campbell recorded his conviction that the Methodist Church could not survive without her cries of "*glory!* glory! glory!" "Her periodical *Amens,*" he said, "dispossess demons, storm heaven, shut the gates of hell, and drive Satan from the camp." [5]

In time the shouting Methodists did die, leaving a subdued progeny to sing more sophisticated lyrics. Their spiritual descendants at Foundry Methodist Church in Washington, D.C., which I have visited on occasion, probably are unaware that securely buried in the cornerstone of their sanctuary is a copy of, yes, "The Methodist." I point no finger of accusation at them; a glance at early Adventist hymnals reveals a number of songs that self-respecting Adventist choir directors long ago buried. As for shouting, that, too, is largely in the past, though we yet sing, but perhaps not so energetically as once—

In my immortal flesh I'll rise
To seize the everlasting prize.
And shout while passing through the air,
"Farewell, farewell, sweet hour of prayer!" [6]

To understand the religion of our forefathers we must understand the religious milieu out of which they came. Many belonged to denominations born in the pietist revivals of the seventeenth and eighteenth centuries. And, it should be remembered, even denominations with roots in the Reformation had something other than embalming fluid coursing through their veins in the early and mid-1800's. An account of the Kentucky Revival in 1801 records a meeting at Cane Ridge during which a Presbyterian minister behaved "much like a Methodist"—preaching in a most lively and ecstatic manner. Peter Cartwright later commented that "Presbyterian, Methodist, and Baptist ministers" were "all united in the blessed work" at Cane Ridge. [7]

The "blessed work" included generous portions of shouting. "Shout, shout, we're gaining ground," the saints sang. "We'll shout old Satan's kingdom down." [8] As Hudson observes, shouting was not mere noise, but rather praise, or, as it was often called, rejoicing. The rejoicing took many forms in addition to shouting: dancing, jerking the head, clapping of hands, ecstatic singing and preaching that often left the church floor covered with "sinners slain," shaking hands while singing, leaping, jumping and falling, calls to the "pen" (a railed off area before the pulpit) and the altar, or, later, the "anxious bench."

Such bodily exercises were not confined to the frontier. Cane Ridge was only a tributary of the rollicking revival that surged through many parts of the United States and abroad, reaching flood stage prior to 1844 under the preaching of William Miller and associates, who expected the Lord's return in that year. The prophetic calculation that led to the great Disappointment and the subsequent light from God on the Sabbath and the sanctuary are part of what history has called the Great Advent Awakening.

In this chapter we are going to see how our Adventist pioneers came to strike a delicate balance between ecstatic feeling and practical godliness. The conclusions they drew about the objectives of the Spirit's work in us, and the function of the Word as a safeguard against deception, say something meaningful to all who are perplexed at how to respond to pentecostalism's rattling of the church gates.

As might be expected, Adventist pioneers who came out of the revival tradition—including not a few former Methodists —were not a silent lot. Among them were those who shouted and gloried and fell prostrate under the power of the Holy Spirit, in the process proving to be quite a trial to some of their less emotional fellow believers.

The young Ellen Harmon, later Ellen White, wrote of the early cold war waged by formalists against spiritual exuberance. She goes back to her girlhood days before she received her first vision:

"For six months not a cloud intervened between me and my Saviour. Whenever there was a proper opportunity, I bore my testimony, and was greatly blessed. At times the Spirit of the Lord rested upon me with such power that my strength was taken from me. This was a trial to some who had come out from the formal churches, and remarks were often made that grieved me much. Many could not believe that one could be so overpowered by the Spirit of God as to lose all strength. My position was exceedingly painful. I began to reason with myself whether I was not justified in withholding my testimony in meeting, and thus restraining my feelings, when there was such an opposition in the hearts of some who were older in years and experience than myself." [9]

But the Holy Spirit had a work to do in the hearts of those who were to become the pioneers of the remnant, and He did it. "Cold formality began to melt before the mighty influence of the Most High." [10] Those who had opposed the work of the Spirit acknowledged their wrong, and united with their brethren. Wrote Ellen: "Unity and peace now dwelt among our people who were looking for the coming of the Lord." [11]

The succeeding years saw scores of manifestations of the Spirit's presence. There were messages confirmed by supernatural signs, [12] church members prostrated by the power of the Spirit, [13] healing, [14] shouting, [15] "a baptizing time, not with water, but with the Holy Ghost" [16]; a child of 13 who was healed praised God for three hours[17]; and, as we have noted in a preceding chapter, there were a few instances of tongues. There is no question: Our pioneers were a joyous people who knew experientially what it means to be filled with the Spirit.

After failing in his first strategy, which was to bring spiritual gifts into question, the devil sought to turn God's people from their eminently practical day-by-day witness for Christ to a subjective, self-focused experience in which feeling predominated. Gradually, as this assault on the senses intensified, God inspired His messenger to meet it with cautions. As early as 1849 she warned of some who fell "prostrate and helpless not by the power of the Holy Ghost . . . but by the power of Satan breathed upon these agents [ministers who had rejected God's truth] and through them to the people." [18]

God revealed to her the influence of previous religious orientation on early Adventist religious "exercises." Requoting a message given in 1850:

"I saw that the exercises were in great danger of being adulterated, . . . former opinion and knowledge governing in a measure their exercise, therefore implicit confidence could not be placed in these exercises. . . .

"I saw that we should strive at all times to be free from unhealthy and unnecessary excitement. I saw that there was great danger of leaving the word of God and . . . trusting in exercises. . . . I saw danger ahead." [19]

One wonders to what extent the previous religious orientation of the Corinthians, with its possible practice of ecstatic utterance, shaped the misuse of tongues in their services.

In 1861, Ellen White (she was married to James White on August 30, 1846) put "shouting" and true piety in perspective:

"I saw that religion did not consist in making a noise. . . . To be a Christian is to be Christlike, and the habit Brother H. has of shouting is no evidence that he is a Christian, for his shouting is regarded by God as no shouting. Half of the time he himself knows not what he is shouting at." [20]

When the Adventists in Portland, Maine, began speaking "gibberish," she not only rebuked the exercise as "manufactured by men and women, aided by the great deceiver," [21] but counseled the church on broader aspects of a sound religious experience:

"Fanaticism and noise have been considered special evidences of faith. Some are not satisfied with a meeting unless they have a powerful and happy time. They work for this and get up an excitement of feeling. But the influence of such meetings is not beneficial. When the happy flight of feeling is gone, they sink lower than before the meeting because their happiness did not come from the right source. . . .

"Impressions and feelings are no sure evidence that a person is led by the Lord. Satan will, if he is unsuspected, give feelings and impressions. These are not safe guides. . . ." [22]

In another message she highlighted the danger of counterfeit gifts:

"Whenever and wherever the Lord works in giving a genuine blessing, a counterfeit is also revealed, in order to make of none effect the true work of God. Therefore we need to be exceedingly careful, and walk humbly before God, that we may have spiritual eyesalve that we may distinguish the working of the Holy Spirit of God from the working of that spirit that would bring in worldly license and fanaticism. 'By their fruits ye shall know them' (Matt. 7:20). Those who are really beholding Christ will be changed into His image, even by the Spirit of the Lord, and will grow up to the full stature of men and women in Christ Jesus. The Holy Spirit of God will inspire men with love and purity; and refinement will be manifest in their characters." [23]

How was the church to deal with spurious exercises? When fanaticism arose in Michigan, James White assured fellow church leaders:

"If a straightforward course is taken, and those who still hold on to their false impressions and strange exercises are disfellowshipped by the brethren, the unholy leaven will soon be entirely purged out." [24]

Still, care was to be exercised in appraising gifts, for the Holy Spirit works as He wills, not as men dictate. Thus:

"While we should be careful not to go into human excitement, we should not be among those who will raise inquiries and cherish doubts in reference to the work of the Spirit of God; for there will be those who will question and criticize when the Spirit of God takes possession of men and women, because their own hearts are not moved, but are cold and unimpressible." [25]

Beginning in the 1880's there came a series of messages emphasizing the rationality of true religious experience:

"The rational thought and the right feelings and the faultless life come from the same source and are quiet and strong and sensible in their operation. To possess and enjoy the Spirit of God, there must be a conformity of the life, the actions to the will of God; the heart must be prepared; the soul temple cleansed from the defilement of self and sin; then the power of grace comes in and God works with His ministers." [26]

When confronted with a group who thought "that religion consists in a noise," Ellen White wrote:

"They shout and bellow and foam and act like men bereft of their reason. This was called the power, but I told them there was no religion in it. It was a spurious article. This is a modern sanctification, but it is as opposite to the genuine sanctification as light is in contrast with darkness. . . .

"The Lord keep His dear people from fanaticism and heresies which are so prevalent everywhere." [27]

Of a genuine revival in South Lancaster, Massachusetts, at which the "glory of God" swept like a "tidal wave" through the congregation, Ellen White observed:

"There were no wild demonstrations, for the praise of God does not lead to that. We never hear of . . . Christ . . . jumping up and down and around, and screaming and hollering. No, God's work appeals to the senses and reason of men and women." [28]

"Softly and silently the power of the divine Spirit does its work, wakening the dulled senses, quickening the soul and arousing its sensibilities, until each member of the church shall indeed be the light of the world." [29]

A letter of counsel, written in 1900, just prior to the birth of pentecostalism, seems especially pertinent today:

"Every influence will be set in operation by satanic agencies, to divert minds from the genuine work that will place men as laborers together with God. . . . We must . . . be very watchful and prayerful, that we may . . . [distinguish] the voice of the deceiver from the voice of Him who always speaks in truth. Those who are worked by the Holy Spirit are not led by a feeling of enthusiasm, which soon goes out in darkness. The spell of Christ's influence is abiding. 'Be still and know that I am God.' This is a solemn, abiding quietude in God.

"There is danger that all of us will have too much zeal, and too little of Christ's sound wisdom and unquestionable prudence. Every one must stand individually as an active, working agency for the Master, beholding his work as it is given in

His word for our practice. Individually, they must think for themselves. With an open Bible before them, they must study under the influence and presence of Jesus Christ, inquiring and knowing for their individual selves what is the way of the Lord." [30]

In the response of our Adventist pioneers to charismatic manifestations I find three emphases appearing repeatedly: (1) Practical godliness rather than ecstatic feeling is the objective of the Spirit's work in us; (2) the Word of God is to be the test of charismatic manifestations; (3) the Spirit works to make men law abiders, not law breakers. (A fourth area, that of unity among believers, is discussed in chapter 13.) Let us consider each of these points of emphasis at length:

1. The Holy Spirit is not an ethereal "ghost" in the Attic of the Universe, but a living presence in our world, touching life in the here and now. Through Him we are given the power and wisdom to face practical problems in day-by-day living. When our gospel shoes pinch, He points out the cause and heals the blister. When our ego swells, He is there to restore perspective. When we are called to witness for Christ, He is there to inspire word and act.

Though great emotion may accompany the infilling of the Holy Spirit—which infilling is to be a daily experience—daily conformity to the character of Christ rather than feeling is the objective of the Spirit. Pentecostals, both classic and neo, have done the cause of God no good by accenting feeling rather than the faithful daily walk with Christ, with its quiet progress toward the goal of godliness. The late Donald Gee of the British Assemblies of God acknowledged that "there is something radically wrong with the experience that gives you gifts and doesn't give you holiness." [31] But we are left with a question: What *is* holiness? Stressing its practical nature, Ellen White said: "Holiness is not rapture: it is an entire surrender of the will to God; it is living by every word that proceeds from the mouth of God; it is doing the will of our heavenly Father; it is trusting God in trial, in darkness as well as in the light; it is walking by faith and not by sight; it is relying on

God with unquestioning confidence, and resting in His love." [32]

All gifts of the Holy Spirit, tongues included, are bestowed for practical use in witnessing for Christ successfully. As an Adventist editor has commented, they are not given "to gratify ambition, to build a stratified elitist spiritual society, or to race one's emotional motors." [33]

2. Though the Word of God is to be the test of charismatic manifestations, many pentecostals consider it almost blasphemous to question their experience. To go to the Bible is to engage in "theological nit-picking," a phrase used by one pentecostal leader to explain his refusal to consider scriptural evidence that would invalidate his experience. [34] But one point should be kept in mind by those who wish to discriminate between the true and the false: *The Word and the Spirit are agreed.* Paul calls the Word of God "the sword of the Spirit" (Eph. 6:17). The two work in perfect-pitch harmony. Their cooperative relationship is witnessed to in 1 Thessalonians 1:5: "When we brought you the Good News," wrote Paul, "it was not just meaningless chatter to you; no, you listened with great interest. What we told you produced a powerful effect upon you, for the Holy Spirit gave you great and full assurance that what we said was true" (Taylor). It is those who "have said 'no' to the truth," who refuse "to believe it and love it," who will be tricked by "strange demonstrations" and "great miracles" (2 Thess. 2:9, 10, Taylor). The classic pentecostal often subordinates the Word to the manifestation; the Catholic pentecostal often subordinates it to the church. An example of the former can be found in the testimony of Vinson Synan, author of *The Pentecostal Holiness Movement,* at the June, 1972, meeting of Roman Catholic charismatics at the University of Notre Dame. He rejoiced "at the growth of Catholic Pentecostalism," the Minneapolis *Star* quoted Synan as saying, and "the Spirit of God told me it was real." [35] The question is, What says the Word of God? Does the Word say it is real? And what if it says it is not? Then what are we to do with the testimony of the Spirit? The answer must be that the testi-

mony originates in someone other than the Spirit of truth, which is ever in harmony with the Word.

The Catholic, on the other hand, believes that gifts are not ministered by the Spirit through the Word, but through the sacramental system of the church.

The Catholic believes his church is, and always has been, filled with the Holy Spirit; he seeks the gifts, therefore, from the priest who dispenses them through the seven sacraments. Thus, in seeking the baptism of the Holy Spirit, Catholic pentecostals are only seeking to actualize what they have already received through the sacraments.[36] The Protestant who really understands the centrality of the Bible in his faith cannot accept this explanation. The baptism of the Holy Spirit comes not through the sacramental system of the Roman Catholic Church but through the Word. And it is to be tested by the Word. A measure of classic pentecostalism's exaltation of experience over Scripture is the degree to which it has accommodated to the Catholic position.

It is only fair to say, however, that many old-line pentecostals are having as hard a time placing a "genuine" label on Catholic pentecostals as an Adventist would. For they, too, believe that fellowship with Christ changes the life-style. Yet here are priests—pipe-smoking priests, wine-drinking priests, mass-celebrating priests—claiming the baptism! How *can* they have the baptism when they continue to desecrate their bodies, the old-line pentecostal wonders.

This unease seems to have been behind a statement on the charismatic movement issued in August, 1972, by the Assemblies of God, which said: "It is important that we find our way in a sound scriptural path, avoiding the extremes of an ecumenism that compromises scriptural principles and an exclusivism that excludes true Christians." [37]

The problem is, of course, that the pentecostal is locked in by his own unscriptural insistence that the gift of tongues is *the* sign of baptism in the Holy Spirit. Having committed himself to this position, and having exalted experience above the Word, he is trapped in a dilemma of his own making.

The Word is truth. It is our safeguard against being deceived. Wrote Ellen White:

"The light from the Word is shining amid the moral darkness; and the Bible will never be superseded by miraculous manifestations. The truth must be studied, it must be searched for as hidden treasure. Wonderful illuminations will not be given aside from the Word, or to take the place of it. Cling to the Word, receive the ingrafted Word, which will make men wise unto salvation. . . . We shall encounter false claims; false prophets will arise; there will be false dreams and false visions; but preach the Word, be not drawn away from the voice of God in His Word. Let nothing divert the mind." [38]

"Our only safeguard against the wiles of Satan is to study the Scriptures diligently, to have an intelligent understanding of the reasons for our faith, and faithfully to perform every known duty." [39]

The centrality of the Bible not only in testing the spirits but in true revival is emphasized:

"In many of the revivals which have occurred during the last half century, the same influences have been at work, to a greater or less degree, that will be manifest in the more extensive movements of the future. There is an emotional excitement, a mingling of the true with the false, that is well adapted to mislead. Yet none need be deceived. In the light of God's word it is not difficult to determine the nature of these movements. Wherever men neglect the testimony of the Bible, turning away from those plain, soul-testing truths which require self-denial and renunciation of the world, there we may be sure that God's blessing is not bestowed. And by the rule which Christ Himself has given, 'Ye shall know them by their fruits,' it is evident that these movements are not the work of the Spirit of God." [40]

3. No movements within Christendom have done more to discount God's law than Catholicism and pentecostalism, the former through church authority, tradition, and a false doctrine of justification; the latter through subjective experi-

ence. Catholicism tampered with the law itself, substituting Sunday for God's seventh-day Sabbath, thus "teaching for doctrines the commandments of men" (Mark 7:7). The pentecostal often assures men that the law no longer needs to be kept; we live now by faith rather than by works. Ignored is Paul's emphatic assertion that law is established through faith: "Do we then make void the law through faith? God forbid: yea, we establish the law" (Rom. 3:31). To deny the authority of God's law is to pervert faith into presumption and love into permissiveness.

It is not the Spirit's work to free men from law keeping, but from the penalty of transgression. Wrote Paul:

"There is no condemnation for those who are united with Christ Jesus, because in Christ Jesus the life-giving law of the Spirit has set you free from the law of sin and death. . . . So that the commandment of the law may find fulfilment in us, whose conduct, no longer under the control of our lower nature, is directed by the Spirit" (Rom. 8:1-4, N.E.B.).

It is not the Spirit-filled mind, then, that is at enmity against God. It is the carnal mind, the mind with which we are born. This mind "is not subject to the law of God, neither indeed can be" (Rom. 8:7). Paul pleads, "Let this mind be in you, which was also in Christ Jesus" (Phil. 2:5). That mind, the mind of Christ, delights to do the will of the Father (see Ps. 40:8). Christ was obedient even to the cross, where He paid the penalty of God's broken law. He did not die for His sins, for He had committed none, but for ours—for our disobedience to God's eternal law. "I have kept my Father's commandments," He testified (John 15:10).

Whatever the name of the movement, if it excuses disobedience to God's law, beware of it. "To the law and to the testimony, if they speak not according to this word, it is because there is no light in them" (Isa. 8:20). The Saviour who came to "magnify the law, and make it honourable" (Isa. 42:21), who assured His disciples that not one dotting of an *i* or crossing of a *t* would pass from His law until all things were fulfilled (see Matt. 5:17, 18), who said, "If ye love me, keep my command-

ments" (John 14:15), and who described His remnant people
as those keeping "the commandments of God and the faith of
Jesus" (Rev. 14:12), is not the inspiration of a movement that
excuses disobedience.

Wrote Ellen White:

"The nature and the importance of the law of God have
been, to a great extent, lost sight of. A wrong conception of
the character, the perpetuity, and the obligation of the divine
law has led to errors in relation to conversion and sanctification, and has resulted in lowering the standard of piety in the
church. Here is to be found the secret of the lack of the Spirit
and power of God in the revivals of our time." [41]

"It is only as the law of God is restored to its rightful position that there can be a revival of primitive faith and godliness
among His professed people." [42] "It is the work of conversion
and sanctification to reconcile men to God by bringing them
into accord with the principles of His law." [43]

"By prayer and confession of sin [transgression of God's
law— 1 John 3:4] we must clear the King's highway. As we do
this, the power of the Spirit [of Pentecost] will come to us.
We need pentecostal energy. This will come; for the Lord has
promised to send His Spirit as the all-conquering power." [44]

Thus the Spirit and the Word and the divine law combine
to bear witness that there is cause indeed to question the source
of the rattling at the church gates. But the Spirit and the
Word and the divine law combine also to bear witness that
Seventh-day Adventists—for all their rich legacy of Spirit-
filled witness—have no cause to mount the throne called hol-
ier-than-thou and point the finger of condemnation. Indeed,
of all churches, that one given divine direction through the
spirit of prophecy has least excuse for spiritual dereliction:

"And unto the angel of the church of the Laodiceans write;
These things saith the Amen, the faithful and true witness,
the beginning of the creation of God; I know thy works, that
thou art neither cold nor hot: I would thou wert cold or hot. So
then because thou art lukewarm, and neither cold nor hot, I
will spue thee out of my mouth. Because thou sayest, I am

rich, and increased with goods, and have need of nothing; and knowest not that thou art wretched, and miserable, and poor, and blind, and naked: I counsel thee to buy of me gold tried in the fire, that thou mayest be rich; and white raiment, that thou mayest be clothed, and that the shame of thy nakedness do not appear; and anoint thine eyes with eye-salve, that thou mayest see. As many as I love, I rebuke and chasten: be zealous therefore, and repent. Behold, I stand at the door, and knock: if any man hear my voice, and open the door, I will come in to him, and will sup with him, and he with me. To him that overcometh will I grant to sit with me in my throne, even as I also overcame, and am set down with my Father in his throne. He that hath an ear, let him hear what the Spirit saith unto the churches" (Rev. 3:14-22).

References

[1] *The Chorus,* compiled by A. S. Jenks and D. Gilkey (Philadelphia, 1860), Nos. 55, 241. At least seventeen such Methodist songbooks were published between 1805 and 1843, according to Charles A. Johnson, *The Frontier Camp Meeting* (Dallas, 1955), p. 193.

[2] Johnson, *Frontier Camp Meeting,* pp. 204; 296, note 30. The song, No. 108 in Mead's *Hymns and Spiritual Songs,* had numerous versions and as many as twelve stanzas.

[3] Winthrop S. Hudson, "Shouting Methodists," *Encounter* 29:73, 74, Winter, 1968.

[4] W. W. Sweet, *Religion on the American Frontier,* Vol. IV, *The Methodists* (Chicago, 1946), pp. 176, 200.

[5] Johnson, *op. cit.,* p. 233.

[6] William B. Bradbury, "Sweet Hour of Prayer," *Church Hymnal,* official hymnal of the Seventh-day Adventist Church (Washington, D.C.: Review and Herald Publishing Association), p. 316.

[7] Peter Cartwright, *Autobiography,* W. P. Strickland, ed. (Cincinnati, 1856), p. 31.

[8] George P. Jackson, *White and Negro Spirituals* (New York, 1943), p. 319.

[9] Ellen G. White, *Testimonies for the Church,* vol. 1, p. 44.

[10] *Ibid.,* p. 48.

[11] *Ibid.*

[12] ———, *Life Sketches* (Mountain View, California: Pacific Press Publishing Association, 1915), pp. 70, 71.

[13] ———, *Spiritual Gifts* (Battle Creek, Michigan: Published by James White), vol. 2, p. 84.

[14] ———, *Life Sketches,* p. 74.

[15] Letter 28, 1850. See A. L. White in *Review and Herald,* March 15, 1973.

[16] White Estate Document File 105. Letter from Winchester, Massachusetts, Nov. 7, 1851.

[17] Joseph Bates in *Review and Herald,* Sept. 2, 1852, p. 69 (Cleveland, Ohio, Aug. 26, 1852).

[18] Ellen G. White, *Early Writings* (Washington, D.C.: Review and Herald Publishing Association), pp. 43, 44.

[19] Manuscript 11, 1850. Quoted by A. L. White in *Review and Herald,* March 23, 1973.

[20] Letter 14, 1861. A compilation of materials relating to charismatic experiences, pp. 55, 56.

[21] Ellen G. White, *Testimonies for the Church,* vol. 1, p. 412.

[22] *Ibid.,* pp. 412, 413.

23 ———, *Selected Messages*, book 1, p. 142.

24 *Review and Herald*, June 9, 1853, report of conference in Tyrone.

25 Ellen G. White, letter 27, 1894, *Selected Messages*, book 2, p. 57.

26 Letter 24, 1880.

27 Letter 42, 1880.

28 Manuscript 49, 1894.

29 Ellen G. White, letter 85, 1889.

30 ———, letter 77, 1900.

31 Donald Gee, *Now That You've Been Baptized in the Spirit* (reprinted by Gospel Publishing House, 1972), quoted in *Christianity Today*, "Tests for the Tongues Movement," by Harold Lindsell, Dec. 8, 1972, p. 10.

32 Ellen G. White, *The Acts of the Apostles*, p. 51.

33 Kenneth Wood, "None Need Be Deceived," *Review and Herald*, July 6, 1972, p.2.

34 Oral Roberts, *The Fourth Man*, p. 17.

35 Quoted by Harold Lindsell, "Tests for the Tongues Movement," in *Christianity Today*, Dec. 8, 1972, p. 10.

36 See Jesuit scholar Donald L. Gelpi's "Understanding 'Spirit Baptism' " in *America*, May 16, 1970.

37 Lindsell, *op. cit.*, p. 12.

38 Ellen G. White, *Selected Messages*, book 2, pp. 48, 49.

39 *Ibid.*, p. 58.

40 ———, *The Great Controversy*, pp. 464, 465.

41 *Ibid.*, p. 465.

42 *Ibid.*, p. 478.

43 *Ibid.*, p. 467.

44 ———, *Gospel Workers* (Washington, D.C.: Review and Herald Publishing Association), p. 308.

10
Miracles, Miracles, Miracles

Water turned to wine . . . the sick healed . . . the dead raised to life . . . food multiplied . . . walking on water . . . a cloud overhead by day to shield from the sun and a light in the heavens to guide by night.

Miracles of Bible days?

Not at all. Everyday occurrences during the 1964-1967 Indonesian revival, according to Mel Tari, 24, one-time member of a youth evangelistic team on the island of Timor. A featured speaker on the Full Gospel Business Men's Fellowship circuit, Mel describes what happened when the Holy Spirit descended with charismatic power.

His stories, compiled into a book, *Like a Mighty Wind,* by Cliff Dudley of Creation House, Incorporated, have a charming simplicity:

★ "Since October of 1967, every time we have communion in our church [on Timor] we just take water, pray over it, and the Lord turns it into wine. More than sixty times He has performed this miracle." [1]

★ Idols collected from Baal worshipers were burned

by a "sharp crashing bolt of fire—like lightning—which hit only the pile of images and burned them to ashes" when team members challenged God to settle a confrontation with Baal priests.[2]

★ Clouds followed team members like umbrellas, to shield them from the hot sun; a light "like the landing light of an airplane" would guide them through the jungle at night[3]; "team members are protected from the rain: We see the rain ten feet in front of us, ten feet behind us, ten feet to the right, and ten feet to the left. But not one single drop comes on our bodies." [4]

★ Twenty team members were fed by four cassava roots at a home in Nikiniki, when God miraculously multiplied the food until all were filled; all twenty had up to two and three glasses of tea from a small pot that continued to pour until all had had enough to drink.[5]

★ Dirty clothes were cleaned by prayer, day after day, when the team was in a village without laundry facilities.[6]

★ Every member of a team walked across a 20-30-foot-deep river, in response to a prayer of faith, without the water going above their knees. Natives "almost drowned" when they sought to follow.[7]

★ Many people were given the gift of visions. "We just go to them and ask them to watch God's 'television.' He shows them future events just as though they are on a screen." [8]

★ The Lord promised some children, as they were praying, that if they sang beautifully He would give them a surprise and play back their voices to them, so that they could hear how they sounded. "Of course," says Tari, "the children did not have a tape recorder." When the song was finished, "the Lord said, 'Now, if you will be quiet, I will play back your voices for you.' So they all were quiet, and suddenly music filled the air. The children were amazed and very happy.

" 'Oh, there is my voice,' one said. Then another exclaimed, and another as they picked out their voices. It was a real thrill for them as the music came right out of the air." [9]

But most dramatic is Tari's account of the resurrection of a man dead two days, whose body already had begun to decompose. Before more than a thousand people, says Tari, the team, in obedience to God's command, stood around the body and sang—though the stench was hardly bearable. On the sixth song, the man began to move his toes. When the team of youth evangelists sang the "seventh and eighth songs, that brother woke up, looked around, and smiled."

Opening his mouth, he said, " 'Jesus has brought me back to life! Brothers and sisters, I want to tell you something. First, *life never ends when you die.* [Italics supplied.] I've been dead for two days and I've experienced it.' The second thing he said was, 'Hell and heaven are real. I have experienced it. The third thing I want to tell you is, if you don't find Jesus in this life you will never go to heaven. You will be condemned to hell for sure.' " [10]

To discourage the easily cultivated belief that all miracles happen in primitive cultures somewhere at the end of an $800 air ticket, let me add two of the home-grown variety. The first is the story of a resurrection—and if it stretches imagination, be forewarned that in the next chapter is a resurrection story that will take the imagination past the breaking point.

It happened in Longview, Washington, a picturesque, planned city of 30,000 on the Columbia, sixty miles northwest of Portland, Oregon. The resurrected: A millwright in the cable plant of Reynolds Aluminum. According to the account in the October, 1972, *Voice* (which, you will remember, speaks for the Full Gospel Business Men's Fellowship International [FGBMFI]), the millwright was "without breath for *not less* than ten minutes, and more probably at least fifteen," after being trapped in the cable roll of a mill machine. In response to the fervent prayer of the president of the Longview chapter of the FGBMFI—"Lord, put life back into this body"—the man not only was fully restored to life, and without brain damage, but was up and walking around three days later!

"We had been told," says the author, John Foreman, "that the injured man had a broken arm, a skull fracture, and three broken ribs." [11]

"I prayed for a dead man," says Foreman, "and literally saw . . . a life loved back." [12]

If this miracle, even though home grown, is still a bit "much," relax with one of a different nature that seems eminently susceptible to proof or disproof. During Oral Roberts' ten-day healing crusade in Danville, Virginia, in May, 1956, reported the evangelist's magazine, *Abundant Life,* "crime and violent death took a holiday."

According to Author George E. Fisher, "The city . . . went the entire ten-day period of the campaign without a crime being committed. . . . A ten-day period of grace, without accident, without crime, at a time when thousands of visitors were jamming every hotel, tourist court, and private rooming house available for miles in and around Danville. . . . A city without crime! A city without accident! . . . Ten glorious days, with crime and highway tragedies operating somewhere else! . . . The Danville Police Chief generously credits the Oral Roberts' campaign with this crime-free, accident-free ten days. We thank the Chief for the credit, and we thank God for the record. . . . This is a sample of what would happen in the nation if the whole nation were to turn to God." [13]

The implications of this type of miracle, if it is valid, are stupendous. Extend this power to the crime centers of America and the world. Extend it to the Middle East and Vietnam, those tortured lands that have challenged the best peace-making efforts of the world's top diplomats and spiritual leaders. Schedule such crusades in Jerusalem, Cairo, Damascus, Saigon, Hanoi. (One does not have to be a Christian to be impressed by miracles!) Move Oral Roberts ahead of Billy Graham on the list of the nation's ten most admired men. Let's face it: No Seventh-day Adventist evangelist has produced such a dramatic impact on a community as the Roberts' crusade allegedly did on Danville.

I have the feeling that it is time for station identification. Just what do I wish to achieve in this chapter?

For one thing I shall not attempt to prove that miracles

occur. To cite proof texts for miracles is a futile pursuit; those who are convinced miracles do not happen will begin by begging the question, an unproductive fallacy of logic. Nor can experience confirm miracles, for seeing is not believing; if we doubt the possibility of miracles we shall simply doubt our senses (and sometimes with good reason, as we shall see). Neither will historical inquiry prove miracles; history does not serve up mathematical certitude; we are left yet with that which is possible but immensely improbable. I would suggest that the person concerned with proving miracles begin by considering the philosophical presuppositions he may have. *

If not to prove the possibility of miracles, what do I wish to accomplish? First (and superficially to be sure), to define miracles, to examine their relationship to natural law, to explore how they may work, and why they may occur. And by so doing to prepare the way for a look at faith healing—a form of miracle—in the next chapter. But I have another purpose: To testify both to my faith and doubts in miracles.

The extraordinary thing about miracles, as Gilbert K. Chesterton said, is that they happen. But the very term *miracle* suggests that they are not everyday occurrences. Wrote C. S. Lewis: "God does not shake miracles into Nature at random as if from a pepper-caster. They come on great occasions: they are found at the great ganglions of history—not of political or social history, but of that spiritual history which cannot be fully known by men." [14]

Adventists, too, believe in the principle known as "the economy of miracle," as the *Seventh-day Adventist Encyclopedia* observes. That is, "at least under ordinary circumstances, God does not employ supernatural means to accomplish that which man himself may achieve by natural means at his command." [15]

But economy of miracle does not mean that Scripture skimps on miraculous accounts. If we were to excise all miracles from the Bible, we would be left with a *Reader's Digest*-sized volume of incomparably less interest. In Mark, probably

* If you have doubts in this area read *Miracles*, by C. S. Lewis (The Macmillan Co., 1948).

the first of the Gospels, the first ten chapters all contain stories of miracles. So mingled are miracles with the ministry of Christ as to defy separation. The New Testament word most commonly used for miracles is *dunamis,* "power," which is residual both in Christ and in the gospel. Observing a miracle, Mark and Luke speak of power going out of Jesus (Mark 5:30, N.E.B.); Paul describes the gospel as the "power of God unto salvation" (Rom. 1:16).

As a Christian, I suffer no intellectual hang-up when confessing my faith in miracles. In fact, I have witnessed miracles—though none so incredibly incredible as a resurrection from the dead, nor so ordinarily incredible as having dirty clothes cleaned by an agent of some celestial laundromat. And if my faith is tinctured with skepticism, it is because of the nature of the miracle reported rather than the essential rationalism of my outlook; if I insist on documentation, it is not that I would thrust my hand into my Lord's side with Thomas before believing, but rather that I am jealous for the reputation of extraordinary events. Scoffers nurtured by Ms. Science deserve the best in miracles rather than dubious and undocumented accounts of something that supposedly happened half a world away.

During the Middle Ages miracle mongers sponsored a daily three-ring circus of supernatural feats. Like the daring young man on the flying trapeze, Joseph of Cupertino flew through the air with the greatest of ease, his walking stick flying wing man. St. Teresa of Avila, though not a featherweight, flew with such consummate ease that she had to be held down forcibly. Bodies were exhumed, undefiled and fresh, and sometimes they bled—St. John of the Cross did, when someone amputated his finger. St. Catherine of Siena was so favored of God that the Host at Mass leaped of its own accord into her mouth. With such real-life miracles reported from all around, who was to question when pictures of the virgin Mary shed tears until some offering was oversubscribed!

In those days you believed or else. Even today Roman Catholics must believe in miracles, though without becoming heretics they may doubt all but the Immaculate Conception, the virgin birth, and the resurrection of Christ. Protestants of the liberal variety, and Jews, are left to believe as they see fit. Most do not see fit. The burden miracles impose on twentieth-century mentality is heavy. Too heavy, I believe, to add the weight of overly imaginative accounts that awaken memories not of Jesus in Galilee but of Alice in Wonderland.

We come to the question, What *is* a miracle?

Among answers commonly given are: Something we cannot understand. A supernatural phenomenon. Something contrary to natural law. An effect wrought in nature directly by God.

If the first answer is correct, then television is a miracle to most of us, and even a flashlight is a miracle to the savage. A supernatural phenomenon may be supernatural only in the sense that we do not understand the operation of the natural laws involved. If a miracle is something contrary to natural law, then we have God, who established natural law, annulling them, thus appearing to act contrary to His own instruments.

What of the last definition—an effect wrought in nature directly by God? The definition seems reasonable—if God does not, in fact, work directly in nature in its everyday operations. But this is the problem with this definition: He always works directly in nature.

"It is not to be supposed that a law is set in motion for the seed to work itself, that the leaf appears because it must do so of itself. . . . It is through the immediate agency of God that every tiny seed breaks through the earth, and springs into life." [16]

"Not by its own inherent energy does the earth produce its bounties, and year by year continue its motion around the sun," says an Adventist textbook, *Education*. "An unseen hand guides the planets in their circuit of the heavens." [17] So, unless one is willing to define the passage of the earth through space and the growth of seeds as miracles, the last definition also is inadequate, for God daily works effects directly in nature. Nature is not wound up and left to perform on its own.

Natural law is simply God's way of accomplishing His will in the physical world. Natural law is regular in its functioning not because it is inherently regular, but because it reflects the design of a God of regularity.

Writes Ellen White:

"In dwelling upon the laws of matter and the laws of nature, many lose sight of, if they do not deny, the continual and direct agency of God. They convey the idea that nature acts independently of God, having in and of itself its own limits and its own powers wherewith to work. . . . It is supposed that matter is placed in certain relations and left to act from fixed laws with which God Himself cannot interfere; that nature is endowed with certain properties and placed subject to laws, and is then left to itself to obey these laws and perform the work originally commanded.

"This is false science; there is nothing in the word of God to sustain it. God does not annul His laws, but He is continually working through them, using them as His instruments. They are not self-working. God is perpetually at work in nature. She is His servant, directed as He pleases." [18]

To summarize: Nature is not self-sustaining, but requires a constant flow of power from God. Natural law or action only describes the constant condition; "miracle" describes the occasional condition when the Mind that directs nature as its instrument interferes either because interference is desirable or necessary.

Adventist scientist and writer H. W. Clark adds to our understanding of miracles: "In some cases they appear to be normal processes speeded up. In other cases they appear to be the interposition of one natural law against another in such a manner as to bring about a result that is out of the ordinary course of events." (As, for example, says Clark, when the law of friction operates against the law of acceleration whenever you depress the brake to slow acceleration of your automobile down a hill.)

"In still other cases," says Dr. Clark, "they [miracles] appear to involve creative power resulting in the production of new, healthy tissue, or the destruction of diseased tissue, or the giving of life to a lifeless body." [19]

Dr. Clark does not believe that miracles deny the natural order and system to which mankind is accustomed.

"Suppose," he says, "we are driving a car along a level road. Then we come to a hill and we find that the production of power in the motor is not sufficient to propel the car farther. What do we do? We simply shift gears and go on our way up the hill.

"Has any principle or law been violated? By the laws of mechanics, a certain size of piston supplied with a certain amount of fuel will produce a certain amount of power. When the hill becomes too steep this amount of power is insufficient to carry the load farther. But by shifting gears we apply that power more slowly, and the laws of mechanics make it possible by this changed rate of application to perform what was impossible before the change was made. No law has been violated, but simply a new combination of forces has been made.

"Miracles," concludes Dr. Clark, "do not deny the natural order or system of the universe, but are as it were gearshift mechanisms through which God may at times perform acts that may be different from those to which we have become accustomed." [20]

According to Dr. Clark, then, a miracle may be produced by (1) speeding up natural processes; (2) interposing one law against another to bring about an extraordinary result; (3) creating healthy tissue or destroying diseased tissue, all without denying natural law.

Can most or all miracles of Scripture be fitted into one or the other of these categories? The answer seems to be Yes.

1. *Crossing the Red Sea* (Exodus 14).

The record says that God "caused the sea to go back by a strong east wind" (Ex. 14:21). The miracle was not accomplished contrary to natural law, but through the utilization of natural forces. It was out of the ordinary, yes, but no problem to the God who controls air pressure. The stilling of the tempest on Galilee likely was accomplished in a similar manner.

Laws governing gravitation and surface tension may have been manipulated to enable Jesus to walk on water.

2. *Healing Hezekiah's boil* (2 Kings 20).

Directed by Isaiah to put a lump of figs on his boil, Hezekiah did so and was healed. Here natural remedy is utilized to help produce a miraculous healing. The lesson seems to be that God wants us to do what we can with the resources available; when these, in themselves, are insufficient to accomplish the desired objective, He assists the natural process.

3. *Turning water into wine* (John 2).

Here the God who works a miracle every day through production of earth's harvests (see Ellen G. White, *The Desire of Ages,* p. 367) speeded up those processes to produce wine in a moment.

In the usual process God combines carbon dioxide and water, compounds the sugars and starches, and, with the addition of a touch of nitrogen, the proteins. The process goes on from planting until harvest. At Cana, God speeded it up.

"Once, and in one year only, God, now incarnate, short circuits the process: makes wine in a moment: uses earthenware jars instead of vegetable fibers to hold the water. But uses them to do what He is always doing. The Miracle consists in the short cut; but the event to which it leads is the usual one." [21]

Though we know something of the physical and chemical forces at work in a vineyard, neither in the normal growth of grapes nor in the miracle at Cana can we explain just what happens. Both take the "immediate agency" of God.

Multiplication of the bread and the fish fits into the same category of miracles. Every year God multiplies little fish into big fish, a few fish into many fish; every year He makes seeds into corn; the seed is sown and in due course there is increase. What God did in multiplying the bread and the fish into a meal to feed the five thousand, He does every day in the process of feeding His children. The more we learn of what happens, the more we are brought to acknowledge the essential operation of Divine power.

4. *The raising of Lazarus* (John 11).

It is one thing to massage a stopped heart and watch pink tint livid flesh into the pastel of virility, as blood flows again into starved tissue. It is another thing to bring life again to decomposing tissue. Required is the same creative power breathed into a lump of dust in the beginning.

Dr. Clark's definition of miracles seems valid, in that it accommodates the miracles we have referred to from Scripture and gives us insight into their relationship to natural law.

But to understand *how* miracles may work is not to understand *why* they occur. The purpose of many of the miracles of the Old Testament was to prove the existence of God and His loving concern for a people who did not know Him. What of the miracles of Christ? Five main purposes are discernible, with more than one sometimes motivating a miracle.

1. *To demonstrate His divinity, as in the raising of Lazarus:*
"Then Jesus looked up to heaven and said, 'Father, thank you for hearing me. (You always hear me, of course, but I said it because of all these people standing here, so that they will believe you sent me.)' Then he shouted, 'Lazarus, come out!' "

And, says the record, "Lazarus came" (John 11:41-44, Taylor).

2. *To raise questions concerning His identity and purpose.* When Jesus changed water into wine at the marriage feast in Cana, He created the opportunity for His disciples to answer questions raised by guests about His identity and purpose. As a consequence of the miracle, priests and elders in Jerusalem, who had heard of it, began to search the Scriptures to see whether He might not be the Messiah. He did not, however, satisfy the curiosity of the Pharisees and others who sought a sign. Nor did He ever perform a miracle to benefit Himself. His wondrous works were ever for the good of others.

3. *To direct minds from nature to the God of nature.* By feeding the 5,000 He sought to direct the minds of those present from belief in natural forces to the God who directs those forces for the good of His children.

4. *Compassion, love.* Of His reason for raising the son of

the widow of Nain (Luke 7) the Bible says, He "had compassion on her." Concern for the hungry was also a motivation in His feeding of the multitude.

5. *To teach truth.* To clarify His purpose in the Sabbath commandment He performed many of His healings on the Sabbath. By healing the man at Siloam (John 9) He taught that it is lawful to do good on the Sabbath, thus rebuking the false accretions that had made His day a burden.

Though one might safely assume that the same purposes would govern performance of miracles today, we cannot safely assume that all miracles are performed by God. The Bible establishes clearly three points concerning Satan and miracles:

1. *Satan is able to perform miracles.* He deceives "them that dwell on the earth by the means of those miracles which he had power to do" (Rev. 13:14). The antichrist acts as "Satan's tool, full of satanic power, and will trick everyone with strange demonstrations, and will do great miracles" (2 Thess. 2:9, Taylor).

Says Ellen White: "Before the close of time he [Satan] will work still greater wonders. So far as his power extends, he will perform actual miracles." [22] Referring to Revelation 13:14, she says, "Something more than mere impostures is brought to view in this Scripture." [23]

2. *He counterfeits miracles he cannot perform.*

Satan is called a deceiver for a reason. When God performed miracles through Moses that Satan could not duplicate, he counterfeited them through the priests, producing so far as observers could determine, the same results as Moses. "But there is a limit beyond which Satan cannot go; and here he calls deception to his aid, and counterfeits the work which he has not power actually to perform." [24]

As I shall show in the next chapter, he is able to make men and women sick by his power, and then, by releasing them, make it appear that a miracle of healing has been wrought.

Particularly, in the time of the end he will work through spiritualism:

"Many will be confronted by the spirits of devils personating beloved relatives or friends, and declaring the most dangerous heresies. These visitants will appeal to our tenderest sympathies, and will work miracles to sustain their pretensions. We must be prepared to withstand them with the Bible truth that the dead know not anything, and that they who thus appear are the spirits of devils." [25]

"Through the agency of Spiritualism, miracles will be wrought, the sick will be healed, and many undeniable wonders will be performed. And as the spirits will profess faith in the Bible, and manifest respect for the institutions of the church, their work will be accepted as a manifestation of divine power." [26]

So powerful are these deceptions that Christ speaks of them as capable of deceiving all but "the very elect" (Matt. 24:24).

"Satan can lead deceived souls to great lengths. He can pervert their judgment, their sight, and their hearing." [27]

"Satan is Christ's personal enemy. He is the originator and leader of every species of rebellion in Heaven and earth. His rage increases; we do not realize his power. If our eyes could be opened to discern the fallen angels at work with those who feel at ease and consider themselves safe, we would not feel so secure. Evil angels are upon our track every moment. We expect a readiness on the part of bad men to act as Satan suggests; but while our minds are unguarded against his invisible agents, they assume new ground, and work marvels and miracles in our sight. Are we prepared to resist them by the word of God, the only weapon we can use successfully?" [28]

3. *Satan cannot give life.* Repeatedly Christ sets Himself forth as the Lifegiver, alone possessing the keys to the grave. Only through Christ can these bodies which are "mortal . . . put on immortality" (1 Cor. 15:53). Says Ellen White: "The prince of evil, though possessing all the wisdom and might of an angel fallen, has not power to create, or to give life; this is the prerogative of God alone." [29] But, as we have observed, through spiritualism agents of Satan will impersonate the dead themselves! The lie of Lucifer to earth's parent is repeated: "Ye

shall not surely die" (Gen. 3:4).

We are reminded of Mel Tari's story, wherein a dead man is reported to have sat up and said, "Brothers and sisters, I want to tell you something. First, life never ends when you die."

Having been returned by the caprice of composition to Timor, let us take a second look at events on that island and throughout Indonesia during the 1964-1966 revival. Was there a revival at all? And, if so, was it characterized by miracles?

"Most of the reports are greatly overplayed," says Alvin M. Bartlett, liaison secretary for the Indonesian Union of Seventh-day Adventists, who has been in Indonesia since 1948. "It is true that in the wake of the abortive [Communist] coup of September 30, 1965, and the bloody reaction which followed, many Mohammedans as well as Animists and other groups did turn to Christianity in some areas, and, of course, our church was also affected. Within just two or three years we baptized nearly 2,000 people from Islam. I know that this figure is not large compared with that claimed by some of the other Christian churches, but I think the difference is in our insistence on a personal conversion and commitment to a new way of life rather than a mere profession.

"The sad part of this story is that many of those that were baptized, even into the Adventist Church, are no longer faithful. Other church leaders here in Indonesia are very much disappointed also over the lack of real conversion among those baptized during that period. As the hysteria of those troubled years has passed, the desire for a Christian way of life has waned."

Continues Bartlett:

"I am sorry to have to report things in this way, for I know it would be wonderful if I could write a glowing report of the way things are happening in Indonesia, but sometimes it is better to tell it like it really is. Our work is going well among the Mohammedans of Central and East Java; that is, it is going well considering the conditions in those areas. However, I am afraid I must be frank in stating that this is certainly not the outpouring of the Holy Spirit which we are expecting to bring in the loud cry and to finish the work. We must take every advantage of the opportunities that are open for us and work carefully and steadily, but the great awakening, if it can be called such, which started a few years ago, was sparked by fear, rather than by the Holy Spirit." [30]

So there was a revival of sorts on Timor and throughout Indonesia, though of considerably less magnitude and from a different motivation than is commonly reported. Should it be a surprise to us that whenever and wherever God is active in revival, so also is Satan, seeking to twist it to his ends and leave those who responded to God's Spirit in a worse condition than before it began? Warned Ellen White, writing of revivals past and future: "There is an emotional excitement, a mingling of the true with the false, that is well adapted to mislead." [31]

Inhabitants of Timor were particularly susceptible to deception. They were, in the main, Animists (worshipers of spirits), with a nominal Islamic overlay. Their centers of religion were not only deficient spiritually but had incorporated idolatrous practices into their worship. The youth evangelists with whom Mel Tari witnessed were themselves spiritual infants. Most were illiterate. Naïve, simplistic, oriented to spirit worship, they saw supernatural elements in common occurrences. What one team reported of the miraculous, others felt it necessary to exceed. And, at last, immorality crept in. The same voices that had directed young men and women to go here and there, directed them to sleep together. Pride grew, and some sought to collect money for the "miracles" they could perform.

A committed Christian, Dr. Pearl K. Englund, anthropologist at Mankato (Minn.) State College, visited Timor during 1972 to investigate the Tari stories. While confirming that thousands of people have experienced healings and that whole villages have become Christian, Dr. Englund reported that in most cases Tari's stories were not only unsubstantiated but repudiated, and further, a source of embarrassment to his pastor and fellow youth evangelists.[32] Her account parallels the conclusions of W. Stanley Mooneyham, a Methodist clergyman who has written about the revival on Timor. Mooneyham released his views through the Associated Church Press after numerous letters and telephone calls questioned an implied endorsement by him in the foreword to Tari's book. The statement, said Mooneyham, was "lifted out of context from a story I wrote in 1967. I do not endorse the book." [33]

Dr. Englund told me the story behind the turning of water into wine. "I found," she said, "that the story had its beginning in an experience with an old Animist woman, not even a Christian, who, unobserved, poured a liquid, which she said was water, into a pot. She covered it and asked the youth evangelists to pray a prayer over it, which she recited to them. When they did so, she removed the cover and lo, there was wine! Draw your own conclusions," said Dr. Englund.

And what of the walking on water? Team members told Dr. Englund that a light revealed rocks under the surface on which they were able to ford the river. Natives not aware of the hidden ford may well have fallen in and nearly drowned. The multiplied cassava root story grew from the testimony of youth among whom the food was divided, that they had had "enough." Both Dr. Englund and Mooneyham report that the dramatic resurrection incident simply did not happen.

Of all Tari's reported miracles, those in connection with fetish burnings seem to have the most basis in fact. Around the fetishes, says Mooneyham, "in earlier days the witch doctors had done their own miracles. How appropriate that God would demonstrate His power as the fetishes were being burned!" [34]

Significant it is, however, that of the tens of thousands on Timor who claim a new relationship with Christ only a handful witness to having experienced any miracle other than the new birth. And sources on the island report that if miracles are occurring on Timor today, they are doing so in no greater frequency than in the United States.

And what of the United States, specifically of the two

"home-grown" miracles, cited earlier? Do they warrant more credence than we have given Mel Tari's report? Let's stop for a page or two in Longview, Washington. Was the millwright trapped in a machine at Reynolds Aluminum really without breath for not less than ten minutes, as John Foreman reports? Was he actually prayed back from the dead? Did he have a broken arm, skull fracture, and three broken ribs, as Foreman said "we had been told"?

With the assistance of Quentin Qualley, pastor of the Longview Seventh-day Adventist church, I asked the millwright, Allan Fruend, what really happened. Was he actually dead?

"Not in my opinion," Mr. Fruend responded.

(Had he been, Author John Foreman's theology would have demanded that he have gone either to heaven or hell. Would Mr. Foreman accept Mr. Fruend's report that he was "unconscious" as evidence that he could not have been dead?)

Fruend also maintains that, contrary to the article, he was given artificial respiration, and thus was not without breath for an extended period.

Did he have a broken arm and a skull fracture, as Foreman says "we had been told"? The answer is No.

Fruend was, however, seriously injured, which led him to point up another inaccuracy in the *Voice* account. He was not, as the article says, up "three days after the accident, . . . walking around the halls, and the doctors could not find a thing wrong with him." "Completely misleading," he snorts. "I was in intensive care for one week, then moved to another room for another week. My heart is just now [January 28, 1973] back to normal; the muscle in my arm will never be one hundred per cent all right again. I am still bothered with pleurisy." [35]

It surely would not have taken much research on Mr. Foreman's part to improve the accuracy of his story. And for the editor of the *Voice* to print it without verification is inexcusable. Given this degree of careless reporting, even on the details of Mr. Fruend's injuries, I feel no pang of remorse in confessing my inability to accept the resurrection account. Should the

Lord decide to resurrect someone from the dead this side of His return, I suspect the trimmings will rival the main event *and* stand up under examination!

By their very definition, miracles are the exception. They are not manufactured on a Detroit assembly line and driven off, thousands a day, to take the place of pedestrian norms. Nor are they the norm of revival.

Many of the greatest revivals of history have seen no miracle other than that of the transformed life. John the Baptist, a "voice" crying in the wilderness of his day, performed no miracles (John 10: 41), yet he was one of the greatest of the prophets. God's people of the last day, His remnant, will be known not so much for the miracles they perform as for the truth they preach and live. A comparison of Revelation 12:17 and 14:12 shows that they have three characteristics: They keep the commandments of God, they keep the faith of Jesus, and they have the testimony of Jesus. Miracles are not mentioned.

In Christ's day many people desired signs from heaven to confirm their faith, but Jesus said, "There shall no sign be given . . . but the sign of the prophet Jonas" (Matt. 12:39). Then He began to quote from the Word of God. Here is the real test of a movement's source. Does it square up with the Word of God? What is its fruit? It is by the Word that pentecostalism, both neo and classic, must be evaluated, not by its miracles—though its reported "miracles" may, indeed, say something about it. And, let us not forget, the Word is *Truth*. Voices crying "Miracle! miracle!" in the spiritual wilderness of our day (yes, even that *Voice* speaking for the FGBMFI) must be measured not by the quantity of their crying but by the quality of their truth.

Mistakes of fact may creep into any publication—including this book; but make no mistake in this: Habitual hyperbole and uncritical charisma do not bear the stamp of heaven. The copy editor's credo—verify, verify, verify—would put scores of miracle mongers out of business. When it comes to reporting miracles, pentecostalism might well take a lesson

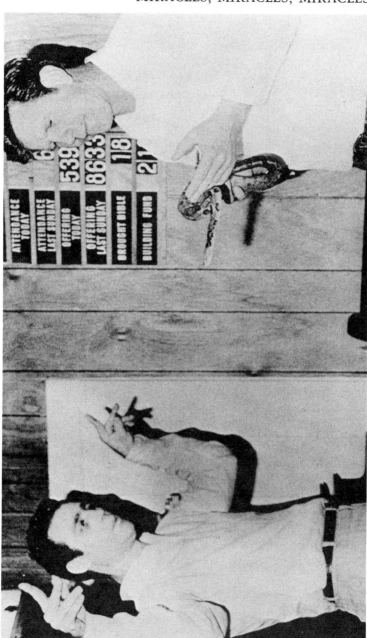

RELIGIOUS NEWS SERVICE PHOTO

Pastor Liston Pack handles a rattlesnake while another man undergoes a "religious trance" during a service of a Holiness sect in North Carolina. Mr. Pack's brother and another man died in April, 1973, after drinking strychnine in a "demonstration of faith."

from the Catholic Church. Of 1.5 million pilgrims who visit Lourdes each year, only a handful—for example, five in 1968—were even *tentatively* certified by church officials as having been cured. The dictionary makes a clear-cut distinction between credibility and gullibility. So should the Christian.

We stop, in conclusion, at the site of our last cited homegrown miracle, Danville, Virginia, where in May of 1956 all crime and accidents took a holiday during the ten-day visit of the Oral Roberts crusade, a miracle that the Danville Major Chief of Police was said to have "generously" credited to the crusade's influence.

In my possession is a letter from J. C. Garrett, then Major Chief of Police in Danville. Addressed to Chaplain Davis A. Thomas* and printed on the stationery of the Department of Police, City of Danville, Virginia, it reads:

"Dear Sir:

"In answer to your letter dated October 5, 1956, I would like to say first of all that I have never made a statement to Mr. Roberts or anyone else regarding crime conditions in the city of Danville, before, during, or after the Oral Roberts Revival held here in Danville, May 4 through May 13, 1956.

"I believe the following figures will answer your questions concerning the ten-day period that the Oral Roberts campaign was in Danville:

OFFENSES	PERSONS ARRESTED
Aggravated Assault	3
Other Assaults	4
Larceny-Theft	4
Embezzlement and Fraud	1
Weapons, Carrying, Possessing, etc.	1
Offenses against family and children	13
Liquor Laws	2
Drunkenness	43
Disorderly Conduct	9
Driving While Intoxicated	3
Reckless Driving	7
Fail to Yield Right of Way	5
Pass Red Light	3
Speeding	3

* Davis A. Thomas is currently a chaplain at Florida Hospital, Orlando.

Improper Passing	1
No City Strip	1
No Operator's License	4
Improper Muffler	1
Hit and Run	2
Follow Too Close	2
Misc. Traffic Offenses	1
All other Offenses, Trespass, A.W.O.L., etc.	9
TOTAL PERSONS ARRESTED	122

Concludes the letter:

"Our Police Department records show there has never been a ten-day period when a single crime was not committed . . .

"Sincerely yours,

(Signed) "J. C. Garrett, Major Chief of Police."

Yes, even after writing this chapter, I still believe in miracles. But with Stanley Mooneyham I believe that "the greatest evidence that a work has been done by God's Spirit is found in redeemed lives, not restructured molecules. The Bible teaches that Satan has power to reorder physical elements and thus produce 'miracles.' Only God can change lives redemptively. This, then, becomes the acid test of God's presence in a movement.

"And for people with a mature faith who don't have to seek after a sign, this ought to be enough." [36]

References

[1] Cliff Dudley, *Like a Mighty Wind* (Carol Stream, Ill.: Creation House, 1971), p. 79.

[2] *Ibid.*, p. 97.

[3] *Ibid.*, p. 101.

[4] *Ibid.*, p. 44.

[5] *Ibid.*, pp. 47-49.

[6] *Ibid.*, p. 104.

[7] *Ibid.*, pp. 46, 47.

[8] *Ibid.*, p. 13.

[9] *Ibid.*, p. 54.

[10] *Ibid.*, pp. 76-78.

[11] John Foreman, "A Life Loved Back," Full Gospel Business Men's *Voice*, Vol. XX (Oct., 1972), p. 26.

[12] *Ibid.*, p. 27.

[13] George E. Fisher, "No Crime for 10 Days," *Abundant Life*, Sept., 1956, p. 15.

[14] C. S. Lewis, *Miracles*, The Macmillan Co. (1948), p. 201.

[15] *Seventh-day Adventist Encyclopedia*, p. 506.

[16] Ellen G. White, quoted in *Review and Herald*, Nov. 8, 1898.

[17] ———, *Education* (Mountain View, California: Pacific Press Publishing Association), p. 99.

[18] _____, *Testimonies for the Church*, vol. 8, pp. 259, 260.

[19] *Review and Herald*, May 9, 1957, p. 8.

[20] *Ibid.*, May 16, 1957, p. 5.

[21] C. S. Lewis, *op. cit.*, p. 163.

[22] Ellen G. White, *Testimonies for the Church*, vol. 5, p. 698.

[23] *Ibid.*

[24] *Ibid.*

[25] _____, *The Great Controversy*, p. 560.

[26] *Ibid.*, p. 588.

[27] _____, *Testimonies for the Church*, vol. 3, p. 351.

[28] *Ibid.*, vol. 1, p. 302.

[29] _____, *Patriarchs and Prophets* (Mountain View, California: Pacific Press Publishing Association), p. 264.

[30] Letter to D. S. Johnson, associate secretary, General Conference, dated Dec. 6, 1972.

[31] Ellen G. White, *The Great Controversy*, p. 464.

[32] From a telephone conversation with Dr. Englund during January, 1973.

[33] W. Stanley Mooneyham, "Revival and Miracles: What About Indonesia?" an Associated Church Press release, 1972.

[34] *Ibid.*

[35] Letter from Allan Fruend to Pastor Qualley, dated Jan. 28, 1973.

[36] Mooneyham, *loc. cit.*

11

"People, It's Here!"

No charismatic meeting is complete without its prayers for healing and its stories of miraculous deliverance from disease. Let's slip back to the Phoenix session of the Full Gospel Business Men's Fellowship International to capture the authentic flavor of a healing report. I have not chosen the following account because it is sensational, which it is, but because it is typical of hundreds I have heard. The speaker is identified on tape as a doctor.*

"I had an experience with a lady just a few days ago—it was in a healing meeting in Home Gardens, just outside the city of Riverside. This lady was in this revival meeting, and she had many needs, but she was afraid to tell the evangelist when she was invited up for prayer, and so she just mentioned the fact that she was deaf in her left ear. So the man prayed for her, but God knew her need, and He completely healed this woman. Now she had had 28 operations! She had a steel bar in her back that enabled her to stand up, and she had a steel

* He is a dentist, not a physician.

screen in her to hold her innards together. It's just fabulous, all the other things she had besides this, and she was really at the end of her rope, and the Lord completely healed her. This was on a Monday night. On Wednesday she went to her medical doctor, who had been taking care of her case. He examined her, and her heart and blood pressure were perfect, her heartbeat was perfect, she had no signs of asthma, her diabetes was gone. There was no indication of the presence of the steel bar, so they X-rayed her, and the steel bar had completely disappeared! The steel screen in her was gone, and she was completely healthy!"

"Oh, praise God!" responded the chairman of the meeting, to an accompanying chorus of Amens. "I knew that we farmers used to tell these wild stories, but I never thought doctors would tell any."

In the wild-story category, my favorite, after twenty years of research, is still that of Betty Baxter Heidt, who recounts it at healing meetings. According to Betty, she was born with a curve in her spine. Every vertebra was out of place, the bones twisted and matted together. Her nervous system was wrecked. In addition she contracted St. Vitus' dance and had to be strapped in bed. Her heart was not normal and the dope the doctors gave her made it worse; she came to have one heart attack a week. For hours she would lie unconscious. When the doctor told her she would have to have a new kidney, something snapped inside of her and she became blind and deaf. Her tongue swelled and became paralyzed. Finally, so bent that her head was pressed tightly against her knees, she died and went to heaven. There Jesus healed her, inside and out. Says Betty:

"He placed His hand on the very center of my spine on one of the large knots. All at once a hot feeling, as hot as fire, surged through my body. Two hot hands took my heart and squeezed it, and when those hot hands let my heart go, I could breathe normally, and I knew my heart was normal for the first time in my life. Two hot hands rubbed over the organs of my stomach and I knew my organic trouble was healed. . . . The

hot feeling ran on through my body. Then I looked at Jesus to
see if He would leave me just healed inside. Jesus smiled and I
felt the pressure of His hands on the knots, and as His hands
pressed in the middle of my spine, there was a tingling sensation like I had touched a live wire. I felt this sensation like an
electrical current, and I stood on my feet. . . ." [1]

I am also intrigued by the story of David Pelletier, who,
when nine years old, lost his left eye.

The Pelletiers report that a miracle occurred on July 16,
1971, when David bounded into the living room and shouted,
"Mama, Daddy, I can see out of my bad eye!"

According to the *Voice* of October, 1972, David now has
light perception and can even see objects, forms, colors, movement; *"and he can even read."* It makes no difference says the
Voice, "whether the plastic eye is in or out." Several eye sur-
geons reputedly have verified this miracle. [2]

A picture on page four shows David, patch over his good
eye, describing a man in the audience as "God enables him to
'see' through the plastic eye."

Apart from the fantastic claim that David can see through
his plastic eye, what intrigues me is the similarity of the account to another of my long-time favorites, the story of Ronald Coyne of Sapulpa, Oklahoma. According to the account in
a faith healer publication of February, 1954, Ronald lost his
eye in an accident. When a lady evangelist "Sister Daisy Gil-
lock," prayed over him the prayer of faith—not knowing that
he had been fitted with a plastic eye—Ronald discovered that
he was able to see through his plastic eye, and indeed was able
to see, whether the plastic eyeball was in or out. [3]

I have not chosen the most unbelievable of the accounts in
faith-healer legend. I could have filled this chapter with nothing but stories of resurrections from the dead, all of which
have taken place, it is said, within the past few decades. At
least one faith healer, O. L. Jaggers, claimed to have been resurrected. [4] And, as we learned in the previous chapter, an Indonesian evangelist claims to have been instrumental in raising
from the dead a man whose body already was putrifying. [5]

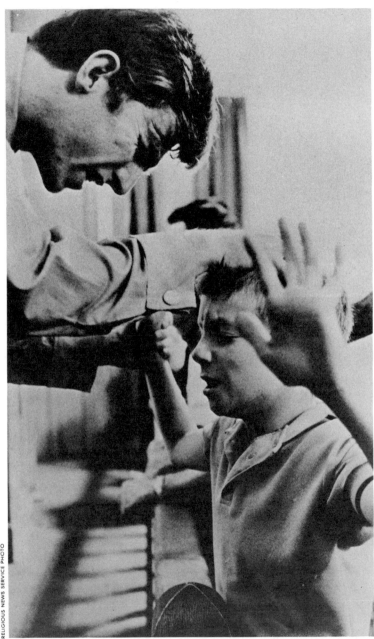

A "healing evangelist" lays his hand on the head of a young supplicant in a Pentecostal revival meeting.

RELIGIOUS NEWS SERVICE PHOTO

There are, of course, more prosaic healings. In vogue are lengthening limbs and filling teeth. The October, 1972, *Voice* reports that in a Copenhagen, Denmark, meeting, "short limbs were lengthened before we could even ask—lengthened right before our eyes, and before the eyes of a lot of amazed people." [6] In an Evangelical church in Vejle, "some who had one limb shorter than the other, saw the limbs lengthened as everyone gathered round and watched." [7] In Stockholm, Sweden, a FGBMFI team member "prayed for a girl with one leg about one and three-fourths inches shorter than the other, and the leg lengthened as we watched." [8] In Bergen, Norway, a left arm five inches short "grew out to equal length." [9] As for teeth, the *Voice* reports on "a gentleman" who was "prayed for who had had a gold inlay fall out of his teeth several weeks ago." Immediately after prayer, "he tried to put his tongue in the hole between the two teeth . . . but he couldn't . . . because Jesus had filled both of his teeth with beautiful fillings." [10] A teen-ager named Yolanda Holley from Globe, Arizona, testifies: "I received fillings in my teeth during a camp meeting." "Why not let God be YOUR dentist?" suggests the story in *Miracle* magazine, published by A. A. Allen Revivals, Inc.[11]

But it is the more sensational healings that fit best into the atmosphere of the pentecostal faith healing service. The following account by Oral Roberts, of a meeting in Jacksonville, Florida, recreates the emotional pitch:

"As I sat there praying, God's power would strike my hand every few seconds. It stung like fire. Then suddenly it struck with tremendous force, and I screamed at the top of my voice, 'People, something is coming! People, something is coming!' . . . In a moment the power of God struck my hand a second time with such force that I shouted at the top of my voice, 'People, it's here! People, it's here!' It seemed like an earthquake shook the tent. I saw the people as a blur before me. My right hand was vibrating and shaking with the presence of God in it. The people leaped to their feet and started streaming down the aisles toward me. People began pulling at my clothes. The voice of the crowd was like the roar of mighty waters.

"I leaped off the main platform on to the lower platform and stood waiting. People started thronging it, and I began laying my right hand upon as many as I could and as fast as I could. It seemed like balls of fire were streaming through my hand and everybody I touched felt the healing power of God. The healing virtue of Jesus would strike them the moment I touched them, and they would go leaping and shouting away. I turned to my right to pray for some people, and there sat a man and a woman in two wheel chairs. They were screaming for someone to let them touch me. I reached out my hand, and they both grabbed it. Without a word they both came out of those wheel chairs, and the last I saw of them they were running down the aisles. Right behind me I heard someone scream that he could see. I whirled around, and it was a blind man who was screaming that he could see the lights, he could see the people's faces. Deaf eardrums were opened, crippled and withered legs were made straight, and people all over the tent were feeling that miraculous power to set them free." [12]

Some call it faith healing. Others refer to it as miraculous healing, divine healing, or spiritual healing. I'll stick with faith healing, the term I have most often heard used in pentecostal services. I should emphasize that this chapter is concerned primarily with the classic pentecostal charismatics, who though no longer having a monopoly on faith healing, surely dominate the field. So far as I am aware, Roman Catholic charismatics, a more restrained group than classic pentecostals, are not presently pitching tents on the faith-healing circuit. They are, however, emphasizing healing at charismatic meetings on Catholic college and university campuses, in private homes, and at interdenominational gatherings, such as those of the Full Gospel Business Men's Fellowship International. (All in addition to the traditional Catholic faith-healing approach at Lourdes and elsewhere.)

Healing was at center stage in the ministry of Jesus. He came that we might have life, and have it more abundantly

(John 10:10). "He 'took our infirmities, and bare our sicknesses' that He might minister to every need of humanity. . . . It was His mission to bring to men complete restoration; He came to give them health and peace and perfection of character." [13]

The concern of Christ for the whole of man was demonstrated in many incidents of His earthly ministry.

He gave sight to the man born blind (John 9:1-7). He loosed the woman bound by Satan (Luke 13:10-13). He enabled the paralytic to walk (John 5:5-9).

In fact, Luke, himself a physician, records that a great multitude came to Him out of Judea and Jerusalem, and He healed them all (Luke 6:19). In every city, every town, every village, through which He passed, He laid His hands upon the sick and healed them. From Him flowed a stream of healing power, and in body and soul and spirit the sick were made whole. Wherever He went the tidings of His mercy preceded Him, and where He had been, the objects of His compassion were found rejoicing in health. There were whole villages where there was not one cry of pain when He passed, for He had healed all their sick.

"His voice was the first sound that many had ever heard, His name the first word they had ever spoken, His face the first they had ever looked upon. Why should they not love Jesus and sound His praise? As He passed through the towns and cities, He was like a vital current, diffusing life and joy." [14]

"The gospel which He taught was a message of spiritual life and of physical restoration. Deliverance from sin and the healing of disease were linked together." [15] As A. J. Gordon has written: "Men believed on Him and were forgiven; men touched Him and were healed. His abounding grace made instant response to the sinner's faith; His abounding life gave instant answer to the sick man's touch. And so blended and interlaced are those two elements in the ministry of our Lord that they are constantly crossing; healing emerging in forgiveness, and forgiveness in healing." [16]

The Saviour devoted more time and labor to healing the

afflicted of their maladies than to preaching. Thus He threw back upon Satan the reproach of the evil that the enemy of all good originated. He showed that Satan is the destroyer, God the restorer. And, unlike in the hospitals and clinics of our day, His ministry was free. It was also practical and educative.

Through His followers today Jesus wishes to continue His work as the Great Physician. It is our work to present the sick and suffering in faith to Him, teaching them to believe in the merits of His atonement, the sureness of His promises. The characters of God and of Satan must again be shown in contrast, their methods made plain. Upon this world's dark night the "Sun of Righteousness" again must shine with "healing in his wings" (Mal. 4:2).

Is Christ's pattern of ministry reflected in the charismatic movement—particularly in that pentecostal segment of it that has become synonymous with the healing tent?

I believe some contradictions are evident. Here are three points on which the majority of faith healers fail to measure up.

First, they promote an unscriptural teaching of the will of God.

Believing that healing is in the atonement, pentecostal faith healers hold that it is God's will for all the sick to be healed.

Says Glenn Clark: "When two agree together in this way in giving any trouble or illness completely into the hands of the Father, He always takes it away." [17] Says F. F. Bosworth: "The greatest barrier to the faith of many seeking bodily healing in our day is the uncertainty in their minds as to it being the will of God to heal *all*." [18]

Adventists believe that all blessings mankind enjoy come through the atonement—the food on our tables, the clothing we wear, the house that shelters us; our very life and health and, yes, healing, all come because Christ took the sins of mankind upon Himself, making available to all who believe at-one-ment with divinity.

An Adventist book on the life of Christ, *The Desire of Ages*, eloquently expresses mankind's daily dependence on Christ:

"To the death of Christ we owe even this earthly life. The bread we eat is the purchase of His broken body. The water we drink is bought by His spilled blood. Never one, saint or sinner, eats his daily food, but he is nourished by the body and the blood of Christ. The cross of Calvary is stamped on every loaf. It is reflected in every water spring. . . . The family board becomes as the table of the Lord, and every meal a sacrament." [19]

So there is no hesitancy among Adventists to approach God by faith, pleading the benefits of the vicarious atonement. But what of the pentecostal insistence that it is the will of God to heal *all*, that He *always* takes illness away?

Must it be emphasized that no one gets out of this world alive? "The wages of sin is death" (Rom. 6:23), and man yet collects his due. Sickness and suffering and eventual death are common to all, saint and sinner, skeptic and faith healer, and will continue to be until death is vanquished at the return of Jesus (1 Cor. 15:23-27).

George Eldon Ladd, professor of Biblical theology, Fuller Theological Seminary, points out that though Christians even now live by faith in the age to come, they still are bound by the frailty and mortality of the old age. Writes Dr. Ladd:

"Your bodies are dead [i.e., dying] because of sin, your spirits are alive because of righteousness" (Rom. 8:10). Death, disease, decay, weakness all belong to the old order. Even though our Lord has 'abolished death and brought life and immortality to life through the gospel' (2 Tim. 1:10), we still live in mortal bodies and, if the Lord tarries, we shall die. The life we experience is primarily in the realm of the spirit; our bodies are still subject to the encroachments of decay and death. . . .

"Jesus' deliverance from both sickness and death are signs of the presence of the Kingdom of God, as well as pledges of ultimate deliverance in the consummated Kingdom. However, they were signs which were not universally exercised, but were outward anticipations, given only in specific instances, of the ultimate promise of the redemption of the body. This final redemption will include creation itself (Rom. 8:21).

"The firstfruits which all believers possess is the indwelling, life-giving Holy Spirit; but in our mortal bodies we continue to groan under the burden of weakness, decay, disease and death, while we await the consummated redemption (Rom. 8:23). This is not to say that God does not still, in isolated instances, perform wonderful acts of healing; however, this blessing, along with deliverance from death, belongs to the age to come, not to the present age." [20]

A further reason why God does not heal all, is that an illness may be God's instrument to prune a branch that it bear fruit (John 15:2). Thus Paul says, "If any man's work be burned, he shall suffer loss; but he himself shall be saved; yet so as by fire." "For our light affliction, which is but for a moment, worketh for us a far more exceeding and eternal weight of glory" (1 Cor. 3:15; 2 Cor. 4:17).

Paul himself stands as Exhibit A that while God *always* answers the prayer for healing, He does not always say Yes. To Paul, who beseeched that his "thorn in the flesh"—probably bad eyesight—be taken away, Jesus replied, "My grace is sufficient for thee" (2 Cor. 12:9).

We should remember both Melita and Melitum; in one Paul healed the father of Publius by his prayers; in the other he left Trophimus sick.

Confusion regarding God's will leads to a second departure from Christ's example—presumption in prayer.

To pray "Thy will be done," insists a faith healer, demonstrates lack of faith and is abhorrent to God![21] "Our faith *makes* God act," asserts another.[22]

To support their thesis, faith healers quote Mark 11:24: "Whatever you ask for in prayer, believe that you have received it, and it will be yours" (N.E.B.). I tried out this promise as an 11-year-old, pleading with God that, as a sign of His power, He remove the mountain from behind our home in Oregon. It did seem a big project, but the evangelist had said faith as large as a pin head could manage it. It didn't. So I prayed for a soapbox car, with an engine. But neither my Father in heaven nor my father on earth saw fit to give it to me.

I would have been saved a good bit of anguished remonstrance with God had someone expanded my proof-text theology with 1 John 5:14, 15 (R.S.V.): "If we ask anything *according to his will,* he hears us. . . . And . . . we know that we have obtained the requests made of him." Some things we deeply desire, including healing, may not be according to His will.

How prayed our Pattern? In Gethsemane, realizing that He was soon to die, Jesus prayed, "O my Father, if it be possible, let this cup pass from me." Jesus does not hesitate to make known His human desires. He asks to be saved from suffering and death. This is an important aspect of prayer. But having made His wishes known, He adds, "Nevertheless, not as I will, but as thou wilt" (Matt. 26:39). Once Jesus had confessed His desire to avoid suffering and death, He then without reserve subjected Himself to the will of the Father.

In prayer for the sick, wrote Ellen White, "It should be remembered that 'we know not what we should pray for as we ought.' We do not know whether the blessing we desire will be best or not. Therefore our prayers should include this thought: 'Lord, Thou knowest every secret of the soul. Thou art acquainted with these persons. Jesus, their Advocate, gave His life for them. His love for them is greater than ours could possibly be. If, therefore, it is for Thy glory and the good of the afflicted ones, we ask, in the name of Jesus, that they be restored to health. If it is not Thy will that they be restored, we ask that Thy grace may comfort and Thy presence sustain them in their suffering.'" [23]

In this submissive yet faith-filled spirit we may press before God the promise of James 5:14, 15: "Is any sick among you? let him call for the elders of the church; and let them pray over him, anointing him with oil in the name of the Lord: And the prayer of faith shall save the sick, and the Lord shall raise him up; and if he have committed sins, they shall be forgiven him."

To recommend that the qualification "If it be thy will" be deleted from our prayers and thoughts is not to make progress in piety, but to retrogress into paganism. Faith healers ought not to forget that the children of Israel were rebuked because they presumptuously committed the sin of putting the Lord to the proof (Ex. 17:7), or, as a paraphrase has it, "tempted him to slay them by saying, 'Is Jehovah going to take care of us or not?' " (Taylor).

In examining the pattern ministry we find a third point at variance with faith healer theology and practice: *Christ linked healing with education and reform, elements usually conspicuous by their absence in today's charismatic ministry.*

At the turn of the century, Seventh-day Adventists faced a perplexing question: Instead of building sanitariums why not just heal the sick as Christ did? The church arrived at two answers that were right to the point: 1. God saw that spurious works of healing through the devil's power would become prevalent, so He "marked out" a medical ministry embracing natural remedies and the teaching of the Bible.[24] 2. Through sanitariums many patients could be educated to right principles of living.

The first reason for building sanitariums came, paradoxically, from a study of the miracles of Christ. Why did He perform them? The answer is not found alone in His compassion for the sick, for He could have healed them by natural remedies or processes. Though slower, this method also would have resulted in healing. And it would have given Jesus time to place even greater emphasis on laws of health. But He did not follow this method. Why?

The reason may lie partly in the shortness of His ministry on earth. What He did, He had to do quickly. But an even more compelling reason was the distinctive witness of miracles. As nothing else could, they certified His divinity. Search the records of the New Testament and you will find little evidence that Satan then used miracles to counterfeit the work of Christ. The lesson of Israel's deliverance from Egypt, in which his every miracle and seeming miracle before Pharaoh was eclipsed, may have made him wary of engaging in another battle of miracles. Whether he dared not risk, or was not permitted even to try to risk, a miracle-working confrontation with the Saviour, the results were the same: Christ's divinity was certified by the miracles He wrought—though, as we learned in the previous chapter, He worked no miracles to prove His divinity to skeptics, but only to satisfy honest doubts.

But Christ having left earth, Satan immediately began to counterfeit His works. Records of the centuries since are replete with counterfeit miracles, many of which are part of church, not pagan, lore. And Satan's campaign of counterfeit miracles will intensify. In the time of the end he will go forth "armed with all the force, wonders, and signs that falsehood can devise. To those involved in this dying world he will come with evil's undiluted power to deceive" (2 Thess. 2:8, 9, Phillips). In judgment Christ will deny working through men who in His name had done "many wonderful works" (Matt. 7:22)—among them, we may be sure, works of healing. Miraculous healings, then, are today no evidence of Christ's divinity, but serve instead, in many cases, to confirm a false christ!

It was with this insight that Ellen White wrote:

"The way in which Christ worked was to preach the word, and to relieve suffering by miraculous works of healing. But I am instructed that we cannot now work in this way; for Satan will exercise his power by working miracles. God's servants today could not work by means of miracles; because spurious works of healing, claiming to be divine, will be wrought." [25]

Confronted with Satan's crusade of the counterfeit, Christ "marked out a way in which His people are to carry forward a work of physical healing, combined with the teaching of the word. Sanitariums are to be established, and with these institutions are to be connected workers who will carry forward genuine medical missionary work. Thus a guarding influence is thrown around those who come to the sanitariums for treatment." [26]

Thus through (1) physical healing, in which patients

would be taught God's laws and how to cooperate with them, (2) the teaching of the Word, with its warnings of counterfeits and criteria for distinguishing truth from error, and (3) the guarding influence of Christians alert to the devil's subterfuges and abilities to deceive, the healing ministry of Christ was to be carried on, adapted by inspiration to meet the unique challenges of our day.

The second reason for a ministry of healing through sanitariums was likewise practical: to relieve sickness through treatment, and to teach right habits of living and how to avoid sickness. [27]

Wrote Ellen White:

"It is labor lost to teach people to look to God as the healer of their infirmities, unless they are taught also to lay aside unhealthful practices. In order to receive His blessing in answer to prayer, they must cease to do evil and learn to do well. Their surroundings must be sanitary. Their habits of life correct. They must live in harmony with the law of God, both natural and spiritual." [28] "In the work of the gospel, teaching and healing are *never* to be separated." [29] "Deliverance from sin and the healing of disease were linked together. The same ministry is committed to the Christian physician." [30]

This philosophy of healing, based as it is on the union of healing and teaching in Christ's ministry, says something essential not only to faith healers but to Christian physicians, nurses, and directors of Christian sanitariums and hospitals. It says that Christian medical institutions are not doing their God-given work if they major more in administering medication than in teaching patients how to live in harmony with God's laws of health. It says that preventive medicine is to occupy a prominent place in the institution's approach to healing. It says that the Christian doctor must not be content to cut out diseased flesh while leaving in debasing habits that lead to disease. It says that the doctor's responsibility in healing does not stop with administration of pills and penicillin, nor with treating the physical man: "Deliverance from sin and healing of disease were linked together" in the ministry of

Christ. It says—and let those in the Adventist ministry of healing especially take note—that *not all false healing takes place in healing tents.*

When Christ healed the sick, He warned many of the afflicted, "Sin no more, lest a worse thing come upon thee" (John 5:14). Thus He taught that man brings disease upon himself by transgression of the laws of God, and that health can be preserved only by obedience. If God were to work a miracle and restore people to health who had brought disease upon themselves by impurity, self-indulgence, and disregard of the laws of health, He would be encouraging sin. Those healed would "pursue the same course of heedless transgression of God's natural and spiritual laws, reasoning that if God heals them in answer to prayer, they are at liberty to continue their unhealthful practices and to indulge perverted appetite without restraint." [31] "God requires all who believe the truth to make special, persevering efforts to place themselves in the best possible condition of bodily health." [32]

In addition to living right physically, men must live right spiritually, if they are to know the healing touch of Jesus. Said our Lord: "Confess your faults one to another, and pray one for another, that ye may be healed" (James 5:16). Thus even the "call for the elders of the church," and the "prayer of faith" that "shall save the sick" are subject to conditions of obedience as well as faith. "If I regard iniquity in my heart, the Lord will not hear me," wrote the psalmist (Ps. 66:18). "Ye are my friends, if ye do whatsoever I command you" (John 15:14), said Jesus. "If ye love me, keep my commandments" (John 14:15). The way God has marked out is the way of reformation—that is, renewed commitment to the laws God has given to keep us living healthfully, happily, and eternally.

When the question was raised, Why not heal the sick as Christ did? Ellen White answered:

"You are not ready. Some have believed; some have been healed; but there are many who make themselves sick by intemperate eating or by indulging in other wrong habits. When they get sick, shall we pray for them to be raised up, that they may carry on the very same work again? There must be a reformation throughout our ranks; the people must reach a higher standard before we can expect the power of God to be manifested in a marked manner for the healing of the sick.

"We talk of the Holy Ghost; we preach of the Holy Ghost; but we need to understand better what the office of the Holy Ghost is. We need to understand that we must cooperate with God in every sense or God can not cooperate with us. 'We are laborers together with God.' " [33]

We are left with a perplexing question. If faith healers commonly misunderstand God's will, presumptuously insist on healing, and fail to link reform and healing, why are they so successful?

They are not so successful as their magazines and radio and television claims would lead us to believe. Many "healings" come under one of the following headings:

1. *Selective "healings."*

Not everyone gets into most healing lines. This was one of the disillusioning discoveries that left me more skeptical of faith healers after my investigation than when I began. Even my visits to my hometown pentecostal church did not prepare me for some of what I have learned.

Several techniques are used to screen applicants for the healing line. All must have a card permitting them to be there. To get this, they must attend a special faith-building service held prior to the evening faith-healing service. There they are given opportunity to respond to a determined offering appeal.

At the healing service card holders may be screened again. All those holding cards numbered from 600 to 650 may be urged to stand. Then a third screening is made. One faith healer walks down the line and chooses those he will treat. Another designates certain afflictions by name, and says they are the only ones he will treat on this night. His favorite groups: Those who are suffering from internal pain "right now."

2. *Chicanery.*

Faith healers like to heal those deaf in one ear and blind in one eye. Most deaf are simply hard of hearing. One healer presses a large pocket watch against the temporal bone. The ticking usually penetrates the auditory nerve by vibrations felt through the bone. Many of the blind can differentiate between light and shadow. The healer will face them into the strong lights shining on the platform and pass his hand slowly back and forth before their face, instructing them to follow his movements. Most are able to do so, much to the enthusiasm of the crowd. "He sees!" the healer will shout, "Hallelujah! Everybody praise God!" The electric organ strikes up, "There Is Power in the Blood," and the faith healer's publicity team chalks up another healing.

Many so-called healings are for diseases that never existed in the first place. The healer may diagnose cancer in a guest seated on the platform. "The Lord has shown me that you have a cancer growing in your stomach. . . ." Ergo: Another healing. The manipulation of short limbs—few people have limbs of exactly the same length—easily gives the impression of growth (though not of five inches of growth, as in the case reported from Bergen).

3. *Undocumented, doubtful, or demonstrably false claims.*

Often reported healings fall into one of these three categories. I investigated the healing of a baby in Nashville, Tennessee, for whom, the mother said, two Adventist physicians could do nothing. She took the baby instead to a prominent faith healer, who, a local newspaper reported, healed the child. The doctors could make no positive diagnosis, for the mother would not permit a biopsy, nor an autopsy after the baby's death, which took place a few months later.

During a week-long crusade in Detroit, Oral Roberts prayed for Mrs. Wanda Beach, 37, of Stanton, Michigan, a diabetic. After the meeting she called her parents and reported she was completely cured. She "felt so good," she told acquaintances, that she "threw away" her insulin. Within 36 hours she was in Mount Carmel Mercy Hospital, in what doctors described as a diabetic coma. She died despite emergency treatment.[34]

When faith healer William Fuller of Florida appeared in Lewiston, Idaho, in June of 1971 with the promise of "dental miracles," the Lewiston-Clarkston Dental Society asked Dr. Russell Radke to check out the claims. Fuller, a Baptist evangelist, was quoted by the Lewiston *Tribune* as saying that fillings would appear "from nowhere." [35] "One instant there is a cavity, the next there is a filling," he said. He also claimed that silver fillings had been changed to gold under his ministry.

Dr. Radke took pictures of the mouths of some 30 people who were to be in the healing line and made dental charts of their teeth. Ten healings were claimed: One a silver filling in a lower right first molar where there had been none; another, gold fillings not previously there; and eight cases in which silver fillings had been turned to gold. Of the eight cases, said Dr. Radke, "I found only what appeared to be old oxidized silver fillings with no gold sheen present as Fuller stated."

On examining his prints, Dr. Radke found that the silver filling in the lower right molar had been there before the service. "When I informed the woman of my finding," said Dr. Radke, "she readily admitted that she had forgotten that the filling was there."

A gold filling miraculously bestowed turned out instead to be tobacco stain. [See Appendix D for Dr. Radke's letter.]

Very few faith healings have been documented by competent medical authorities. This is not to say that they are then false; only that they are undocumented. One must also question the documentation. Faith healers use the term *doctor* loosely. For example, Oral Roberts printed a picture of three men on the cover of his March, 1952, *Healing Waters.* The caption read: "Three Great Medical Doctors Congratulate Oral Roberts for His Ministry of Faith to Suffering Humanity During the Roberts Campaign in Phoenix." The names of the doctors were given as W. A. Cruice of Phoenix, J. H. Miller of Phoenix, and E. B. Froome, North Towne Clinic, Phoenix. Under another photograph of Dr. Miller that appeared inside the magazine was this caption: "Dr. J. H. Miller, outstanding

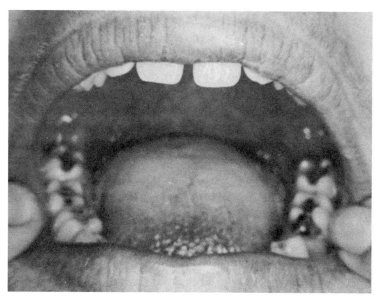

Silver fillings "miraculously turned to gold" turned out to be silver still.

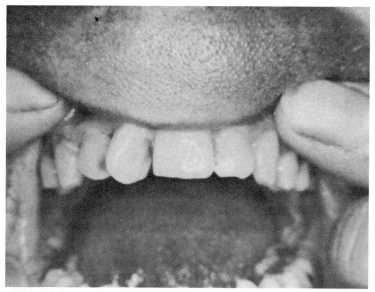

PHOTOS COURTESY OF RUSSELL RADKE, D.D.S.

"Miraculous gold fillings" proved to be only tobacco stains.

medical doctor, president of a medical society of over 20,000 physicians. . . ."

Asked about the three doctors, the American Medical Association replied:

"A careful check of our biographic records (and they are the most complete extant) failed to reveal that any of the three men was a Doctor of Medicine or licensed to practice medicine in Arizona. We could not identify Cruice with any of the cults, and did not find him listed in the Phoenix telephone directory. That directory did list E. B. Fromm of 1040 East Camelback Road as a naturopath. He was not, however, listed under naturopaths in the classified section. Neither could we find any listing for the North Towne Clinic. There were three J. H. Millers listed, but there was no indication that any of them had any connection with medicine or any of the healing cults." [36]

4. *Spontaneous remission of disease.*

Spontaneous remissions of disease, even of cancer, are not a medical rarity. Unexplainable, yes, but they occur, with and without faith, and with and without the ministrations of faith healers.

The mind itself has an almost unbelievable influence upon the body. People make themselves ill by bad thinking and sometimes make themselves well by good thinking. "One doctor at the Mayo Clinic declared that eight out of ten of his patients would get well without medical attention, if they only thought they could." [37] Most physicians would agree that 80 per cent of all disease originates in the mind, and that most of these psychosomatic disorders are curable by right thinking. "In most cases," says a physician of my acquaintance, "we doctors simply help the patient cooperate with nature. In fact, I rather suspect that many patients recover despite medication, not because of it!"

As C. S. Lewis points out: "The magic [of healing] is not in the medicine but in the patient's body—in the *vis medicatrix naturae*, the recuperative or self-corrective energy of nature. What the treatment does is to stimulate natural functions or to remove what hinders them. We speak, for convenience, of the doctor, or the dressing, healing a cut. But in another sense every cut heals itself: no cut can be healed in a corpse." [38] This is not to say, however, that the body heals itself apart from God. Says Lewis: "That same mysterious force which we call gravitational when it steers the planets and biochemical when it heals a live body, is the efficient cause of all recoveries." [39]

5. *Healed despite the healer.*

Some honest supplicants are healed, I am convinced, just as some are converted, despite the source. As Jesus assured a woman, "Thy faith hath made thee whole" (Matt. 9:22). True healing, after all, does not come from the human instrument but from God.

Writing of some church members who had become confused because they received blessings through the prayers and apparent faith of corrupt, but seemingly holy, men, Ellen White said:

"They [the church members] trusted to feeling, to an influence or power that was brought to bear upon their feelings. I saw that many, very many, had been truly converted through the influence of persons who were living in open violation of the commandments of God, their lives vile and corrupt." [40]

Shall we say that God may choose to honor integrity and faith by healing despite the unworthiness of the healer? And do this in the Seventh-day Adventist Church as well as in the faith-healing meeting, through the ministry of corrupt men?

6. *Healed by Satan.*

Not all who are healed are healed by God, as I have emphasized elsewhere in this book. Satan deceives "them that dwell on the earth by the means of those miracles which he had power to do" (Rev. 13:14). What he cannot actually do, he counterfeits. Diseases that he inflicts upon men, he removes.

It is this type of miracle that will bring Seventh-day Adventists "to the test":

"Wonderful scenes, with which Satan will be closely connected, will soon take place," wrote Ellen White. "God's

192 RATTLING THE GATES

Word declares that Satan will work miracles. He will make people sick, and then will suddenly remove from them his satanic power. They will then be regarded as healed. These works of apparent healing will bring Seventh-day Adventists to the test. Many who have had great light will fail to walk in the light, because they have not become one with Christ." [41]

A teacher once said that the best way to ensure a passing grade on a test is to pass out the answers beforehand. Here is an answer that should help the most obtuse Adventist evaluate healings:

"Many make great pretensions of holiness, and boast of the wonders they perform in healing the sick, when they do not regard this great standard of righteousness [God's law]. But through whose power are these cures wrought? Are the eyes of either party opened to their transgressions of the law? and do they make their stand as humble, obedient children, ready to obey all of God's requirements? John testifies of the professed children of God: 'He that saith, I know him, and keepeth not his commandments, is a liar, and the truth is not in him' (1 John 2:4). . . . If those through whom cures are performed, are disposed, on account of these manifestations, to excuse their neglect of the law of God, and continue in disobedience, though they have power to any and every extent, it does not follow that they have the great power of God. On the contrary, it is the miracle-working power of the great deceiver. . . . We must beware of the pretended holiness that permits transgression of the law of God. Those cannot be sanctified who trample that law under their feet, and judge themselves by a standard of their own devising." [42]

"Through Spiritualism, Satan appears as a benefactor of the race, healing the diseases of the people, and professing to present a new and more exalted system of religious faith; but at the same time he works as a destroyer. His temptations are leading multitudes to ruin. Intemperance dethrones reason; sensual indulgence, strife, and bloodshed follow." [43]

We must not forget that it is false *ministers,* not avowedly anti-religious spokesmen, who do this work of deception. Paul makes this truth plain: "For such are false apostles, deceitful workers, transforming themselves into the apostles of Christ. And no marvel; for Satan himself is transformed into an angel of light" (2 Cor. 11:13, 14).

I do not imply that all faith healers are con men. Or that genuine miracles do not occur under their ministry. To echo Chesterton again, "The extraordinary thing about miracles is that they happen." One further facet of the faith-healing ministry does warrant attention, however, before we leave the subject. It is amazing how many healing miracles occur, or are promised to occur, in connection with offerings. "The Scriptures say you got to vow and pay, vow and pay, vow and pay," goes the pitch for a $100 special offering at one healer's faith-building service.[44] The three "Keys for miracles to work," advocated in each issue of *Abundant Life,* are revealing: "1. Make God your Source; 2. Give to God first and . . . 3. Expect a miracle!"[45] The giving to God, to be sure, may be satisfied by a prayer for someone else's healing, but an implied appeal to give to the evangelist can be found nearby.

A typical "seed faith" testimony (the term speaks for itself) in *Abundant Life* will run something like this: "I was facing bankruptcy, but I responded to your appeal and pledged $1,000. God responded to my seed faith by enlarging my business. I now hire fifteen full-time employees. Yes, seed faith was the key to my success." Often an account of a miraculous healing follows the testimony. A chapter in Oral Roberts' *The Miracle Book* is titled "How You Can Become Faith-Centered for Miracles in Your Finances."[46]

As a Seventh-day Adventist who has been accused by pentecostals of having a gospel of works, I stand amazed at the theology of many offering promoters. The difference between a Tetzel hawking indulgences and a score of faith healers hawking healing is one of degree and technique, not of theological substance. I find particularly repugnant the hawking of prayer handkerchiefs and like articles, favorite come-ons of radio evangelists, sent you "free for the asking," but "don't forget to enclose an offering." Prayer handkerchiefs, blessed by the healer, are guaranteed to bring health, wealth, and happiness, and even your husband back to you if he is chasing with other women (just put it under his pillow unknown to him . . .).[47]

Readers familiar with the exposés of "Marjoe," a documentary film made by a pentecostal evangelist on the healing circuit, will recall the scene where Marjoe and the local pastor are backstage counting the offering while the service continues. "You count the big bills," Marjoe says, "and I'll count the smaller ones." As they divide the bills into stacks, the local minister says how much he appreciated the service. "I liked that, boy, I really did. You sure got them going." Or the scene at the dinner table with a pastor and his wife. The pastor speaks of his 800 acres in Brazil and the big deal he has with a canning company to buy his produce. The scene closes as he mentions, incidentally, his plans to build a Bible school on the land someday. Or the scene where Evangelist Sister Taylor, dressed in white, tells the audience, "We don't use God's money for foolishness," as the camera zooms in on her large jeweled brooch and outsized diamond rings.

Marjoe Gortner, who said he made millions for his parents as a child evangelist, is, by his own confession, a small-time con man. But anyone who has investigated the healing circuit will recognize the type. The sad truth is that a faith built largely on emotionalism rather than on reason, and seeking its authentication in miracles rather than in a Thus saith the Lord, invites abuse. It also invites Adventists to the test.

People, it's here!

References

[1] *The Betty Baxter Story*, published by Oral Roberts, The Western Bible Institute, P.O. Box 4032, South Denver Station, Denver 9, Colorado. Quoted by Carrol Stegal, Jr., and Carl C. Harwood in *The Modern Tongues and Healing Movement*.

[2] *Voice*, October, 1972, pp. 38-42.

[3] "The Boy Who Sees," in *The Voice of Healing*, publication of the Last-day Sign Gift Ministries, published by The Voice of Healing, Inc., February, 1954, p. 6. The story appears in greater detail in *When God Smiled on Ronald Coyne*, by Mrs. Lydia E. Coyne, Improved edition, 1970-1971, Ronald Coyne Revivals, Tulsa, Oklahoma.

[4] See O. L. Jaggers, *Bro [sic] Jaggers' Life Story. How God Raised Him From the Dead! Miraculously healed him several times!* (32 pages—$1.00.)

[5] Cliff Dudley, *Like a Mighty Wind*, pp. 76-78.

[6] Raymond W. Becker, ed., "A Report of the 1972 Scandinavian-European Airlift," *Voice*, p. 5.

[7] *Ibid.*, p. 6

[8] *Ibid.*, p. 10.

[9] *Ibid.*, p. 11.

[10] "Convention '72," *Voice*, Nov., 1972, p. 15.

[11] Quoted in *Time*, March 7, 1969, p. 64.

[12] Oral Roberts, *Life Story*, pp. 113-115.

[13] Ellen G. White, *The Ministry of Healing* (Mountain View, California: Pacific Press Publishing Association), p. 17.

[14] *Ibid.*, pp. 19, 20.

[15] *Ibid.*, p. 111.

[16] Gordon, A. J., "The Ministry of Healing," cited in *The Pentecostal Evangel*, June 24, 1956, p. 7.

[17] Glenn Clark, *How to Find Health Through Prayer* (New York: Harper and Brothers, 1940), p. 72.

[18] F. F. Bosworth, *Christ the Healer* (Chas. O. Benham, Pub., 1924), p. 33.

[19] Ellen G. White, *The Desire of Ages* (Mountain View, California: Pacific Press Publishing Association), p. 660.

[20] George Eldon Ladd, "Faith Healing in the Church," a review of *The Healing Ministry in the Church*, by Bernard Martin (John Knox Press, 125 pp.), published in *Eternity*, Aug., 1961, p. 21. Reprinted by permission from *Eternity* magazine, copyright 1961, The Evangelical Foundation, 1716 Spruce Street, Philadelphia, Pa. 19103.

[21] See *Modern Tongues and the Healing Movement*, p. 30, and Wade G. Boggs, Jr., *Faith Healing and the Christian Faith* (Richmond, Va.: John Knox Press, 1956), p. 122.

[22] *Ibid.*

[23] Ellen G. White, *The Ministry of Healing*, pp. 229, 230.

[24] ———, *Medical Ministry* (Mountain View, California: Pacific Press Publishing Association), p. 14.

[25] *Ibid.*

[26] *Ibid.*

[27] ———, *Testimonies for the Church*, vol. 1, p. 561; *Counsels on Health* (Mountain View, California: Pacific Press Publishing Association), p. 247.

[28] ———, *The Ministry of Healing*, pp. 227, 228.

[29] *Ibid.*, p. 141.

[30] *Ibid.*, p. 111.

[31] *Ibid.*, p. 227.

[32] ———, *Testimonies for the Church*, vol. 1, p. 619.

[33] General Conference Bulletin, 1901, p. 25.

[34] Washington, D.C., *Evening Star*, Monday, July 6, 1959, A-13.

[35] Lewiston (Idaho) *Tribune*, June 9, 1971.

[36] Oliver Field, American Medical Association, in a letter to Chaplain Davis A. Thomas, U.S. Navy, dated Jan. 10, 1957.

[37] Murl Vance, "The Greatest Medical Prescription," *Signs of the Times*, Pacific Press Publishing Association, Feb. 21, 1950, p. 6.

[38] C. S. Lewis, *Miracles*, p. 168.

[39] *Ibid.*

[40] Ellen G. White, letter 2, 1851.

[41] ———, *Selected Messages*, book 2, p. 53.

[42] *The SDA Bible Commentary*, Ellen G. White Comments, on Matt. 24:23, 24, p. 1099.

[43] Ellen G. White, *The Great Controversy*, p. 589.

[44] *Time* Magazine, March 7, 1969, p. 64.

[45] *Abundant Life*, Dec., 1972, p. 19.

[46] Oral Roberts, *The Miracle Book* (Tulsa, Oklahoma: Oral Roberts Press), p. 197.

[47] A radio offer of Reverend Ike.

12
I Meet a Ghost

What does it mean to receive the baptism of, or with, the Holy Spirit? Is it the same as receiving the Holy Spirit? Does it come at conversion? At baptism? After baptism? How can we know when we receive it? Is the baptism of the Holy Spirit always accompanied by the gift of tongues, as Pentecostals believe it must be?

When I first met the Holy Spirit, in my boyhood, it was not under conditions conducive to confidence. He was introduced as the "Holy Ghost." Now if there is one condition of humanity that disturbs little boys it is holiness. Girls must occasionally attain it, for some grow into wonderful mothers, but boys? Never! The only boys who try to attain it are insufferable prigs, as every boy who ever bloodied someone's nose will remember.

It wasn't enough, however, that this "third person of the Godhead"—another description that theologians rather than little boys should wrestle with—was holy; He was a "Ghost." Of all the disservices the King James Version does to children, this one is the worst. To talk about ghosts in the security of dad's presence, and even occasionally to scare girls with ghost stories, is one thing; to meet one is another. So in my Sunday school classes it was three cheers for Jesus the Lamb, but a nervous silence for the Holy Ghost who, as I myself observed, made otherwise sensible people lose their reason and talk in gibberish, sometimes while rolling in the church aisles. I have wondered to what degree these early misconceptions influenced my imagery of the Holy Ghost as someone who chases bad people, and when he catches them, takes everything that is fun out of their life.

Even when I walked into the baptismal tank, near the end of my first year of college, I had reservations about permitting Him complete autonomy. He might, after all, want me to become a minister, or to go from door to door selling gospel books—both of which fears were, in time, realized. Or, horrible to contemplate, He might want me to marry a girl who was *not* like the one that "married dear old dad," as the song has it—a fear that was not realized. Maybe the holiness hang-up was still there, but I had a sneaking suspicion that the Holy Spirit didn't approve of girls—even good girls—whose beauty tempted one to think unholy thoughts.

But I had the doctrine down pat:

The Holy Spirit, the third Person of the Godhead, was present at Creation (Gen. 1:2) and is the active agent in re-creation of sinners (John 3:5).

The Spirit is Christ's representative on earth (John 16:7).

He is both the divine Comforter (John 14:16, 17) and the divine Disturber (John 16:8). He disturbs us by reproving sin, through what we often describe as the voice of conscience. He comforts us by bringing our rebellious spirits into harmony with the law of God, which He writes in our hearts (Heb. 10:15, 16). The result: "Great peace have they which love thy law: and nothing shall offend them" (Ps. 119: 165).

The Holy Spirit is our teacher (John 14:26).

He gives us power (Acts 1:8).

He purifies us (2 Thess. 2:13).

He develops our character (Gal. 5:22, 23).

He gives us gifts (1 Cor. 12:4).

He guides us to truth (John 16:13).

He prays for us (Rom. 8:26).

He is the guarantee of our inheritance (Eph. 1:14).

All these facts about the Spirit and His work I knew when I was baptized. But what a chasm there is between knowing and receiving! Before the waters closed over me, I disliked a classmate who lived just down the hall in the dormitory; when I came up, supposedly a "new creature," I disliked him still, and let that dislike rule my words and actions toward him. Before baptism I had wrestled with and been thrown for falls by impure thoughts. Afterward, though I tried new grips and new strategies, sin squeezed me in its old, sensual hammer lock, and pinned my shoulders to the mat. It was two and one-half years of struggle and defeat before the Holy Spirit led me gently through a night of prayer into a dawn of victory, and I experienced the joy of the 110-pound weakling who exercises unseen muscle to throw his heretofore unbeatable opponent. As God's Word promises, I *had* received power after the Holy Spirit had come upon me.

But one infilling of the Spirit does not suffice for life. Sad the story of that man who is yet testifying, "Twenty years ago the Spirit came upon me." Rather our testimony should be that *today* the Holy Spirit has baptized me anew! I have learned that what is needed is daily baptism, daily surrender, daily victory over sin, through a daily baptism of the Holy Spirit.

"Christ was continually receiving from the Father that He might communicate to us. . . . From hours spent with God He came forth morning by morning to bring the light of heaven to men. Daily He received a fresh baptism of the Holy Spirit. In the early hours of the new day the Lord awakened Him from His slumbers, and His soul and His lips were anointed with grace, that He might impart to others. His words were given Him fresh from the heavenly courts, words that He might speak in season to the weary and oppressed. 'The Lord God hath given Me,' He said, 'the tongue of the learned, that I should know how to speak a word in season to him that is weary: He wakeneth morning by morning, He wakeneth Mine ear to hear as the learned.' " [1]

Here is a gift of tongues that all should seek and all might have—words fresh daily from the heavenly courts to ease the burden of the "weary and oppressed." Ellen White, addressing Seventh-day Adventist ministers in Battle Creek, Michigan, spoke of "the necessity of . . . [their] being fitted up day by day with the baptism of the Holy Ghost, before going forth to their labors. Christ has promised it," she said, "why should they not have it? Lay hold by faith." [2]

Few promises of the Bible are more thoroughly documented than the baptism of the Holy Spirit:

Matthew 3:11, "He will baptize you with the Holy Spirit" (N.E.B.). Mark 1:8 and Luke 3:16 repeat the promise.

John 1:33, " 'He [Christ] . . . baptizes with the Holy Spirit' " (R.S.V.).

Acts 11:16, "You will be baptized with the Holy Spirit" (N.E.B.).

The apostle Paul confronted believers with the question, " 'Did you receive the Holy Spirit when you became believers?' " (Acts 19:2, N.E.B.). To the Ephesian believers he wrote, "Be filled with the Spirit" (Eph. 5:18, K.J.V.).

It would be a strange kind of Christian who, faced with such emphatic affirmations, would reject the doctrine of baptism by the Holy Spirit. The tragedy is that so many Christians go so many years with so little power. Through another gift of the Spirit to the church, the spirit of prophecy, Ellen White repeatedly stressed the importance and the blessings of the baptism. To Adventist ministers she wrote:

"An intellectual knowledge of the truth is not enough; we must know its power upon our own hearts and lives. Ministers need to come to Christ as little children. Seek Jesus, brethren, confess your sins, plead with God day and night, until you know that for Christ's sake you are pardoned and accepted. . . . I counsel you to tarry at Jerusalem, as did the early disciples, until, like them, you receive the baptism of the Holy

Spirit. Never feel at liberty to go into the desk until you have by faith grasped the arm of your strength." [3]

And there were words for the laity too:

"No outward forms can make us clean; no ordinance, administered by the saintliest of men, can take the place of the baptism of the Holy Ghost. The Spirit of God must do its work upon the heart. . . . Strife and contention cannot arise among those who are controlled by His Spirit." [4]

"When you have received the baptism of the Holy Spirit, then you will understand more of the joys of salvation than you have known all your life hitherto." [5]

And that is the way it was with me, when I let the Spirit take over the steering wheel of my life. For months I seemed bathed in joy. When I went to bed, my last thoughts were of Christ; I awakened with a smile, confident that God would bring me new victories through the day. But whatever brought these blessings, pentecostals assure me, it could not have been the baptism with the Holy Spirit, because I did not speak in tongues. Everyone, they say, does speak in tongues as the initial *sign* of the baptism, even if one does not receive the *gift* of tongues for daily witness.

"The Baptism of believers in the Holy Ghost," says the Constitution of the Assemblies of God, "is witnessed by the initial physical sign of speaking with other tongues as the Spirit of God gives them utterance."

Carl Brumback cites the following resolution of the Assembly:

"Resolved, That this Council considers it a serious disagreement with the fundamentals for any minister among us to teach contrary to our distinctive testimony that the baptism in the Holy Ghost is regularly accompanied by the initial, physical sign of speaking in other tongues." [6]

Some pentecostal Bible scholars modify this position, but pentecostal evangelists suffer from no such equivocation. Here is the doctrine as it appeared in an ad by the Rainbow Revival, a pentecostal team:

"When Jesus baptizes a Christian with the Holy Ghost,

the Holy Ghost speaks thru *[sic]* that Christian with a language of His own, which is called speaking in tongues." [7]

After giving texts to prove the point (Acts 1, 2, 10, 19; 1 Cor. 12 and 14), the ad cautions:

"Don't ask someone to explain these Scriptures who doesn't have the baptism and has never spoken in tongues, because how can they *[sic]* explain properly something they don't have, can't do, never did, and are in need of themselves?"

The second-class status of Christians who do not speak in tongues is boldly asserted by the same evangelists:

"A Christian who doesn't have the baptism or who doesn't seek the baptism of the Holy Ghost belongs back about 50, 75, or 100 years ago or more. . . .

"We also talk to Him in spiritual languages, which are so much more powerful to use, and bring so much more blessing from God. . . . A Christian whom Jesus has not baptized with the Holy Ghost and who has not spoken in tongues, is like a spiritual baby who has not yet learned to talk. A Christian who has not been baptized with the Holy Ghost with the proof thereof by speaking in other tongues, is a spiritual weakling compared to what he could be, if he were baptized with the Holy Ghost, according to Acts 2:4." [8]

Said a Catholic bishop: "Hearing another leader say 'Tongues are quality control' makes one realize that man's criteria for judging the action of the Spirit are not always reliable." [9] An astute observation!

Catholic pentecostals differ from Protestant pentecostals on baptism theology, holding that tongues is *a* sign rather than *the* sign. Writes Catholic theologian Kilian McDonnell:

"Baptism in the Holy Spirit is considered a decisive moment, but it is not taught that those without the baptism are without the Spirit. Speaking in tongues is a proof that one has had the baptism (Acts 2:1-42; 10:46; 19:6), but Catholic pentecostals almost universally reject the necessary link between the two. For them anyone who asks for the baptism receives it, whether or not he speaks in tongues." [10]

Catholics I have interviewed confirm this understanding.

What does the Bible say on this point? A study of the 18 major accounts of baptism with the Holy Spirit reveals that Catholic pentecostals reflect the Scripture more faithfully than do their Protestant colleagues.

In what Peter calls a prophecy of Pentecost (Joel 2: 28-32), tongues are not among the supernatural manifestations mentioned.

The first mention of tongues as a sign appears in Mark 16:17. Christ has been crucified and resurrected. He now gives marching orders to His disciples, pointing them "into all the world" (verse 15). "And these signs shall follow them that believe" He says; "In my name shall they cast out devils; they shall speak with new tongues; they shall take up serpents; and if they drink any deadly thing, it shall not hurt them; they shall lay hands on the sick, and they shall recover" (verses 17, 18).

Some Bible scholars are unimpressed with these verses because they do not appear in the most ancient and best Greek manuscripts. Aside from the matter of authenticity, they raise an interesting question, for they enumerate *five* signs, all of which do not appear in the lives of all baptized by the Holy Spirit. To choose one sign and make it *the* sign hardly seems evidence of sound thinking.

In four parallel passages—Matthew 3:11; Mark 1:8; Luke 3:16, 17; John 1:33—four men under inspiration of the Holy Spirit describe the same event—John the Baptist's preaching. None say anything about tongues being a sign.

Results of the baptism are stressed in other passages. Jesus tells the disciples they "shall receive power" to witness (Acts 1:8); Elisabeth, who is pregnant with John, is filled with the Holy Spirit and speaks a revelation from God (Luke 1:41); Zacharias is "filled with the Holy Ghost" and prophesies (verses 67, 68); Simeon receives a revelation from the Holy Spirit (chap. 2:25, 26); Jesus is filled with the Holy Spirit and led immediately into the wilderness to be tempted (Matt. 3: 16; 4:1). There is no record that Jesus, on whom God's Spirit was "without measure or limit" (John 3:34, Taylor), spoke in tongues when baptized by the Holy Spirit or afterward. Nor is any mention made of tongues as Jesus confers the Holy Spirit on the disciples in connection with the giving of the Great Commission—"As my Father hath sent me, even so send I you" (John 20:21-23).

On the Day of Pentecost (Acts 2) impressive events occur: the sound of a tornadolike wind is heard; cloven tongues as of fire appear and rest on each disciple; they begin to speak with other tongues—in foreign languages, as we have discussed in a previous chapter. Of eighteen accounts of the baptism this is one of only three that mention tongues.

In Acts 4:31 the Spirit descends with such power that the building is shaken. What is the result? The disciples speak "the word of God with boldness." Not with tongues, but with *boldness!*

In Acts 8:14-17, we read of the evangelistic campaign conducted by Philip in Samaria. Peter and John are sent by the "General Conference from Jerusalem" to instruct the new believers. The disciples lay their hands on the converts and they receive the Holy Spirit. One of the new members, Simon the sorcerer, offers money to buy the gift. Pentecostals surmise that Simon was impressed by the gift of tongues. The Scripture records only miraculous healings that left "great joy in that city" (verse 8). To read tongues into the account is to go beyond what inspiration records.

In Acts 9:17-20 is the account of Saul, who was blinded on the road to Damascus by a revelation of Jesus. The Lord directs Ananias to lay hands on Saul, he is filled with the Holy Spirit, his sight returns, he is baptized, and "straightway he preached Christ in the synagogues, that he is the Son of God" (verse 20). No mention is made of tongues. We know only that Paul told the Corinthians that he spoke in tongues more than them all (1 Cor. 14:18), likely a reference to his ability to converse in foreign languages, a number of which he had learned, though he may have been given additional languages by the Holy Spirit at some time. No reference is made to tongues or any kind of ecstatic babbling when he is filled with the Holy Spirit.

We come now to the second incident in which the baptism of the Holy Spirit and tongues are linked. Peter and some fellow Jews are at the house of Cornelius in Caesarea. They have come in response to a vision given Peter, which teaches them that he "should not call any man common or unclean" (Acts 10:28). In other words, Gentiles as well as Jews are precious to God. Says Peter: "Of a truth I perceive that God is no respecter of persons: but in every nation he that feareth him, and worketh righteousness, is accepted with him" (verses 34, 35). Peter preaches to the Gentiles gathered, and, to the astonishment of the Jews who have come with Peter, the Holy Spirit falls "on all them which heard the word" (verse 44) and they "speak with tongues, and magnify God" (verse 46).

In this incident the baptism of the Holy Spirit comes on them prior to water baptism (verse 47), and as the context indicates, both to qualify them to witness throughout Asia and as a sign to Peter and his Jewish companions of His acceptance of the Gentile converts. Peter, who had been so prejudiced that he would not preach to the Gentiles, and then hesitated to baptize them, hesitated no longer. "Forasmuch then as God gave them the like gift as he did unto us . . . ; what was I that I could withstand God?" (Acts 11:17). The lesson here is not that tongues speaking is *the* sign of Spirit baptism, but that prejudices die hard and greatly hinder God's work on our behalf. Our concern should be with the kind of service we can give God through the indwelling Spirit rather that what the Spirit can do to us to add to our euphoric feeling. In its preoccupation with tongues pentecostalism subtly shifts the emphasis from what a man can do for God to what God can do for a man. The end product of the shift does not contribute to spiritual maturity, which is attained "when the impulse to help and bless others springs constantly from within." [11] The tongues given by God were a tool for evangelism, not an end in themselves.

The account of Peter and the converts at the house of Cornelius is the only one in which tongues stands alone as evidence of the infilling of the Spirit. It is no more consistent with sound exegesis to insist from this account that tongues is *the* sign of Spirit baptism than it is to insist that revelation from God is *the* sign, as in the case of Elisabeth, or prophecy *the* sign, as in the case of Zacharias. The whole matter of signs is put into perspective when we recall that the disciples and their new converts had no New Testament to turn to for authentication; God gave that which was needed to certify their genuineness and to qualify them to spread the gospel through knowledge of foreign languages, the gift of healing, and other gifts, the Holy Spirit "dividing to every man severally as he will" (1 Cor. 12:11).

In Acts 19:1-6 we read of Paul bringing new light about the mission of Christ to converts of Apollos at Ephesus. They are baptized in the name of the Lord Jesus, and as Paul lays his hands upon them the Holy Spirit comes on them and they speak with tongues and prophesy. If tongues is a sign of Spirit baptism, so is prophesying; neither can be *the* sign. This account is the last of the three in which tongues and the baptism of the Holy Spirit are linked. And, as we observed in a previous chapter, the tongues bestowed were a foreign language. The account should not be used, then, in support of ecstatic gibberish as a form of tongues.

There is yet another verse to examine. In Ephesians 5:18-21 we have an exhortation to "let the Spirit stimulate your soul" (Phillips). Paul then instructs those baptized by the Spirit in how to express their joy:

"Express your joy in singing among yourselves psalms and hymns and spiritual songs, making music in your hearts for the ears of God! Thank God at all times for everything, in the name of our Lord Jesus Christ. And 'fit in with' one another, because of your common reverence for Christ."

Of the eighteen incidents that speak of the baptism of the Holy Spirit, fifteen do not so much as mention tongues in the context of the baptism. And those that do, quite obviously concern foreign languages given to prepare the believer for witness to other nationalities. The modern gibberish called tongues would not fit into this scriptural framework. And it seems no great risk to leave it to the reader to decide whether the scriptural evidence is on the side of tongues' being the sign of Spirit baptism.

One thing that comes through clearly in all these passages is that the baptism of the Holy Spirit makes a difference. When a man receives it people know that something has happened. And no wonder, for it is through the agency of the Holy Spirit that man becomes a partaker of the divine nature.

Let us take a closer look now at the term *baptism,* as in "baptism" of the Holy Spirit. Baptism is not a translation of a Greek word; it is a transliteration, which means that we have appropriated the word virtually unchanged from the Greek. *Baptism* means "to immerse," a meaning that has been somewhat obscured by the sprinklings and pourings that masquerade as baptism in some churches. But the reason for John's going to "Aenon near to Salim" to do his baptizing is clearly stated: Because "there was much water there" (John 3:23). To baptize properly, he had to go to a place where there was enough water to immerse his converts. Had baptism meant sprinkling, a barrelful of water would have taken care of everyone converted under the power of the Holy Spirit at Pentecost.

So baptism means to immerse. The baptism of the Holy Spirit, then, suggests that we are immersed by the Holy Spirit into Christ. The two baptisms are linked in Titus 3:5-7: "Then he saved us—not because we were good enough to be saved, but because of his kindness and pity—by washing away our sins and giving us the new joy of the indwelling Holy Spirit whom he poured out upon us with wonderful fullness—and all because of what Jesus Christ our Saviour did so that he could declare us good in God's eyes" (Taylor).

The pentecostal, as Emmanuel Sullivan points out, is in danger of pressing "the distinction of baptism in water and baptism in the Spirit to a point of separation into two baptisms—one of symbol, the other of experience; one a believer's deed, the other God's doing; one a human event, the other divine. From this point it is easy to establish two classes of Christians, again, right across denominational lines." [12]

With theologian Frederick Bruner, Sullivan concludes that "Christian baptism is one spiritual event. There is only one baptism (Eph. 4:6). He [Bruner] takes care to stress that Acts 8 does not teach separation, but the union of baptism and the gift of the Spirit and he rejects interpretations which develop a biblical doctrine of a second reception of the Spirit 'in fullness', either experientially or sacramentally." [13]

One can overdraw the baptism metaphor. The Bible speaks of the same experience as a filling—"They were all filled" (Acts 2:4). Peter finds in Pentecost a fulfillment of the outpouring of the Spirit predicted by Joel rather than the baptism foretold by John. Baptism has the drawback of pointing us to an initiatory rite, usually performed once only. A filling, however, may come daily, as indeed it should.

Scripture uses a number of figures of speech other than baptism to describe the Spirit's entrance into a person's life. Among them are: "The promise of the Holy Ghost" (Acts 2:33), "the gift of the Holy Ghost" (verse 38), receiving the Holy Spirit (chap. 8:17), being filled with the Holy Spirit (chap. 2:4), being endued with power (Luke 24:49), the Holy Spirit comes on (Acts 19:6), the Holy Spirit falls on (chap. 10:44), the Holy Spirit is poured out on (chap. 2:33), the Spirit is given (chap. 8:18).

What appears to be the same experience is described as: Receiving the promise of the Holy Spirit (Gal. 3:14), being sealed with the Holy Spirit (Eph. 1:13), being born of water and the Spirit (John 3:5), ministering the Spirit to us (Gal. 3:5).

The baptism of the Holy Spirit, then, describes what happens to an individual when he first experiences, or experiences with new intensity, the presence and working of the Holy Spirit. The baptism can be synonymous with coming to Christ, or it can be distinct from that experience; the former seems to be the ideal.

A verse often quoted by pentecostals to show a time interval between believing and being baptized, or sealed, with the Holy Spirit—Ephesians 1:13—instead shows the opposite: "In whom also after that ye believed, ye were sealed with that Holy Spirit." The Greek suggests no interval between the believing and the sealing. A better translation is "In whom also believing ye were sealed," or "In whom when ye also believed, ye were sealed with the Holy Spirit."

The Spirit is described as coming on believers before baptism (Acts 10:44-48), following baptism (chap. 19:5, 6) and some undetermined time after baptism (chap. 8:12-17). The purposes of a special spiritual filling after baptism are to renew faith, bring about unity, give power for special challenges, impart specific gifts for the spread of the gospel, and impart that transcendent love without which, though we "speak with the tongues of men and angels," we are "become as sounding brass, or a tinkling cymbal" (1 Cor. 13:1). God is not bound; the Spirit may reveal Himself as He chooses. I assume that my filling came more than two years after baptism because I was not ready before; I was unwilling to surrender my life fully to the Spirit.

The assumption of the disciples as they write to new churches is that their members *have* the Spirit; there is no recognition of an underprivileged group lacking the Spirit and a privileged group having it. Paul wrote to the Romans: "Remember that if anyone doesn't have the Spirit of Christ living in him, he is not a Christian at all" (Rom. 8:9, Taylor).

What solemn words! *All* Christians must be spirit filled! If a man does not have the Spirit in him, he is not a Christian at all! Christ does not acknowledge us to be His unless we know the reality of the Holy Spirit living in us. "To be baptized in the Spirit is to become Christ's," says theologian Frederick Dale Bruner.[14] It is the Holy Spirit who communicates Christ to us. To have the Spirit is to have Christ. As the Spirit leads us from spiritual childhood to maturity, Jesus becomes increasingly the center of our life, for the Spirit leads us to Him, introduces us to Him, immerses us in Him, and, at last, loses us in Him—"For there is none other name under heaven given among men, whereby we must be saved" (Acts 4:12). There is no tension between the "Ghost" and the Lamb. It is the Spirit's purpose to bring the Lamb "great honor" by showing us Christ's "glory" (John 16:14, Taylor). W. H. Aldis once said that "the fulness of the Spirit is not given in order to work miracles, but to make Christians living miracles." [15]

How does a man receive the Spirit and His gifts? Simply by responding to an invitation: "Behold, I stand at the door, and knock: if any man hear my voice, and open the door, I will come in to him, and will sup with him, and he with me" (Rev. 3:20).

The invitation, of course, is from Christ. Were it not for His initiative in extending it, we could not come. To receive Him is to receive the Spirit; to receive the Spirit is to receive Him. One cannot say, Do this, do that, and the Spirit will be given. The Spirit is not given to us because of our *attainment,* someone has said, but because of His *atonement.* It is His act, His invitation. Even before we act, He has acted. Indeed, we could not respond to the invitation were the Spirit not motivating us. First evidence of the Spirit's presence may be simply our awareness that we are outside of Christ and that He is inviting us in.

But here we are faced with a divine paradox, for while it cannot be said that we must do this or that before the Spirit will enter, neither can it be said that we have nothing to do about His entering! The form of the invitation itself—a knock at our heart's door—communicates our potential to refuse the Spirit entrance. He gives us the motive, even to invite Him in, but He will not overrule our will. And we have something to do in cooperation with Him if we want Him to stay, for He will not reside in a dirty house! If the Spirit consented to stay in a thief, a murderer, an adulterer, a liar, He would be sanctioning sin, and this the God who died for sin will not do. Sin and God are incompatible, a fact demonstrated at Calvary.

The Scriptures do give some guidelines on receiving the

14

Holy Spirit, which are often arranged under the headings of repentance, obedience, prayer, and faith.

1. Repentance. "Repent and be baptized, every one of you, in the name of Jesus the Messiah for the forgiveness of your sins; and you will receive the gift of the Holy Spirit. For the promise is to you, and to your children, and to all who are far away, everyone whom the Lord our God may call" (Acts 2:38, 39, N.E.B.).

2. Obedience. "If you love me, you will obey my commands; and I will ask the Father, and he will give you another to be your Advocate, who will be with you for ever—the Spirit of truth (John 14:15, 16, N.E.B.). "The Holy Spirit [is] given by God to all those who are obedient to him" (Acts 5:32, N.E.B.).

3. Prayer. "When they had ended their prayer, [for boldness in preaching, healing power, and miracles and wonders] the building where they were assembled rocked, and all were filled with the Holy Spirit and spoke the word of God with boldness" (Acts 4:31, N.E.B.). " 'If you, then, bad as you are, know how to give your children what is good for them, how much more will the heavenly Father give the Holy Spirit to those who ask him!' " (Luke 11:13, N.E.B.).

4. Faith. "All of us as Christians can have the promised Holy Spirit through this faith" (Gal. 3:14, Taylor). "And what is faith? Faith gives substance to our hopes, and makes us certain of realities we do not see" (Heb. 11:1, N.E.B.).

Ellen White has written:

"There is no limit to the usefulness of one who, putting self aside, makes room for the working of the Holy Spirit upon his heart and lives a life wholly consecrated to God. All who consecrate body, soul, and spirit to His service will be constantly receiving a new endowment of physical, mental, and spiritual power. The inexhaustible supplies of heaven are at their command. Christ gives them the breath of His own Spirit, the life of His own life. The Holy Spirit puts forth its highest energies to work in mind and heart. Through the grace given us we may achieve victories that because of our erroneous

and preconceived opinions, our defects of character, our small-
ness of faith, have seemed impossible." [16]

"The lapse of time has wrought no change in Christ's parting promise to send the Holy Spirit as His representative. . . .
If all were willing, all would be filled with the Spirit. . . . For
the daily baptism of the Spirit every worker should offer his
petition to God." [17]

In the gift of Christ and the Holy Spirit, says Mrs. White,
heaven emptied itself. There was nothing left to give. "In the
great and measureless gift of the Holy Spirit are contained all
of heaven's resources. It is not because of any restriction on the
part of God that the riches of His grace do not flow earthward
to men. If all were willing to receive, all would become filled
with His Spirit." [18]

All heaven is waiting to bestow the power of Pentecost. It
has not come because the promise is casually discussed. There
is no intensity of spirit, no audacity in prayer. But the gift is
for now. [19]

The key to the reception of the Holy Spirit is renunciation
of self. "By prayer and confession of sin we must clear the
King's highway. As we do this, the power of the Spirit [of
Pentecost] will come to us. We need Pentecostal energy. This
will come; for the Lord has promised to send His Spirit as the
all-conquering power." [20]

What poignant words! "All heaven is waiting." "The
gift is for now." "If all were willing, all would be filled."

Oh, the shame that should tinge our cheeks! From bended
knee we should cry out in faith to that One who is faithful to
fill our cup and quench the thirsting of our souls.

When I consider my miserable failure to grasp the promises of God, the self that has ruled unrebuked in my ministry,
my willingness to settle for so little so long, I document the
doctrinal distortions of the charismatic movement with sincere
compassion for its honest-hearted seekers. For the movement
is people, people who for too long have been fed empty words
by empty shepherds.

And what shall I say of the Seventh-day Adventist Church?

Emphatically this: Of all churches the Seventh-day Adventist has least excuse for a spiritless ministry. How deeply concerned each member should be that he "come behind in no gift; waiting for the coming of our Lord" (1 Cor. 1:7).

One night when my son, Douglas, was three, he decided to walk in my shoes. I can see him yet, a curly-haired little man with shy eyes, plodding awkwardly into the front room. "Look, Daddy," he said, "I'm walking in your shoes."

But it was not that easy. Either his feet were too small or the shoes were too big. Whatever the case, when he tried to turn right, the shoes turned left. I untangled him and he tried again—and again.

"Help me, Daddy," he asked at last, lifting his hands. I reached down and took them. When the shoes turned wrong, I steered him right. When he would have fallen, I supported him. And so we walked, a little man in shoes too big no longer, because of the power of his father above.

The promise is for *now*.

References

[1] Ellen G. White, *Christ's Object Lessons*, p. 135.

[2] ———, manuscript 22, 1889.

[3] ———, *Testimonies for the Church*, vol. 5, p. 159.

[4] *Ibid.*, p. 227.

[5] ———, letter 33, 1890.

[6] Carl Brumback, *Suddenly From Heaven* (Springfield, Mo.: Gospel Publishing House, 1961), p. 223.

[7] Newspaper advertisement, Rainbow Revival. Los Angeles, California.

[8] Plunkett, Rainbow Revival Evangelists, from a Bible study on the Baptism.

[9] Bishop Stephen A. Leven, "What I Want for the Catholic Pentecostal Movement," *New Covenant*, vol. 1, No. 5, November, 1971, p. 24.

[10] Kilian McDonnell, "Catholic Pentecostalism: Problems in Evaluation," *Theology Digest*, Vol. XIX, No. 1, Spring, 1971, p. 47.

[11] Ellen G. White, *Christ's Object Lessons*, p. 384.

[12] Emmanuel Sullivan, "Can the Pentecostal Movement Renew the Churches?" *Study Encounter*, VIII, no. 4, 1972, p. 6.

[13] *Ibid.* For Bruner's view see *A Theology of the Holy Spirit* (London: Hodder & Stoughton, 1971), p. 181.

[14] Bruner, *loc. cit.*, p. 160. Cited in *Commonweal*, March 5, 1971, p. 533.

[15] Quoted by Steven Barabas in his *So Great Salvation*, Marshall, Morgan, Scott, p. 134.

[16] Ellen G. White, *The Ministry of Healing*, p. 159.

[17] ———, *The Acts of the Apostles*, p. 50.

[18] ———, *Christ's Object Lessons* (Washington, D.C.; Review and Herald Publishing Association), p. 419.

[19] ———, *Testimonies to Ministers* (Mountain View, California: Pacific Press Publishing Association), p. 174.

[20] ———, *Gospel Workers*, p. 308.

13
A Prophetic
Cartoon Strip

Not long ago a prominent clergyman of a mainline Protestant church called on me. When I heard his voice I knew he was unhappy.

He explained that he had received a questionnaire from a special committee set up by the ruling body of his church. It asked such questions as these: "Are you exercising the priestly as well as the pastoral functions of your ministry?" "Would you mind if your title were changed to Father?"

Not that he was against brotherhood, he assured me.

"It's just that I believe there is a worse sin than the sin of separation. It's the sin of compromise."

He referred with displeasure to a bishop of his church who had returned from a meeting in Rome with a number of St. Christopher medals blessed personally by the pope, which he had distributed to newsmen.

"A few years ago," he grumbled, his bushy eyebrows furrowing into an emphatic line of disapproval, "he would have been asked to turn in his credentials."

Knowing that he had been graduated from an Ivy League school of theology, I suspected that he would not share my Seventh-day Adventist concept of eschatology. But emboldened by his concern, I turned the conversation to Bible prophecy and the viewpoints of our Adventist pioneers. When I told him that as early as 1851 they had predicted the ecumenical developments of our day, as well as other trends in church-state relationships, he stopped me, a look of incredulity on his face.

"Wait a minute. Do you mean to tell me that these viewpoints are on record in books of a hundred years ago? That they predicted then, on the basis of Bible prophecy, what we are seeing now?"

Going to my bookcase I took out several books in which prophetic interpretation was featured, choosing the oldest and most worn looking.[1]

For the next half hour I turned from page to page, reading the prophetic concepts of our pioneers.

"You know," he said at last, "I was raised in an evangelical church that really believed the Bible is the Word of God. But in my theological training I got away from the fundamentals of the faith. Now, day by day, I find myself being driven back to the simplicity and surety of my early belief."

Picking up a book from which I had finished reading, he arched his eyebrows expressively. "Amazing! Absolutely amazing! What a sermon I could preach if I were an Adventist minister!"

He since has read *The Great Controversy* with deepening conviction, and recently authored a book on ecumenism that would fit, without cutting, into the prophetic pattern of the revelator.

Today thousands of Protestants and Catholics, including ministers and priests, are turning to the Bible—and Adventist books—for the explanation of the ecumenical advances that are erasing old battle lines between denominations. As pentecostalism has proliferated, penetrating historic denominations with its charismatic ministry, they have sought an explanation of its role in the movement toward church union. A hundred years ago, with confidence in the "sure word of prophecy" (2 Peter 1:19), our Adventist forefathers already had made a surprisingly accurate projection.

In the middle and late 1800's denominations were proliferating with the gay abandon of rabbits. Of the nearly 300 denominations listed in current rosters of American churches, the majority had their beginnings during that period. Among them were such interesting groups as the Christadelphians; Church of the Living God, the Pillar and Ground of the Truth; Hepzibah Faith Missionary Association; Pillar of Fire; Fire Baptized Holiness Church of God of the Americas; Church of Illumination.[2]

It seemed incredible that the process of fragmentation ever would be reversed. The Baptists alone were dividing and subdividing so prolifically that it was difficult to keep up with the new divisions, among which were the Two-Seed-in-the-Spirit Predestinarian Baptists, Duck River and Kindred Associations of Baptists, Free Will Baptists, General Baptists, General Six-Principle Baptists, Primitive Baptists, Regular Baptists, United Baptists.[3]

Imagine, then, the derision with which the religious world greeted the confident assertion of our Adventist pioneers that a day would come when the trend would be reversed, churches would bridge the theological gulfs that divided them, and, further, seek the aid of the state in enforcing their doctrines. When in 1851 Adventist writers identified the Papacy as the persecuting power of Revelation 13 and predicted the part America would play in closing scenes, hardly an iota of evidence, outside of the Bible, supported their viewpoint.[4] Theologians of the Christian establishment—who looked on Revelation as a closed book rather than as "the Revelation of Jesus Christ, which God gave unto him [John] to shew unto his servants things which must shortly come to pass" (Rev. 1:1)— must have scoffed.

They are not scoffing any longer. They are too busy trying to update their tally sheets of uniting denominations. In the past twenty-five years twenty-two denominations have merged. Nine major denominations—including the Methodist, Episcopal, United Presbyterian, and Congregationalist—have, since 1961, been engaged in merger negotiations intended to lead to a new 22-million-member church. Some thirty-four merger engagements are moving toward the marriage altar in twenty-four countries. And few "offspring" are being produced by these unions: It is as if someone had slipped a denominational birth-control pill into the interfaith communion cup!

Evidence is accumulating that gives fresh impact to our pioneers' interpretation of Revelation 13 and 17, chapters that have influenced both eschatological views and voting records of a generation of Seventh-day Adventists. Let's view what they found there. Having done so, we will be in a better position to evaluate the ecumenical movement and the part pentecostalism may be expected to play in it.

Revelation is a prophetic cartoon strip, an Alfred Hitchcock spine tingler, and a CIA intelligence report, all wrapped up into one coded communication. (Had the revelation not been in code, it would not have survived the censors either of the Roman Empire or the Roman Church.) To understand the message hidden in it, one must first discover the keys to the prophetic cipher. Then, by astute detective work—comparing, sifting, deducing—one can unmask the mysterious international intrigues and master criminals hidden behind its symbols. The process of interpretation may be difficult; sections of the communication may remain obscure; but we can persist in confidence that a blessing is pronounced by its Author on him "that readeth, and they that hear the words of this prophecy, and keep those things which are written therein" (Rev. 1:3). Investigators have testified to the awareness that unseen intelligences from the Counter-Espionage Division of the Universal Empire have been at work to help interpret clues.

In Revelation 13, hidden under the symbolism of a strange animal—much as we today personify nations under such symbols as a bear, eagle, bulldog, et cetera—our pioneers discovered the life story of the Roman Catholic Church and the nations that would help it achieve its lifelong ambition—to control the minds of mankind.*

How excited I was during my first year of college to discover the meaning of the mysterious symbols. Day after day I compared historical events with predictions written long before they happened. The record was irrefutable, and it must therefore, I reasoned, be divine. I could not so much as predict the weather on the weekend; as surely as I looked at the sky and prepared for a picnic, it rained. I recalled that Jesus had chided the religious leaders of His day for being able to discern in the sky the signs forecasting good or bad weather (which put them one up on me), but being unable to interpret the signs of the times (Matt. 16:1-3). His challenge was straightforward: "Now I tell you before it come, that, when it is come to pass, ye may believe that I am he" (John 13:19). So convinced did I become of the "sure word of prophecy" that at the end of my freshman year, I became a Seventh-day Adventist.

During my sophomore year I studied further. I was saddened to learn of the part America ultimately would play in coercing God's people, creating an "image to the beast" (Rev. 13:14)—an intolerant church-state union similar to that which sent many of our forefathers fleeing their homelands. It would force "the earth and its inhabitants" to worship the first beast, whose mortal wound had been healed (verse 12, N.E.B.). Finally, it would "cause all who would not worship the image to be put to death" (verse 15, N.E.B.).

At the end of my sophomore year I changed my course to theology. Today, only a bit over two decades later, I am preaching and writing on prophetic fulfillments that I then

---

*Evidence of its identity was plentiful: 1. The devil, working through pagan Rome, conferred upon it "power and rule and great authority" (Rev. 13:3, N.E.B.); 2. it was a city-state, combining both ecclesiastical and secular functions; 3. for 1260 years its power was exerted throughout Europe (see Rev. 13:5, 12:6); 4. a deadly wound then reduced it to a postage-stamp-sized domain headquartered in Rome; 5. it appropriated divine prerogatives, including the authority to forgive sins (blasphemy, Rev. 13:5; see Matt. 9:2, 3); 6. it would regain such dominance that all nations would follow its lead in "wondering admiration," saying, "Who is like the Beast? Who can fight against it?" (Rev. 13:4, N.E.B.).

could see only by faith. Since the reign of Pope John XXIII and Vatican Council II the Roman Catholic Church has risen to an eminence that did not seem probable even fifteen years ago. Statesmen seek her counsel and approval, and Protestants look Romeward with the nostalgia of an orphan seeking his home.

The ecumenical movement comes more directly into the prophetic script in Revelation 17. There our pioneers discerned that Mother Rome has daughters (verse 5) who follow her profession—spiritual harlotry. The expression used to describe her profession, *porneuo,* used figuratively as here, "refers to an illicit alliance of professed Christians with some master other than Christ, in this instance to a religio-political compact between an apostate church . . . and the nations of earth." [5]

Having gained the support of the nations, which are of "one mind" (verse 13), mother and daughter churches seek to force the inhabitants of the earth to drink the "wine" in her golden cup. The wine is constituted of Satan's addictive falsehoods and miracles, through which he advances his policy of uniting both the religious and the political world. He comes "armed with all the force, wonders and signs that falsehood can devise. . . . With evil's undiluted power to deceive" (2 Thess. 2:9, 10, Phillips). *Undiluted.* Straight demonic vodka! No 7Up to cut the intoxication potential!

In Revelation 16:12-14 John uses another symbol to portray the deceptive agencies. He refers to "three impure spirits" resembling frogs, which he sees hop out of the mouth of the dragon, the beast, and the counterfeit prophet. John identifies the frogs as symbols of "demonic, miracle-working spirits." Adventist prophetic expositors generally have identified the dragon as the non-Christian world (paganism), the beast as the Papacy, and the counterfeit prophet as Protestantism in its final, apostate condition. [6]

Under the reality-distorting effect of miracle drugs *(pharmakeia)* and falsehoods, the nations go forth to the epic final confrontation between Satan and Michael. And then will come those desperate hours when "he causeth all, both small and great, rich and poor, free and bond, to receive a mark in their right hand, or in their forehead" (Rev. 13:16). The place of the mark may imply that the mark effects both belief (the forehead) and action (the hand). Or that either from drugged conviction (the forehead) or coerced conformity (the hand), all must worship according to the dictates of the false religious system. Economic sanctions are involved, with "no man" permitted to "buy or sell, save he that had the mark, or the name of the beast, or the number of his name" (verse 17), the number being, John adds, 666 (verse 18). Following the Reformation an interpretation that gained currency was that 666 came from the numerical value of the letters in *Vicarius Filii Dei,* meaning "vicar of the Son of God," the title Catholics have applied to the pope.*

Our Adventist forefathers were not in doubt about what constituted the "mark." They understood it to be "not a literal brand but some sign of allegiance that identifies the bearer as loyal to the power represented by the beast. The controversy at that time will center on the law of God, and particularly on the fourth command. . . . Hence the observance of Sunday

*V	5
I	1
C	100
A	——
R	——
I	1
V (U)	5
S	——
F	——
I	1
L	50
I	1
I	1
D	500
E	——
I	1
	——
	666

See the *Seventh-day Adventist Bible Commentary* on Revelation 13:18 for a detailed discussion of the title and number. On the chief exponent of this interpretation following the Reformation, Andreas Helwig (1572-1643), see L. E. Froom, *The Prophetic Faith of Our Fathers,* Vol. II, pp. 605-608. The story of how Catholic scholars turned away the prophetic finger of accusation of the pope by evolving and popularizing new methods of prophetic interpretation can be found in Froom's book, pages 484-505.

will constitute such a sign, but only at the time when the beast's power will be revived and Sunday observance becomes a matter of compliance with civil law. Adventists hold that simultaneously the third angel's message will warn against the reception of the mark (ch. 14:9-11). This message, swelling into a loud cry (ch. 18:1-4), will enlighten men as to the issues involved. When the issues are thus clearly before them, and men nevertheless choose to support an institution of the beast, knowing it to be in direct opposition to the command of God, they thereby show their allegiance to the power and receive the mark of the beast." [7]

Adventist pioneers did *not* teach that Sundaykeepers in their day had the mark of the beast.

Adventists today do *not* teach that Sundaykeepers have the mark of the beast.

Only when the false Sabbath (the "mark" of the beast's claimed power to change even divine law) is substituted for God's Sabbath (His mark of creatorship and authority) and enforced by law will Christians who observe it have the mark of the beast. [8]

Successful in his subterfuge, Satan maneuvers church and state into making "war with the Lamb" (Rev. 17:14). Those who reject the authority of the beast at last face death (Rev. 13:15). How tragic the picture! Men and women who in their right mind would be horrified at their actions are so deluded by the addictive sophistries of miracle-working demons that they strike out, like drunkards unable longer to distinguish friend from foe, at the Lamb and His followers. No longer shielded by "the truth which could have saved them," they "put their faith in an utter fraud" (2 Thess. 2:10, 11, Phillips).

The consequences to the earth and its inhabitants are as sure as the reason for their happening: "The land suffers for the sins of its people. . . . The people have twisted the laws of God and broken his everlasting commands. Therefore the curse of God is upon them" (Isa. 24:4-6, Taylor).

Then occur the horrifying scenes that usher in the battle of

Armageddon. Ellen White has pictured them:

"And then the great deceiver [Satan] will persuade men that those who serve God are causing these evils. The class that have provoked the displeasure of Heaven will charge all their troubles upon those whose obedience to God's commandments is a perpetual reproof to transgressors. It will be declared that men are offending God by the violation of the Sunday sabbath; that this sin has brought calamities which will not cease until Sunday observance shall be strictly enforced; and that those who present the claims of the fourth commandment, thus destroying reverence for Sunday, are troublers of the people, preventing their restoration to divine favor and temporal prosperity." [9]

"Those who honor the Bible Sabbath will be denounced as enemies of law and order, as breaking down the moral restraints of society, causing anarchy and corruption, and calling down the judgments of God upon the earth. Their conscientious scruples will be pronounced obstinacy, stubbornness, and contempt of authority. They will be accused of disaffection toward the government. Ministers who deny the obligation of the divine law will present from the pulpit the duty of yielding obedience to the civil authorities as ordained of God. In legislative halls and courts of justice, commandment keepers will be misrepresented and condemned. A false coloring will be given to their words; the worst construction will be put upon their motives.

"As the Protestant churches reject the clear, scriptural arguments in defense of God's law, they will long to silence those whose faith they cannot overthrow by the Bible. Though they blind their own eyes to the fact, they are now adopting a course which will lead to the persecution of those who conscientiously refuse to do what the rest of the Christian world are doing, and acknowledge the claims of the papal sabbath. . . . Liberty of conscience, which has cost so great a sacrifice, will no longer be respected. In the soon-coming conflict we shall see exemplified the prophet's words: 'The dragon was wroth with the woman, and went to make war with the remnant of her seed, which keep the commandments of God, and have the testimony of Jesus Christ' " (Rev. 12:17).[10]

There it is, the prophetic picture, lacking only the assurance that "the Lamb shall overcome them" (Rev. 17:14). Our Adventist forefathers put it together piece by piece, prayer by prayer. While the world scoffed, they preached and watched. Go through Adventist publications of the late 1800's and the early 1900's and you will find them tracing the outline.

Some of the "more prominent steps leading toward union of church and state in the United States," were reviewed by an Adventist leader, Elder W. A. Colcord, in 1908. Here are eight of his entries, as they appeared in *Liberty*, a magazine of religious freedom:[11]

"1. 1811—First petition to Congress for laws prohibiting the carrying of mails on Sunday.

"6. 1863—First organization to change the Constitution of the United States (Xenia, Ohio).

"7. 1864—Permanent organization formed, called the 'National Reform Association,' with the avowed object to secure a religious amendment to the Constitution of the United States.

"8. 1864—Motto 'In God We Trust,' placed on coins at suggestion of a Pennsylvania minister, being authorized by Act of Congress, April 22.

"9. 1884 (Dec. 11)—First offer of National Reformers to join hands with Catholics.

"13. 1888 (May 21)—Senator H. W. Blair's bill for a National Sunday Rest Law. . . .

"17. 1889 (Nov. 12)—Catholic Congress at Baltimore resolved to unite with Protestants in movement for 'proper Sunday observance.'

"25. 1908 (Sept. 14)—Mr. Samuel Gompers officially announced the American Federation of Labor as in favor of Sunday rest, and as having 'done as much, if not more, than any other organized body of men and women to enforce the observance of the Sunday rest day.' "

Adventists did not impugn the motives of the men seeking

church union. They knew that many were motivated by sincere concern over division of the church—the body of Christ—into competing camps. But they knew also that it was not for coerced uniformity that Christ had prayed, but rather that His followers might be one in heart with the Spirit of truth:

"Holy father, keep the men you gave me by your power that they may be one, *as we are one.* . . . Make them holy by the truth for your word is the truth" (John 17:11-17). Added Jesus: "I have given them the honor that you gave me, that they may be one, as we are one—I in them and you in me, that they may grow complete into one, so that the world may realize that you sent me and have loved them as you loved me" (verses 20-23).

Spiritual oneness was not evident in the formative ecumenical movement, nor is it today. Men speak of disunity of the church as the scandal of Christendom, but they do not seek on their knees that commitment to truth that is the mark of the Spirit's working. Rather than studying points that divide them, with determination to discover and follow truth at whatever cost, ecumenical leaders often stress only those beliefs they hold in common.

On another point, too, church leaders gave evidence that their work did not bear the seal of Heaven. They sought support from the state, seeking to enact Sunday legislation and even to rewrite the Constitution to force all citizens to give allegiance to their concept of Christian duty. The first Seventh-day Adventist religious liberty magazine, *The American Sentinel,* was founded to meet the threat of the Christian Amendment and the drive for a national Sunday law.

And what of those Christians who wished to preserve separation of church and state, who remembered Christ's words to Peter, "My kingdom is not of this world" (John 18:36), who placed emphasis upon changing the heart rather than the Constitution of the State? The Reverend E. B. Graham, vice-president of the National Reform Association, had the program for them:

"If the opponents of the Bible do not like our government

and its Christian features, let them go to some wild, desolate land, and in the name of the devil, and for the sake of the devil, subdue it, and set up a government of their own on infidel and atheistic ideas; and then if they can stand it, stay there till they die." [12]

Another Protestant leader urged the government to "lay its hand on any religion that does not conform to it [moral law]." [13]

But these movements came to nothing. God commissioned angels to hold back the winds of strife (Rev. 7:1, 2) until the servants of God were sealed "in their foreheads" (verse 3), that is, until their submission to truth was so complete that the character of Christ was perfectly reproduced in them. Supreme Court decisions emphasized minority rights and separation of church and state—though the justices, in 1961, held that Sunday laws had outgrown their religious roots and had civil and health rationales compatible with religious freedom. [14]

So it went, year by year. Adventists continued to watch, confident that the sure word of prophecy would not fail. When the Federal Council of Churches was organized in 1908 by 28 denominations to act "in their common interest," Adventist publications analyzed the new organization in the light of Bible prophecy. The World Council of Churches, organized in 1950 by 34 Protestant and Orthodox bodies, received the same searching scrutiny. When the Federal Council of Churches became the National Council of Churches, and when the League of Nations and later the United Nations were organized, articles in the Adventist press explored their potential role in prophetic events.

Then came December 2, 1960, and the visit of Dr. Geoffry Fisher, the Archbishop of Canterbury, to the pope in Rome. My clergyman friend pointed up the significance. When he left my study, he may not have realized just what a sermon he could preach if he were an Adventist minister, but he is learning fast.

"You remember," he said, "that the Archbishop greeted the pope by saying, 'Your holiness, we are making history.' Don't you think it would have been more accurate had he said, 'Your holiness, we are fulfilling prophecy'?"

I suspect that before the final prophetic scenes become reality, not a few ministers and church members—all those "other sheep" of Christ—will be echoing his observation. If I am not mistaken, however, they also will be placing another character within their prophetic parameters—pentecostalism, in both its historic and its new forms. It is to today's ecumenical movement and pentecostalism's emerging role in it that we shall look in the next, and concluding, chapter.

References

[1] Uriah Smith, *Revelation*, originally published in 1873; Ellen G. White, *The Great Controversy*, 1888 (originally published as *Spiritual Gifts*, in 1858).

[2] Frank S. Mead, *Handbook of Denominations in the United States* (New York: Abingdon-Cokesbury Press).

[3] *Ibid.*

[4] *Review and Herald*, Aug. 5, 1851; Aug. 19, 1851.

[5] *The SDA Bible Commentary*, on Rev. 17:2.

[6] *Ibid.* See, for example, comments on Revelation 16.

[7] *Ibid.*, on Rev. 13:16.

[8] Ellen G. White, *Evangelism* (Washington, D.C.: Review and Herald Publishing Association), p. 234.

[9] ———, *The Great Controversy*, p. 590.

[10] *Ibid.*, p. 592.

[11] *Liberty* (Washington, D.C.: Review and Herald Publishing Assn.), Vol. III (third quarter, 1908), pp. 28, 29.

[12] *Ibid.*, Vol. V (third quarter, 1910), p. 15.

[13] *Ibid.*

[14] See *McGowan* v. *Maryland*, 366 U.S. 420 (1961); *Gallagher* v. *Crown Kosher Super Market*, 366 U.S. 617 (1961); *Braunfeld* v. *Brown*, 366 U.S. 599 (1961); *Two Guys From Harrison* v. *McGinley*, 366 U.S. 582 (1961).

14
Pentecostalism's Emerging Role

A film, *Another Pilgrim,* prepared for showing at a World Council of Churches (WCC) assembly in Sweden, features a Protestant minister removing his clothing while conducting a worship service. The WCC said the scene depicts "in poetic form the exhilaration of modern man, as well as his bewilderedness in a world where the only permanent factor is change."

Only decades ago churches found the answer to change in One who changes not. In confidence congregations sang:

"Change and decay in all around I see;

O Thou, who changest not, abide with me!" [1]

But today even man's approach to God has changed. In their attempt to recapture the allegiance of contemporary man, clergymen are putting on performances to rival the off-Broadway theaters. Items:

★ In the Los Angeles "World Church," one night a few months ago, cages occupied by booted girls performing various popular dances were let down from the ceiling. The minister descended in another golden cage to offer "the hottest sermon ever preached in Los Angeles." Its title: "Youth A-Go-Go." [2]

★ Washington, D.C.'s staid National Cathedral (Episcopal) hosted 3,000 youth for a "Spirit in Sound Song and Dance Fest." A rock group beat out the melody as youth danced before the altar in Bethlehem Chapel.

But still attendance drops at Sunday services, as polls of church-going habits show. For all the theatrics, something is missing—power to change lives. Power to testify that man is not alone on Planet Earth. Power to link man to Pentecost and the God of Pentecost and the promises of Pentecost.

Says one man of his church attendance:

"I have sat a hundred times waiting for words that would show me meaning and point me to someone greater than myself. I have heard instead philosophy, literature, and theology, but never have I heard the word of God."

A Jacksonville, Florida, college youth says:

"It is hard for us to trust, much less have faith in, traditional religion when we see its proponents and its institutions. There must be a re-examination."

Disillusionment grows, along with determination to recapture the reality behind religious symbols. The Jesus movement has captured the allegiance of hundreds of thousands of youth. Hare Krishna devotees stand on street corners seeking ecstatic experience through repetitiously chanting the name of their god:

"Hare Krishna, Hare Krishna, Krishna Krishna, Hare Hare, Hare Rama, Hare Rama, Rama Rama, Hare Hare. . . ."

Orthodoxy is, in a sense, "the heresy" of our day. It is a departure from the living church and the living Word. It confuses correctness of theology and living faith. It intellectualizes the simple, though not simplistic, truths of the gospel. Instead of an altar at which hearts warmed by the promise of salvation can melt into new patterns of right conduct, it offers a formalism so cold that church members can skate up the center aisle. Its vitals eaten away by modernism, secularism,

Members of the Hare Krishna movement on the streets of New Orleans. These and others joined in a revolt against the cold formalism that characterizes much of Christianity.

RELIGIOUS NEWS SERVICE PHOTO

existentialism, universalism, and relativism, it presents a hollow shell to hollow men, who close "their ears to the truth" and wander off after "man-made fictions" (N.E.B. and Phillips of 2 Tim. 4:3, 4).

Within the hollow shell of the historic institutional church, two great movements are incubating: Ecumenism, with its hopes of brotherhood and oneness, and pentecostalism, with its promise of power. Ministers unprotected by the "whole armour of God" remove their clothes to depict their exhilaration and bewilderedness. Bewilderment seeks brotherhood; exhilaration feeds on ecstasy. Thus have ecumenism and pentecostalism become religious phenomena to be reckoned with by the student of Bible prophecy.

In chapter 13 we identified the central characters of a prophetic cartoon strip and followed their story up to the Archbishop of Canterbury's historic—and prophetic—visit with Pope John on December 2, 1960. In this chapter we continue the story from that event, having noted the part man's alienation from God plays in the developing prophetic drama.

By 1960 merger negotiations were multiplying. Churches were uniting. Both the World Council of Churches and the National Council of Churches had risen to new pinnacles of prestige and power, numbering among their membership the historic churches descended from the Protestant Reformation. Through lobbyists, they pressed views on government that seemed far removed from the moral issues on which a church organization might be expected to speak. Increasingly, church programs reflected dependence on legislative reform. A new theology was emerging: Evangelism no longer meant reaching out to convert hearts to the gospel. Rather it meant changing the social structure of society.

Within Catholicism, too, social action was receiving increasing emphasis. Two religio-political encyclicals, *Rerum Novarum* ("Of New Things," 1891)* and *Quadragesimo Anno* ("Fortieth Year," 1931), laid the foundation for translating

---

* "Workingmen's associations . . . must pay special and chief attention to the duties of religion and morality, and social betterment should have this chiefly in view," because the "foundation of social laws is thus laid in religion."

Catholic doctrine into social mores and through labor unions making them the law of the land. *Mater et Magistra* ("Mother and Teacher," May 15, 1961) contained a demand that workers, public authorities, and employers observe Sunday:

". . . The Church has always demanded an exact observance of the third precept of the decalogue: 'Remember that thou keep holy the Sabbath day.' Religion, morality, and hygiene, all unite in the law of periodic repose which the Church has for centuries translated into the sanctification of Sunday. . . . It is with great grief that we must acknowledge and deplore the negligence of, if not the downright disrespect for, this sacred law and the consequent harmful results for the health of both body and soul of our beloved workers.

"In the name of God and for the material and spiritual interests of men, We call upon all, public authorities, employers, and workers to observe the precepts of God and His church, and We remind each one of his grave responsibilities before God and society." Added the pope: "This presupposes a change of mind in society and the intervention of the powers of the state"!

Pacem en Terris ("Peace on Earth," April 11, 1963), in the tradition of Augustine's *The City of God*, spoke of an evolutionary kingdom of God on earth, and a supernational authority to preserve peace. Hubert Humphrey, then Vice-President, referred to the encyclical as "a public philosophy for a nuclear era." He added:

"It represents not a utopian blueprint for world peace, presupposing a sudden change in the nature of man. Rather, it represents a call to leaders of nations, presupposing only a gradual change in human institutions."

Still another encyclical, *Humanae Vitae* ("Human Life," July 25, 1968), insisted that "governments must be persuaded to take positions 'in favor of Catholic morality.'" [3] In cooperative social action, Catholics and Protestants find common objectives on which they can cooperate despite doctrinal differences.

But until the mid 60's ecumenism was largely a Protestant concern, for the Roman Catholic Church refused to come on stage so long as it was not given the star billing, i.e., recognition as the unique and authoritative voice of Christendom. Then, in a tactical coup, Pope John XXIII wrote a new script. At Vatican Council II Protestant heretics became "separated brethren," baptism administered in Protestant churches was called "valid." The recrimination that had characterized the old dialog was replaced by benevolence. The pope spoke of efforts to "continue the loving invitation to our dear separated brothers, who also carry on their forehead the name of Christ." [4]

Richard Cardinal Cushing put the objectives of the Papacy into focus: "For the past several centuries there has been either a great silence or a species of embittered argument between us and those who, like us, bear the Christian name. Whether in silence or in recrimination, there has been a great gulf between us. That gulf we set ourselves to bridge." [5]

Since Vatican Council II ended in December, 1965, more advance toward union between Roman Catholics and Protestants has been made than in the previous four hundred years. Perhaps the most incredible high light of the new climate occurred on October 4, 1965, when Pope Paul, addressing the United Nations, claimed to speak not only for the Catholic family but "also in the name of these 'Christian brethren' who 'so kindly charged us explicitly to be their spokesman here.' " [6]

In 1965 a former Roman Catholic priest who had become professor of New Testament Greek and Latin at Augsburg College, Minneapolis, Minnesota, expressed amazement at ecumenical advances:

"It would have been unthinkable fifteen years ago to imagine that the time would come in my own generation when some of the highest authorities of the Roman Catholic Church would turn with a friendly attitude toward non-Roman Catholic Christians by calling them brethren in Christ. I would have never expected, in my generation at least, that the work of a Protestant evangelist [Billy Graham] would receive the blessings of a Roman Catholic cardinal [Cushing]; that Roman Catholic and non-Roman Catholic theologians would engage in friendly discussions and would exchange their views in the same books and magazines; that a Roman Catholic priest would give the main address at a Reformation festival; that Protestant theologians would be called to teach in Roman Catholic institutions; that a Roman Catholic archdiocese would officially join the local Council of Churches; that a Roman Catholic cathedral would apply for membership at the National Council of Churches; that Roman Catholic and non-Roman Catholic Christians would use the same edition of the Bible; that, in Spain and South America, Roman Catholics would join Protestants in praying for the unity of the Christian Church; that Roman Catholic observers would be present at denominational and interdenominational gatherings of non-Roman Catholic Christians." [7]

Who would have predicted, at the beginning of the 60's, that the Roman Catholic Church would set up a working group to cooperate officially with the World Council of Churches? It happened in 1965.

Who would have anticipated that the pope and the late ecumenical Patriarch Athenagoras· I, spiritual leader of 160 million Orthodox Christians, would issue a joint declaration expressing penitence for past faults, including the mutual exchange of excommunications in A.D. 1054? It happened on December 7, 1965. (It was this act that made it possible for Orthodox priests to participate in the service conducted around the bier of the late James Cardinal Spellman in St. Patrick's Cathedral, New York City.) *Rapprochement* proceeds: Some 300 documents exchanged by Rome and Constantinople during the past few years were published in 1972. [8]

In Belgium, in 1971, Catholics and Protestants issued a common declaration on baptism.* In England, in 1971,

---

*Though described as a "common declaration" by Cardinal Leo Joseph Suenens, a source at the Catholic University reference library describes the agreement as a "mutual recognition," which is one or two diplomatic steps down the ecumenical ladder.

Anglicans and Catholics released the historic agreement of Windsor Castle on the eucharist; in France, during the same period, the agreement of Dombes arrived at similar conclusions. In 1971 a report was published summing up the work of a mixed Lutheran-Roman Catholic study commission on "The Gospel and the Church." Reconciliation is being carried on by the Protestant community of Taize, France, and in Germany at the ecumenical village of Ottmaring, near Augsburg. The latter is an experiment in Christian living, shared by Lutherans and Catholic members of the Focolarini movement.[9]

The *Information Service* of The Secretariat for Promoting Christian Unity (Roman Catholic) for January, 1973, reports on dialog with the World Alliance of Reformed Churches and the World Methodist Council; relations with Pentecostals, the Anglican Communion, the World Lutheran Federation; meetings of working groups with the World Council of Churches, the International Catholic-Jewish Liaison Committee; and staff activities that involve another half-dozen religious groups.

Who would have predicted that Catholic, Protestant, and Orthodox Churches would cooperate in Key 73, a "concerted Christian evangelism effort" "calling our continent [America] to Christ"?

Seventh-day Adventists, that's who! And not only fifteen years ago, but fifty, and, in broader prophetic outline, one hundred years ago and more! Nor, having predicted on the basis of Biblical prophecy in 1888 that "Protestants . . . will reach over the abyss to clasp hands with the Roman power, . . ."[10] are they surprised to observe what the epidemic of merger fever is doing to Protestant speech:

Norman Vincent Peale states that what Protestants "are shooting for now is organic unity bringing to an end the old denominations and blending them together into a new church. It will take some time to accomplish this, but no doubt it's on its way. It's the wave of the future, religiously speaking."[11]

John Sutherland Bonnell, a Presbyterian churchman, has

suggested that Protestants be given opportunity for private confession to their minister as a mark of a "spiritual advance in Protestantism." [12]

Dr. Hans Christian Asmussen, a top Lutheran clergyman in Germany, began in the late 1950's an effort to lead his church back to recognition of the authority of the pope. His movement, *Die Sammlund* ("The Gathering"), would also have Protestants place increasing emphasis on saints and sanctity, and especially on the virgin Mary. The trend Dr. Asmussen espouses is so strong that almost every German city now has churches where Lutherans can go to confession. [13]

Episcopal* Bishop C. Kilmer Myers on June 4, 1967, at Grace Cathedral in San Francisco, called on Christians to acknowledge the pope as "the chief pastor of the Christian family . . . and joyfully acclaim him as the Holy Father in God of the universal church." [14]

Little wonder *Time* magazine observed: "On certain thin-aired uplands where theologians graze, it is growing increasingly difficult to tell a Protestant from a Roman Catholic." [15]

And so the *rapprochement* set in motion by Pope John rolls Romeward with a full complement of Protestant leaders who have forgotten why Protest is part of their name. Naturally, Catholic leaders are not grieving at the response, for only as *Protestantism* changed could union become a reality; Rome might change *tactics* but she could not change her *nature* and remain Rome.

The Catholic version of a basis for union was set forth by the late Gustave Wiegel, foremost Catholic ecumenist, in a comment on the World Council of Churches. The Roman Catholic, he said, wants the World Council "to bring all of its churches into the Catholic Church. He considers the Council good and grace-inspired insofar as it will bring the 'other sheep' into the fold of the one Shepherd, visibly represented by His one vicar. . . .

"The Catholic must say to the Protestant that the Church was substantially right, and therefore any endeavor toward re-

---

*Episcopalians are not, in fact, Protestant; but then, who is anymore?

union will be a return to her unreconstructed, unreformed unity." [16]

Yes, long-term wounds are being healed; around the world a new tide of brotherhood is covering the scars of a thousand conflicts. Already some religious observers are hailing the imminent end of that great split in the Western soul called the Reformation. Not that divisions between denominations are going to end overnight. It may take a prophetic day or two for that!—and the intervention of fallen angels performing "unbelievable miracles" (Rev. 13:13, Taylor). But, as Dr. Peale observed, "It's on its way."

Where does pentecostalism fit into the picture?

The past few years have witnessed not only ecumenical advance but disturbing setbacks. In 1972 Pope Paul dashed cold water on hopes that the Roman Catholic Church will soon join the World Council of Churches. COCU—that blueprint for merger of the major Protestant denominations, born with such optimism in 1960—has become just four letters in a rapidly cooling alphabet soup. Debates over the nature of inspiration and revelation are threatening to dismember historic denominations. Hundreds of congregations are splitting away from their parent churches, charging them with apostasy. Is it coincidental that at this critical time a miracle-working third force is emerging on the ecumenical scene?

As we have noted, pentecostal leaders believe that the movement has been commissioned to break down the barriers dividing the religious world and to unite mankind at last under the Holy Spirit's charismatic cape. For this purpose, says Oral Roberts, he was given in 1968 a "mantle of leadership"; for this purpose, says David J. Du Plessis, a world pentecostal leader, the spirit bade him go; he characterizes pentecostalism's role as "spiritual ecumenicity," in contrast to the "institutional ecumenicity" of the World Council of Churches. Another pentecostal booster suggests that the movement, with its "experience of the charismata," is the missing line of an ecclesiastical triangle, through its "perfect experience" uniting the system and order of Catholicism with the doctrine of Protestantism.

A prominent Catholic Cardinal, Leo Joseph Suenens of Malines-Brussels, Belgium—himself reported by Catholic charismatics to have received the baptism of the Holy Spirit—speaks of the ecumenical significance of neo-pentecostalism, which he refers to as "charismatic renewal." Said the Cardinal in an interview in the *National Catholic Reporter* for January 19, 1973:

"Ecumenism must be a constant concern of all Christians, whether or not theologians. The more a Christian accepts the gospel with the soul of a child, the more accessible he will be to the Lord's command 'that they all may be one.' This special openness to the spirit, which is proper to real Christians, should be particularly treasured. This is why a certain number of 'manifestations of the Spirit' which are taking place before our eyes among the people of God hold an extraordinary ecumenical importance for me.

"I am thinking in particular of the ecumenical contribution of the 'charismatic renewal' which began in its Catholic form in America in 1966-67, and at this moment is spreading in Europe and elsewhere in an impressive way. Everything that opens Christians to a new, experimental sense of the spiritual life is a push toward unity."

Unfortunately, as we have observed from the Word of God, not everything that opens Christians to a new, experimental sense of the spiritual life is a push toward unity *in Christ*. Not with miracle-working demons confirming a counterfeit religious experience! And those demons are presently *within* fallen Christendom, if the revelator's account is to be believed, for he saw them, in the final crisis, coming out of, rather than going into, the mouth of the dragon, the beast, and the counterfeit prophet.

We dare not, then, point to charismatic manifestations as proof of discipleship. In fact, both true revivals and false revivals may possess not only supernatural manifestations but also sincerity, enthusiasm, and even love. The false revival, the false movement, will be distinguishable only in this: *Its re-*

fusal to give God obedience. Thus God can distinguish His remnant by their keeping of His commandments (see Rev. 12:17).

It is not "theological nit-picking" to insist on the importance of doctrine:

"Anyone who goes ahead and does not abide in the doctrine of Christ does not have God; he who abides in the doctrine has both the Father and the Son. If any one comes to you and does not bring his doctrine, do not receive him into the house or given him any greeting" (2 John 9, 10, N.E.B.).

Nor are tongues the mark of discipleship. For everyone the test "of the doctrine of Christ in the spirit of Christ" must be applied. As Harold Lindsell, editor of *Christianity Today,* has pointed out: "No matter how many tongues a man speaks or how many times he does it, if his doctrine is defective, his tongues will not sanctify his aberration. The baptism in the Spirit cannot serve as a cover for heterodox belief or sanctify the denial of scriptural truth. . . . Even love," says Lindsell, "in the short run can be simulated, just as tongues can be counterfeited." [17]

Asked Ellen White:

"Is it possible for men to be holy, in accord with the will and character of God, without coming into harmony with the principles which are an expression of His nature and will, and which show what is well pleasing to Him?" [18]

To many Christians, religion consists of an experience. "To them a happy emotion is godliness. They say, 'Come to Jesus, and believe in Him. It makes no difference what you believe so long as you are honest in your belief.' They do not seek to make the sinner understand the true character of sin. . . .

"Satan is willing that every transgressor of God's law shall claim to be holy. This is what he himself is doing. He is satisfied when men rest their faith on spurious doctrine and religious enthusiasm; for he can use such persons to good purpose in deceiving souls. There are many professedly sanctified ones who are aiding Satan in his work. They talk much of feeling; they speak of their love for God. But God does not recognize their love; it is a delusion of the enemy." [19]

It is "a wrong conception of the character, the perpetuity, and the obligation of the divine law" that "has led to errors in relation to conversion and sanctification, and has resulted in lowering the standard of piety in the church. Here is to be found the secret of the lack of the Spirit and power of God in the revivals of our time." [20]

On its distorted concept of God's law Catholicism has superimposed a distorted concept of justification, which substitutes a system of works for Christ's imputed righteousness. Catholicism teaches that men are justified because they *are* righteous. The Bible teaches, and the Reformers reflected, the truth that men are justified because *Christ* is righteous. Man is unrighteous, but when he by faith accepts the righteousness of Christ as his, he is counted to be righteous. Thus the perfect law is satisfied by the perfect righteousness of Jesus. To offer the imperfect righteousness of man and his works to satisfy the transgressed law is to offer another gospel. For "a man is not justified by the works of the law, but by the faith of Jesus Christ" (Gal. 2:16). Said Paul: "Though we, or an angel from heaven, preach any other gospel unto you than that which we have preached unto you, let him be accursed" (Gal. 1:8). Thus we see that the Word of God is the arbiter of orthodoxy even among angels. We are left to wonder whether many pentecostals, Catholic and Protestant, would deny the evidence of their senses (which have been so conditioned to uncritical acceptance of supernatural manifestations) should an angel bring them a false gospel—which, indeed, has been done.

Scarcely better off than Catholicism in its approach to justification is Protestantism as a whole. Particularly in historical pentecostalism the emphasis is so experience-oriented that most church members cannot distinguish between God's outward work in justifying the sinner and the Spirit's inward work in the new birth. In addition, pentecostals subordinate justification to the "higher experience" of sanctification, which in turn can be attained, according to them, only through a second work of grace.

Catholic pentecostals in particular must grapple with these doctrinal issues, at the center of which is justification. Not even ecstatic utterance has sufficed to gloss over the great gulf between their church's vision of salvation and what the Bible teaches. The distinction, as we have observed, has also created tensions between classic pentecostals and their more ecumenically inclined colleagues of neo-pentecostalism. Ultimately the Catholic pentecostal will have to decide whether to repudiate his church or his experience. For in all the sure word of prophecy there is no hint that Catholicism will correct its wrong concepts of the character and perpetuity of God's law or of the Christian's obligations to it, or of the justification by works that constitutes another gospel. Nor can we anticipate that classic and neo-pentecostalism will subordinate experience to the Word of God, exalt the law, renounce false concepts of conversion, the baptism of the Holy Spirit, tongues, and sanctification, and fill the prophetic mold of God's remnant church, which keeps the commandments of God and the faith of Jesus.

Should we be surprised, then, that the picture of fallen Christendom drawn by divine inspiration is done in charcoal?

"And after these things I saw another angel come down from heaven, having great power; and the earth was lightened with his glory. And he cried mightily with a strong voice, saying, Babylon the great is fallen, is fallen, and is become the habitation of devils, and the hold of every foul spirit, and a cage of every unclean and hateful bird. For all nations have drunk of the wine of the wrath of her fornication, and the kings of the earth have committed fornication with her, and the merchants of the earth are waxed rich through the abundance of her delicacies. And I heard another voice from heaven, saying, Come out or her, my people, that ye be not partakers of her sins, and that ye receive not of her plagues. For her sins have reached unto heaven, and God hath remembered her iniquities" (Rev. 18:1-5).

In concluding our look at ecumenism and pentecostalism in prophetic perspective, it seems to me that eight points drawn from the above verses and others examined in this chapter are important.

1. The last true revival will lighten the world by enlightening members *within* fallen Christendom to their true spiritual condition.

2. Christ's followers in Babylon are not called to reform the system, but to *come out of it.*

3. They are directed to God's remnant people, a movement keeping the commandments of God and the faith of Jesus, two marks of such distinction that John uses them as guideposts. It is obvious that if a number of churches could be so identified, the marks would not clarify, but confuse. Therefore, we can expect that the line between commandment keepers and commandment breakers will be sharp and distinctive. It may not be now, but it *will* be! As to the faith of Jesus: It will indeed be a mark of distinction to have such faith in the Word of God that when confronted with deceptive miracles confirming false doctrines, and even with a decree of death, the follower of Christ will respond as Jesus did in the wilderness of temptation, by saying simply, "It is written."

4. Doctrine will be a crucial issue in the confrontation between truth and error, for the fallen religious system is pictured holding out a golden cup in which are combined miracles of deception and false doctrines, while God's remnant are characterized not by miracles but by their faith and fidelity to God's commandments.

5. Movements appealing to experience rather than the will of God are suspect, for it is a counterfeit experience that deceives. Those who shall say, "Lord, Lord, did we not *[in thy Name] prophesy,* and in thy name cast [demons] out,—and [in thy name] many works of power perform?" (Matt. 7:22, 23, Rotherham), rest their case on experience, not obedience. To them Jesus says, "Never have I acknowledged you—*depart from me, ye workers of lawlessness!"* (verse 23, Rotherham). "Lawlessness" is a literal rendering of the Greek word *anomia,* translated "iniquity" in the King James Version.

6. Movements that look to the state to sustain their reli-

gious concepts—demanding Constitutional amendments to make God's will the law of the land, urging compulsory religious observances in the public schools, promoting Sunday laws (or for that matter, *Sabbath* laws!)—should be regarded with suspicion.

7. Many sincere Christians must be scattered throughout fallen Christendom, because God's last revival message calls them out. One should not, therefore, attempt to judge a person's commitment to Christ by his denominational affiliation. One might expect to find in the charismatic movement not only spiritual enthusiasts placing a premium upon the spectacular but also honest hearts repelled by the spiritual apathy of their institutional church, to whom the movement seems to offer vitality, warmth, love, and often—in a shrewd and appealing substitute for the Christian warfare against self—instant sanctification, confirmed by speaking in tongues.

8. Truth, as revealed in the Word of God, is our shield against deception. God will perfect His love in the person who seeks truth, and who conforms his life to truth. The blessing pronounced on those who "read and understand" the prophecies of the Revelation of Jesus Christ consists in being forwarned of deception and its masquerades so that they are able to build intellectual and spiritual defenses against it.

Another church in another age once responded to a rattle at its gates. And an apostle, himself a walking gift of God (Eph. 4:11), given to help them "attain to the unity inherent in . . . [their] faith and in . . . knowledge of the Son of God" (verse 13), wrote them words of counsel. Time was, he pointed out, when they had obeyed the "promptings" of their "own instincts and notions" (Eph. 2:3, N.E.B.), becoming, as a consequence, like children "tossed by the waves and whirled around by every fresh gust of teaching, dupes of crafty rogues and their deceitful schemes" (Eph. 4:14, N.E.B.).

Then, in now-familiar words of counsel, he told them how to arm themselves against the charismatic forces of the air, "the spirit . . . at work among God's rebel subjects" (Eph. 2:2, N.E.B.):

"Find your strength in the Lord, in his mighty power. Put on all the armour which God provides, so that you may be able to stand firm against the devices of the devil. For our fight is not against human foes, but against cosmic powers, against the authorities and potentates of this dark world, against the superhuman forces of evil in the heavens. Therefore, take up God's armour; then you will be able to stand your ground when things are at their worst, to complete every task and still to stand. Stand firm, I say. Fasten on the belt of truth; for coat of mail put on integrity; let the shoes on your feet be the gospel of peace, to give you firm footing; and, with all these, take up the great shield of faith, with which you will be able to quench all the flaming arrows of the evil one. Take salvation for helmet; for sword, take that which the Spirit gives you—the words that come from God. Give yourselves wholly to prayer and entreaty; pray on every occasion in the power of the Spirit. To this end keep watch and persevere, always interceding for all God's people; and pray for me, that I may be granted the right words when I open my mouth, and may boldly and freely make known his hidden purpose, for which I am an ambassador—in chains. Pray that I may speak of it boldly, as it is my duty to speak" (Eph. 5:10-20, N.E.B.).

Boldly he spoke, even unto death. And his words assure us that, like the church at Ephesus, "we have nothing to fear for the future except as we shall forget the way the Lord has led us." [21]

References

[1] Henry F. Lyte, "Abide With Me," *Church Hymnal*, p. 50.

[2] Quoted in *Christian Century,* Aug. 10, 1966, p. 992.

[3] Quoted in *Time,* Feb. 1, 1971.

[4] Christmas Message, Dec., 1958; *Our Sunday Visitor,* Dec. 17, 1961, p. 3.

[5] Pastoral Letter, "The Christian and The Community," March 6, 1960, p. 26.

[6] *Liberty,* Vol. 61, No. 1 (January-February, 1966), p. 20.

[7] Reprinted by permission from *American Lutheran* (now *Lutheran Forum*), May, 1965, p. 10.

[8] "Seeds of Unity Are Found in Charismatic Renewal," an interview with Cardinal Leo Joseph Suenens of Malines-Brussels, Belgium, *National Catholic Reporter,* Jan. 19, 1973, pp. 8, 9.

[9] Incidents described in this paragraph are cited by Cardinal Leo Joseph Suenens as evidences of ecumenical advance. See Suenens, *loc. cit.*

[10] Ellen G. White, *The Great Controversy,* p. 588.

[11] Norman Vincent Peale, "Confident Living," a syndicated newspaper column, Jan. 22, 1961.

[12] Religious News Service, April 25, 1960, p. 17.

[13] *Time* Magazine, Sept. 22, 1961, p. 87.

[14] *Christian Century*, June 21, 1967, p. 803.

[15] *Time* Magazine, "The New Protestantism," May 30, 1960, p. 43.

[16] Gustave Wiegel, *A Catholic Primer on the Ecumenical Movement* (Westminster, Maryland: The Newman Press, 1957), pp. 50, 51, 66. Cited in *SDA Bible Students' Source Book*, article 663, p. 371.

[17] Harold Lindsell, "Tests for the Tongues Movement," *Christianity Today*, Dec. 8, 1972, p. 12. Copyright 1972 by *Christianity Today*; reprinted by permission.

[18] Ellen G. White, *The Great Controversy*, p. 471.

[19] ————, *Evangelism*, p. 597.

[20] ————, *The Great Controversy*, p. 465.

[21] ————, *Testimonies to Ministers*, p. 31.

.

Appendices

Appendix A

"Interpret"? Or "Translate"?

Are ἑρμηνεύω and its derivatives correctly translated only "interpretation," and never "translation"? Lexicographers say No. They recognize the following variation of meanings: Translate, interpret, explain, expound, put into words, express, describe, write about, speak clearly, articulate. (William F. Arndt and F. Wilbur Gingrich, *A Greek-English Lexicon of the New Testament and Other Early Christian Literature* [Chicago: University of Chicago Press, 1957], p. 310. [Book by Arndt and Gingrich is a translation and adaptation of Walter Bauer's *Griechisch-Deutsches Wörtenbuck zu den Schriften des Neuen Testaments und der übrigen urchristlichen Literatur.*] Henry Liddell and Robert Scott, *A Greek-English Lexicon* [Oxford: Clarendon Press, 1968], p. 690.)

ἑρμηνεία   This word occurs in 1 Corinthians 12:10; 14:26.
                 The word is used to head a Greek translation of a will
                 originally written in Latin. (James Hope Moulton and
                 George Milligan, *The Vocabulary of the Greek Testament*
                 [Grand Rapids: Wm. B. Eerdmans Publishing Co.,
                 1972], p. 254.)

ἑρμηνευτής   In Genesis 42:23 this word is used in the Septuagint
                 for the person who served as a translator between
                 Joseph and his brothers.

                 A derivative of this word occurs in 1 Corinthians 14:28
                 (διερμηνευτής).

ἑρμηνεύω   ἑρμηνεύω is used in Papius 2:16 to refer to a translation
                 of Matthew's work. (Arndt and Gingrich, p. 310.)

διερμηνεύω   This occurs in 1 Corinthians 12:30; 14:5, 13, 27.

                 In Acts 9:36 the Aramaic name, Tabitha, is διερμηνευ -
                 ομένη   λέγεται Δορκάς.

Appendix B

Editorial Guidelines

In three editorials Kenneth Wood, editor of the *Advent Review and Sabbath Herald** provided "information and some guidelines" as to "how Seventh-day Adventists should relate to the neo-pentecostal movement." Following are ten guidelines he suggested:

1. Christ promised to pour out the Holy Spirit on His followers.

"Being assembled together with them, [Jesus] commanded them that they should not depart from Jerusalem, but wait for the promise of the Father, which, saith he, ye have heard of me. For John truly baptized with water; but ye shall be baptized with the Holy Ghost not many days hence. . . . Ye shall receive power, after that the Holy Ghost is come upon you" (Acts 1:4, 5, 8).

a. "The lapse of time has wrought no change in Christ's parting promise to send the Holy Spirit as His representative." [1] "The promise of the Holy Spirit is not limited to any age or to any race." [2]

b. God's people should earnestly desire and pray for the bestowal of the Spirit in His fullness. "Why do we not hunger and thirst for the gift of the Spirit? Why do we not talk of it, pray for it, and preach concerning it? . . . For the daily baptism of the Spirit every worker should offer his petition to God." [3]

"Near the close of earth's harvest, a special bestowal of spiritual grace is promised to prepare the church for the coming of the Son of man. This outpouring of the Spirit is likened to the falling of the latter rain; and it is for this added power that Christians are to send their petitions to the Lord of the

---

*Kenneth H. Wood, "The Charismatic Movement," *Review and Herald*, June 22, 1972, p. 2; "Testing the Spirits," June 29, 1972, p. 2; "None Need Be Deceived," July 6, 1972, p. 2.

harvest 'in the time of the latter rain.' In response, 'the Lord shall make bright clouds, and give them showers of rain.' 'He will cause to come down . . . the rain, the former rain, and the latter rain.' " [4]

2. In the last days there will be a genuine charismatic movement among the people of God. "Before the final visitation of God's judgments upon the earth there will be among the people of the Lord such a revival of primitive godliness as has not been witnessed since apostolic times. The Spirit and power of God will be poured out upon His children." [5]

"In visions of the night, representations passed before me of a great reformatory movement among God's people. Many were praising God. The sick were healed, and other miracles were wrought." [6]

The purpose of this bestowal of power will be to gather in the honest in heart. "At that time many will separate themselves from those churches in which the love of this world has supplanted love for God and His word. Many, both of ministers and people, will gladly accept those great truths which God has caused to be proclaimed at this time to prepare a people for the Lord's second coming." [7]

3. Before the genuine outpouring of the Spirit, Satan will introduce a counterfeit. "In those churches which he can bring under his deceptive power he will make it appear that God's special blessing is poured out; there will be manifest what is thought to be great religious interest. Multitudes will exult that God is working marvelously for them, when the work is that of another spirit." [8]

4. The religious world of the last days will be characterized by miracles and great signs and wonders (see Rev. 13:13, 14; Matt. 24:23, 24).

a. The purpose of some impressive phenomena will be to deceive (see Rev. 13:14).

b. So persuasive will be the "signs and wonders" that if it were possible even "the very elect" would be deceived (Matt. 24:24).

5. Miracles and other supernatural phenomena may not be

of divine origin, nor do they prove genuine discipleship (see chap. 7:22, 23).

"Satan is working with everyone who is not under the control of the Spirit of God. It is the lying wonders of the devil that will take the world captive, and he will cause fire to come down from heaven in the sight of men. He is to work miracles; and this wonderful, miracle-working power is to sweep in the whole world." [9]

6. Spiritual ecstasy does not prove that a person is a Christian. [10]

7. Some Christians will label as fanaticism even the genuine baptism of the Holy Spirit. "The baptism of the Holy Ghost as on the day of Pentecost will lead to a revival of true religion and to the performance of many wonderful works. Heavenly intelligences will come among us, and men will speak as they are moved upon by the Holy Spirit of God. But should the Lord work upon men as He did on and after the day of Pentecost, many who now claim to believe the truth would know so very little of the operation of the Holy Spirit that they would cry, 'Beware of fanaticism.' " [11]

8. Not all "spirits" are of God, hence the spirits must be tested. (See 1 John 4:1.)

a. One test is whether the spirit acknowledges "that Jesus Christ is come in the flesh" (verse 2).

b. Another test is whether the spirit relates properly to God's law and revelation. "To the law and to the testimony: if they speak not according to this word, it is because there is no light in them" (Isa. 8:20). [12]

c. A third test is the fruitage. "By their fruits ye shall know them" (see Matt. 7:15-20). Does the spirit lead to godliness or worldliness? Does it lead to love for Christ or love for the world? Does it lead to obedience to the Word or dependence on emotion and feeling? "If those through whom cures are performed, are disposed, on account of these manifestations, to excuse their neglect of the law of God, and continue in disobedience, though they have power to any and every extent, it does not follow that they have the great power of God. On the contrary, it is the miracle-working power of the great deceiver." [13]

9. The Holy Spirit is given to those who obey, not to those who ignore, reject, or oppose God's law. "And we are his witnesses of these things; and so is also the Holy Ghost, *whom God hath given to them that obey him*" (Acts 5:32).

10. There is a genuine gift of tongues (see Acts 2:1-13). This gift at Pentecost enabled the apostles not only to break the language barrier in preaching the gospel but "from this time forth the language of the disciples was pure, simple, and accurate, whether they spoke in their native tongue or in a foreign language." [14]

a. There also is a false gift of tongues. When this appeared among a fanatical group of early Adventists, Ellen White wrote: "Some . . . have an unmeaning gibberish which they call the unknown tongue, which is unknown not only by man but by the Lord and all heaven. Such gifts are manufactured by men and women, aided by the great deceiver. Fanaticism, false excitement, false teaching in tongues, and noisy exercises have been considered gifts which God has placed in the church. Some have been deceived here." [15]

b. The gift of tongues, like all other gifts of the Spirit, is bestowed at the discretion of the Spirit, not of the individual. It is only one of several gifts, no more unique than other gifts, and, like the others, is given selectively, not to all (see 1 Cor. 12:28-31).

c. Love is greater than either the gift of tongues or the gift of prophecy (see chap. 13:1, 2).

d. To prophesy (say something spiritually edifying) is more desirable than to speak in tongues (see chap. 14:1-5, 9).

e. *Order must prevail* (verses 33, 40).

FOOTNOTES

[1] Ellen G. White, *The Acts of the Apostles*, p. 50.
[2] *Ibid.*, p. 49.
[3] *Ibid.*, p. 50.
[4] *Ibid.*, p. 55.
[5] ———, *The Great Controversy*, p. 464. (See also *The Acts of the Apostles*, p. 54.)
[6] ———, *Testimonies*, vol. 9, p. 126.
[7] ———, *The Great Controversy*, p. 464.

[8] *Ibid.*

[9] Ellen G. White, *Selected Messages,* book 2, p. 51.

[10] See White, *The Acts of the Apostles,* p. 51, and *Selected Messages,* book 2, p. 26.

[11] Ellen G. White, *Selected Messages,* book 2, p. 57. (See also *Gospel Workers,* pp. 170, 171.)

[12] See White, *Selected Messages,* book 2, p. 49, and *Gospel Workers,* pp. 300, 301.

[13] *Ibid.,* pp. 50, 51.

[14] Ellen G. White, *The Acts of the Apostles,* p. 40.

[15] ———, *Testimonies,* vol. 1, p. 412.

Appendix C

Adventists and Tongues

A number of incidents, not corresponding to the Biblical gift of tongues, seem to have been used of God to communicate His word through Seventh-day Adventists. Here are eight of the better-documented reports, all cited by W. E. Read in *The Ministry*, August, 1964, pages 18-23.

1. Calument, Massachusetts, 1919: An Adventist minister spoke fluently in Portuguese, of which he knew but little; 2. India, prior to 1954: A postal inspector who had prayed that God would confirm the Sabbath was convinced when he heard a short message spoken in his dialect by a missionary who did not know his language; 3. Hanford, California, 1904: Mrs. E. G. White preached in English but was understood in German by a non-Adventist German lady present; 4. Singapore Mission, 1926-1931: A young Batak worker of Sumatra was heard in Chinese though he was speaking in Malay; 5. South Africa, prior to 1954: An Adventist minister spoke in Afrikaans but was heard, by one person present, in Spanish; 6. Newark, New Jersey, 1946: An Adventist minister preached in English, understood by a Czechoslovak Adventist sister in her native tongue; 7. Teheran, Persia, in early days of our work: An Adventist minister preached in Turkish and was translated into Russian by a worker who did not understand Turkish; 8. London, some years ago: A minister gave a message in English but a few sentences spoken in Chinese were understood by three seamen present; 9. California, a "good many years ago": An Italian bought *The Great Controversy* in English, which he could not speak or read, but found he could understand it and read it through.

Appendix D

Dental Miracles in Lewiston, Idaho

The following is the text of a letter from Dr. Russell Radke, D.M.D., concerning his investigation of dental miracles performed by healer William Fuller at Faith Tabernacle in Lewiston, Idaho, June 8-10, 1971.

"Because of letters of invitation to witness dentistry miracles to be performed by evangelist William Fuller at Faith Tabernacle in Lewiston, I was asked by the Lewiston-Clarkston Dental Society to investigate. I therefore sought and was granted permission to take pictures of the teeth of those people who were to seek healing. I did this prior to the services, so that I would have a record of their dental problems. In all I examined twenty-eight persons and recorded, on my charts and color film, forty dental problems at the first and last of three services.

"The healing line was formed at the third meeting. Each person was instructed to tell the evangelist what his problem was. Mr. Fuller then quickly went down each line clasping each person's head between his hands. In a rapid and almost unintelligible burst of words he said, 'In the name of Jesus Christ be thou healed.'

"Fuller then asked each person to open his mouth, and, with a dental probe and common flashlight, sought to document healings. After finding some ten examples of dental miracles, he invited me to come forward and examine them, and give my professional opinion. In eight mouths, he said, silver fillings had been turned to gold. I found only what appeared to be old oxidized silver fillings with no gold sheen present as Fuller had reported observing.

"In another mouth, gold fillings miraculously bestowed turned out instead to be tobacco stains (see picture no. 2). I felt certain that if the Master Healer were involved, He would produce a more esthetic job than that!

"As diplomatically as possible I reported my findings to the audience, adding that further testing would be necessary for me to make a conclusive diagnosis.

"After the service a lady who had claimed a dental healing asked me to re-examine her mouth and note the new silver filling in her lower right first molar, where, she said, there had been only a cavity. After my prints of her mouth came back, I examined them and discovered that she had had the silver filling prior to the healing service. When I informed her of my finding, she readily admitted that she had forgotten that the filling was there.

(Signed)
"Dr. Russell Radke, D.M.D.
"Clarkston, Washington"